DATE DUE

In the Best of Families

ALSO BY DENNIS McDOUGAL

Angel of Darkness
Fatal Subtraction

IN THE BEST OF FAMILIES

THE ANATOMY OF A TRUE TRAGEDY BY
DENNIS McDOUGAL

WARNER BOOKS

A Time Warner Company

Grateful acknowledgment is made for permission to reprint from the following:

Sexual Personae: Art and Decadence from Nefertiti to Emily Dickinson by Camille Paglia. Reprinted by permission of Yale University Press. Copyright © 1990 by Camille Paglia.

Thou Shalt Not Be Aware: Psychoanalysis & Society's Betrayal of the Child by Alice Miller, translated by Hildegarde and Hunter Hannum. Translation copyright © 1984 by Alice Miller. Reprinted by permission of Farrar, Straus & Giroux, Inc.

President Reagan: The Role of a Lifetime by Lou Cannon. Copyright © 1991 by Lou Cannon. Reprinted by permission of Simon & Schuster, Inc.

Editorial, "Useful Silence," *Palos Verdes Peninsula News,* 31 March 1983.

Warner Books, Inc., 1271 Avenue of the Americas, New York, NY 10020

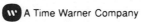 A Time Warner Company

Printed in the United States of America
First Printing: June 1994
10 9 8 7 6 5 4 3 2 1

Library of Congress Cataloging-in-Publication Data

McDougal, Dennis.
    In the best of families : the anatomy of a true tragedy / Dennis McDougal.
    p. cm.
    ISBN 0-446-51672-4
    1. Murder—California—Palos Verdes Estates. 2. Parricide—California—Palos Verdes Estates. 3. Murder victims—California—Palos Verdes Estates—Family relationships. I. Title.
HV6542.M33 1994
364.1'523'0979493—dc20   92-50534
                                        CIP

Book design by Giorgetta Bell McRee

For Carl and Lola,
the best of parents.

ACKNOWLEDGMENTS

The journey through time and fact that a book represents is almost never a solo voyage. Coauthors may be as few as the patient spouse who trudges through the first draft without wincing, or the close friends and family who spot an inconsistency or a jarring phrase in the second, third or fifteenth revision. In fact, a book without acknowledgments is a book with a missing chapter.

My chapter of thank-yous for the help I had in writing *In the Best of Families* begins with the best of families: my remarkable wife and partner, Sharon McDougal; my unceasingly supportive parents, Carl and Lola McDougal; my wonderful, opinionated sister, Colleen Seliger; my brothers, Neal and Pat; my children, Jennifer, Amy, Kate and Fitz, who have taught me so very much about human nature.

Friends and professional peers who demonstrated their understanding of the unrelenting angst of the professional journalist/author by never giving in to the impulse to hang up on me while I was whining: Pat Broeske, Bill Knoedelseder, Bryn Freedman, Katherine Lowrie, Julie Payne, Dorothy Korber, Paul Ciotti, Brian Zoccola, David Levinson, Larry Lynch, Kathy Cairns, Bob Sipchen, Steve Weinstein, John Horn, Tim Fall, Wayne Rosso, Jamie Masada, Richard Lewis, Laurie Pike, Daniela Wild, Jill

Stewart, Corinne Lynch, Ray Richmond, Lisa Sonne, Mark Glad-stone, Pierce O'Donnell, Tom Szollosi, Brian Taggert and Zazi Pope.

A special thanks to Janet Kaye, a splendid reporter, who gave generously of her time, memory and notes in helping me piece together an eleven-year-old murder mystery. Her former professional home, the late and lamented *Los Angeles Herald Examiner*, was the conscience of L.A. journalism. Its demise has brought predictable journalistic sloth to a one-newspaper town.

Thanks to my researchers Marina Lakhman, Anna Shen and Alexandra Matisoff, whose on-the-job training as young reporters helped me chip away at the concrete wall of family denial and the awesome power of a major law firm. Their jobs, as well as my own, would have been sorely limited without the cooperation of the library staffs at the *Los Angeles Times*, *South Bay Daily Breeze* and the *Long Beach Press-Telegram*. My gratitude, too, to the staffs of the Hannold Library at the Claremont Colleges, Claremont Heritage Association, Dartmouth College library, Stanford University law library, Drake University library, the Palos Verdes public library and Iacobani Library in Lakewood, California.

Thanks to Frank Dana, the unofficial archivist of the American Institute of Hypnosis, who opened up his treasure trove of documents to me, and retired Sgt. Al Sett of the Los Angeles Sheriff's Department, whose cynical sense of humor is matched only by his genuine compassion for the victims of horrifying crimes. Thanks to Dep. District Attorney Richard de la Sota, who went the extra mile at my request to get the Michael Miller case file unsealed. And thanks to Judge Cecil Mills of the Los Angeles Superior Court, who finally let me examine the story of a murder that was tried in virtual secrecy in the public court system.

Thanks to Dave Johnston, who believed that the story of the Miller family was as important a tale of our dysfunctional times as I did and coaxed me on when doors were slamming in my face at every turn. Thanks to Leo Hetzel, crusader with a camera and my photographic mentor. Thanks to Michelle Winterstein, whose professional detachment gave perspective, but whose personal compassion never wavered. And, though their hands were tied by a legal system that prizes privacy over truth, staff members at Patton

State Hospital, as well as Drs. Saul Faerstein and Michael Maloney, deserve my thanks and gratitude for their insights into the dark recesses of the human psyche.

To my editors, Rick Horgan, who launched and molded the project through its early stages, and Anne Milburn, who picked up the book midway when Rick moved on to another publishing house and brought as much enthusiasm and skill to the mission as her predecessor. To William Betts, a copy editor with an eagle eye and a CD-ROM memory for detail. To Alice Martell, that rare and special agent who stands by clients in good times and bad and actually does what she says she will do.

And thanks, as always, to Irv Letofsky—still the best editor I've ever worked with in my life.

INTRODUCTION

On most Sunday mornings, Roy Miller can be found in one of the forward pews of the United Methodist Church on Colorado Boulevard in downtown Pasadena. He prays silently and listens attentively to the sermon and sings along with the choir when the time comes to stand and join in the hymns. Sometimes he'll share a word or two after the service with other church members or with his pastor. But he rarely displays emotion, and some mistakenly describe him as cold, numb, or mechanical. He is not.

Roy Miller has always placed his faith in logic and God, though not necessarily in that order. He is a lawyer and not one for small talk. A man of reason, he cloaks his private pain in perfunctory remarks about the news or the weather. Casual conversation is as foreign to his nature as blunt passion. It is reason that keeps his heart well hidden. It is reason that has made him a survivor.

A decade has gone by since his tragedy. With each passage of another year, fewer and fewer of his acquaintances recall the dim details of his nightmare. His is the story of the American dream, fallen, twisted and baptized in blood. As a father, son and husband, he did everything right, yet still his life and family were torn apart.

As a father, son and husband, I empathize with Roy Miller. I marvel at his will. Most of all, I am touched to the quick by his tragedy—a tragedy so profound that it defies comprehension and lingers somewhere just beyond the emotional grasp of most human hearts. One must return to ancient mythology or the Old Testament Book of Job to find analogies.

Roy Miller *is* Job, circa 1994. His heart must brim, though few have glimpsed its overflow. He has been to hell and back.

Most parents maintain that there is no task more demanding, more draining or more rewarding, than raising a child. And doubtless there is no grief more wrenching than bearing witness to that child, at the very threshold of his or her adult life, cut down and destroyed.

But few parents must live with the knowledge that their child can succumb utterly to evil; that they can kill as well as be killed—and make their victim their own mother or father.

Roy Miller lives with such knowledge.

When my own children were in their early adolescence, their mother and I were divorced. It was wrenching and it was painful for all of us. My eldest daughter once remarked that it was the worst tragedy that had ever befallen her, or that she could imagine would ever befall her.

I disagreed.

We parents who grapple with garden-variety disappointments and uneasy truces with our children cannot know Roy Miller's private hell. We spouses who have flirted with lust, despair, rage and jealousy will never fully understand. We sons and daughters who have quarreled bitterly with our parents and sworn never to see or speak to them again have no frame of reference.

Our hearts have been broken and scarred. Those we have held dear may have drifted past our dreams, beyond our love and sometimes out of our reach forever. Our sons and daughters may have left us hurt, humiliated and disillusioned, and our elders may have disowned us. But we get past it. Hopefully, we learn something from our private pain and we move on.

How Roy Miller has been able to move on and keep his faith is nothing short of a miracle.

Before I ever started researching this book, I knew the story of the Miller family. I had written about the bare-bone details of the tragedy when I was a daily newspaper reporter, and I covered the court hearings that followed. From a distance, I followed Roy Miller's career, watching as he helped President Ronald Reagan and First Lady Nancy Reagan through the decade that will forever be synonymous with their names.

In the aftermath of his own anguish, Miller became a quiet force for good. Working for environmental causes, hospitals, the Los Angeles Music Center, higher education and, of course, his church, Roy Miller has grown to become an even more staunch pillar of his community in the decade since his family self-destructed. But the wound to his heart will never heal.

He is just a few years younger than my own father. They share a common heritage in modest Southern California beginnings. They both survived the Great Depression, a World War and a Cold War, and went on to excel and make a real contribution to their respective professions. They both were, and are, conservative to a fault. They were family men. They remained wed most of their adult lives to the same women.

Our family has had its trials and troubles, but it has not been cursed with insanity. My parents have witnessed their share of human misery, but rarely within the confines of their own family and certainly not to a degree approaching the immensity of Roy Miller's torment.

Shamans and physicians dating back to the time of the Greeks have warned us that we are the authors of our own destinies. Beware of hubris, they said: excessive pride.

Yet, how is excessive pride the key to the story of the Millers? How could hubris dismantle a family that had everything, gave generously to peers and poor alike, and still bent down to worship their God with Biblical regularity on the seventh day of every week?

How, indeed.

Perhaps the real answer to the riddle of the perfect family rent asunder remains locked inside the mind of Roy Miller—the stoic, stony man of reason.

But it is more likely that he is still searching for that answer himself, every Sunday morning, when he sits in a forward pew at the United Methodist Church on Colorado Boulevard in downtown Pasadena, and prays silently from the unfathomable depths of a broken heart.

He could not sleep. He had been up most of the night, arranging and rearranging the collection of knives and swords that his grandparents had given him. He was haunted by thoughts of power and sex and blood and weapons.

He was tall and dagger-thin, like his parents and their parents before them. His fingers were musician's fingers: long, slender and delicate, but extremely strong. His hair was brown and wavy. His teeth glinted in orthodontically precise rows when he smiled in the bathroom mirror. He had filed them down smooth and even over the years. They were perfect teeth.

His eyes gleamed in a tortured radiance, like a gloomy portrait by El Greco. They were eyes that masked a deep anguish that he carried within the very core of his being. Sometimes his eyes would go blank and he would stare into the distance at nothing at all for long, uncomfortable moments. Then, without any cue, he would click back into present tense, turning those doleful eyes into alert eyes, and his perfect teeth would curve into a smile.

His mother was still in bed when he entered her room. He sat on the edge of the bed and told her he was feeling dizzy. He asked her if he could crawl into bed with her. She told him to go back to his room and get into his own bed.

He couldn't, he told her. He had wet his bed. He opened his mouth and pointed to the back of his jaw, where he could feel his wisdom teeth crowding in on his perfect smile. He asked his mother to look at them. She ignored him. She got up and went to the next room to use the phone. After chatting with someone animatedly, she giggled a high-pitched girlish giggle, said good-bye and hung up. Then she went to the bathroom and shut the door behind her.

He removed his clothes. He left them in a pile next to the lamp in the living room. Then he strode naked through the house.

"It would be convenient to do what I wanted to do," he said later. "I could make love to her. I was dark under the eyes."

He had found an Alaskan fishing club in the family room. Like the knives, it had been a gift from his grandparents. He hefted it in one hand. He thought that he could use the club to coerce her. He would go into her bathroom and threaten her, right then. If she failed to submit to his desires, he could hover over her until she did. No. No, he would wait until she came out of the bathroom. Then he would surprise her.

He hid in a closet in her bedroom and waited.

"I had animal, primitive, physical, demonic feelings," he recalled. Crouched inside the closet, he decided that he would not chicken out. He would actually do it. This would be no dress rehearsal. She would not stop him.

When she emerged from the bathroom, she saw his reflection in her mirror. He stood naked with his club half-hidden beside him, peering out from behind the closet door.

She had seen this before. She was not going to put up with his foolishness. She told him that she was not going to look at his vulgar nakedness. She told him that he should be discussing his problem with his therapist. She refused to acknowledge this absurd behavior. Then she marched out of the bedroom.

He followed her to the living room. When she turned and faced him, hands on hips in mild annoyance, he started to pull her down to the carpet.

"What are you doing?" she screamed.

He raised his club and hit her on the head. She cried out. He hit her again. He hit her again. And again. It might have been five times. It might have been a dozen times. He couldn't remember exactly. In the

tangle of fury and adrenaline and terror that followed, he remembered
her well-reasoned admonitions about discussing his feelings with his therapist. He remembered those admonitions giving way to a more primal
objection. What he was doing was "not right," she shrieked while he
pounded her into submission. He remembered her hands pushing him
away and flailing at his chest.

"What are you trying to do?" she howled.

Those had been her last words.

After the final blow, she lay still. Then he was upon her.

FATHERS

Ye fathers, provoke not your children to wrath.

EPHESIANS 6:4

— 1

Marguerite Miller decided to sleep in late.

The night before, Roy Miller told his wife that he'd be leaving for the law office at daybreak. His regular Thursday morning breakfast meeting convened in downtown Los Angeles at 7 A.M. and it was a good thirty-minute drive from Palos Verdes, if the traffic was light. Beating the heavy morning commute required getting an early start.

Roy tried not to disturb her frail form as she lay in her flannel nightgown, still curled beneath the comforter on her side of the bed. He crept quietly out of the bedroom, shaved, put on a starched white shirt and tied his tie—all with as much stealth and silence that a tall, angular man like himself could hope to muster.

Towering, gaunt, not particularly dashing in appearance, even in his youth Roy Miller had learned to live with his craggy six-foot-plus carriage and his awkward form. He became a gentle giant early, substituting a warm, empathetic intensity for fluid movement. Through example, he tried passing on his giant's grace to his sons.

It was still dark outside when he stepped into the kitchen at a few minutes past 6 A.M., but Roy was not the only one awake. The toast popped up and, across the room, his son Michael smiled at him. The boy was dressed in pajamas, robe and mukluks. Roy was mildly surprised that the boy was up so early, but Michael surprised him even further when he cheerily announced that he was cooking oatmeal for his father.

While Roy good-naturedly went along with his wife's nutrition regimen at home, he wasn't a fanatic about it. Marguerite, on the other hand, was a walking, talking nutrition devotee, and her belief in a proper diet was contagious. Virtually all of her friends shared her faith in health food, and both of the Millers' sons, Michael and Jeffrey, had caught the health food bug as early as junior high school. Marguerite and Michael both believed passionately that "you are what you eat." From time to time, Michael tried to proselytize his father, with the same mixed results that his mother had achieved.

As his son fussed over the stove, mixing up the oatmeal, Roy couldn't help but feel that this might be one of those times.

Still, it seemed odd. The boy was depressed a good deal of the time these days. He rarely got up before nine and never made breakfast. Marguerite usually did that.

But Roy was pleased that Michael had come out of his funk long enough to break bread with his old man, so he nibbled the toast that Michael had slathered in butter and took a few diplomatic bites of oatmeal, even though the amount of sugar and butter Michael had doused it with revolted him.

Roy gave his younger son an A for effort, but a silent F for cooking skills. But it was the thought that counted.

Roy had always avoided displays of affection, even though he assumed his son understood that he cared deeply for him. Michael had been in and out of counseling for years, perpetually trying to discover what it was he wanted to do with his life.

There were other troubles beyond his chronic identity crisis, though. There was little doubt in the Millers' minds that their son was quite neurotic. After years spent in rounds of ineffective treatments, for close to eight months Michael had been regularly visiting a good therapist with apparently positive results. The boy's attempt at making breakfast looked like a good sign that the strained relationship between father and son was improving.

Roy Miller smiled at his boy . . . well, no longer a boy really. Michael was twenty now and a young man, despite his impulsive behavior and his mother's fluttering attentions.

He seemed disappointed that his father hadn't eaten more. Michael implored him to take a few more bites. Roy declined, pointing out that he had yet another breakfast to eat when he got downtown. He broke away long enough to pop in and kiss his sleeping wife a good-bye peck on the cheek. Then he hugged Michael and hurried out the front door, into the first glimmerings of morning.

From his front yard, when the Peninsula wasn't socked in by fog, Miller could see the Pacific Ocean all the way to Santa Monica, thirty miles to the north. To the east, the snow-tipped San Gabriel Mountains peeked above the gray overcast that hung over the Los Angeles Basin. The island of Santa Catalina, twenty-six miles off the western shore of Palos Verdes, often seemed so distinct from a rise just a half a mile down the street from the Millers' house that, on bright summer days, Roy and his neighbors along Via Visalia almost felt like they could reach out and touch it.

In many ways, Palos Verdes Estates was the culmination of the Millers' American Dream—close enough to the heart of Los Angeles to enjoy its benefits, but far enough removed to avoid the crime and poverty. With its broad, winding avenues centered with shade trees and flowers and its spectacular hilltop vistas of the ocean and the mountains, Palos Verdes could have been a million miles away.

Los Angeles in the spring of 1983 had its own synergistic magic. There was power in Los Angeles, and at the age of fifty-three, Roy Miller had become a part of it.

He was a senior partner at Gibson, Dunn and Crutcher—the oldest, largest and arguably the most influential law firm in the western United States. It was a quiet, deliberate source of civilized power in an increasingly uncivilized city. It was the law firm headed by William French Smith, who had taken a leave of absence in 1981 to become Attorney General of the United States.

After World War II, real power in the United States had shifted from the Atlantic seaboard to the Pacific. Wall Street and Washington were understandably reluctant to acknowledge this hard truth. Easterners resisted it for decades. But by March 1983, the facts were overwhelmingly clear to the professionals, businessmen and political leaders who lived in the Golden West. The torch John F. Kennedy had lit in 1960 had been passed across the country to Southern California, where a new generation was calling the shots.

The power shift had forged Roy David Miller—as much as he'd helped create it. Miller was, however, a private man. He shunned notoriety and didn't especially like the public notice often attached to his work. But it was difficult, he had learned, to remain a private man while acting, in addition to heading Gibson, Dunn and Crutcher's taxation department, as personal lawyer to the President of the United States.

Miller had been passed this torch by Ronald and Nancy Reagan's friend and attorney William French Smith. It was Miller who handled the sale of the Reagans' California home so that they could move into the White House. It was Miller who advised the First Couple on the more lucrative aspects of estate planning and the tax law loopholes that allowed Mrs. Reagan to write off her designer gowns as museum donations. And it was Miller who prepared and signed the President and First Lady's Form 1040 tax return each spring.

But while his clients moved to Washington, Roy preferred to stay in Los Angeles. That was where Roy Miller had everything he wanted.

On this particular Thursday morning in March 1983, Roy had a meeting at the California Club in downtown L.A. He was a dedicated member of the Economic Round Table, an exclusive group of about fifty conservative L.A. business executives who met for breakfast at the California Club on the fourth Thursday of each month to talk politics, commerce and law.

The club itself was rich, exclusive, all-male and baronial, housed in a sturdy fortress at Fifth and Flower with long carpeted corridors, grand dining halls and the dark walnut anterooms reminiscent of Newport's Bellevue Avenue mansions or the country homes of Oxford dons.

For Roy Miller, however, the club represented only one of the conservative Southern California power centers where he operated. Church, hospital, chorale, college, orchestra . . . if a board or advisory group needed a hand, Roy Miller lent his without hesitation. Of his many civic duties, however, the Round Table meetings remained one of his favorite. The group was comprised exclusively of successful middle-aged white men—usually bankers, brokers or lawyers like himself.

Since his birth one month before the stock market crash of 1929, Roy Miller had lived a life of privilege on the comfortable outskirts of Los Angeles. Though Southern California had always been his family's home, it was a California of prosperous conservatives and landed gentry.

He grew up in the rustic college community of Claremont in the hills east of L.A., long before those hills became lost in the smog. Claremont was a rural town when he was born, barely inside the Los Angeles County border. The Great Depression had been a vision of orange groves, freight trains and eternal sunshine for Roy and his younger brother, Marvin. Their parents' own middle-class affluence acted as a buffer against economic disaster. Their father was a citrus wholesaler and their mother a lifelong teacher in the Claremont public school system. The Miller boys never felt the sting of chronic unemployment and poverty that had destroyed so many other lives.

By the time Roy entered grade school in the mid-1930s, he was already used to the Los Angeles mirage. It was a big city, somewhere off to the north and west. Claremont was small-town America. The county fair, held each autumn in neighboring Pomona, was about as close as the Millers came to a taste of Los Angeles urbanity. Still, L.A. was very vivid to Roy even then. His parents passed on to him and his brother the picture of Los Angeles as a hub of prosperity and influence where the whole nation's future might eventually be forged.

And the years advanced kindly for Roy and his brother. When World War II was gobbling up young soldiers and sending them back to L.A. as cripples or heroes or not at all, Roy was still in high school. He celebrated V-J Day with a promise of college, paid for by his own hard work and his parents instead of by the G.I. Bill. When it came time for law school in 1951, he went to Stanford, not Korea.

His timing was blessed, but his life was never devoid of striving and sacrifice. The Miller boys were conscious of their good fortune and thankful for it, but ever vigilant too. Roy and Marvin learned quiet efficiency from their mother and midwestern values from their conservative father, who began driving the Protestant ethic deep into the boys before they even learned to walk.

Getting into Stanford was one thing. Staying in required far more than the goodwill accorded by proud, well-heeled parents.

Though born with a silver spoon in his mouth, Roy Miller turned it to platinum with his own dedication to the study of law. He worked hard, was elected to Phi Beta Kappa, made the staff of the *Stanford Law Review* and passed the California bar the first year after he graduated.

He did a short stint in the army in Oklahoma to satisfy his military obligation. Then he and the high school sweetheart he'd married while at Stanford returned to Southern California to live briefly in West Los Angeles, where their first son, Jeffrey, was born. They then moved to the Pasadena foothills, ten miles north of Los Angeles, where they lived for close to fifteen years in a quiet upscale suburb. Meanwhile, Roy moved from associate to partner at Gibson, Dunn and Crutcher, continuing to study and pass the necessary tests to become a certified tax specialist.

While he climbed the career ladder, his wife, Marguerite, made a home for him. Unlike the stone and glass seaside homes that jutted out over the Pacific in Palos Verdes, twenty miles south of downtown Los Angeles, Pasadena represented old-style California affluence, with a gentrified patrician populace that matched the understated architecture. Their first real home was a subdivision ranch-style house within two blocks of the elementary school that Michael and Jeffrey attended.

As the years advanced, so did the Millers' standard of living.

In 1969 Roy moved his family to Palos Verdes, where Ronald Reagan's own children once attended Chadwick, the Peninsula's exclusive prep school. The Miller boys went to public schools, but in Palos Verdes a public school was very nearly as good as any private one. Besides, public schools were good enough for Roy and Marguerite; they were good enough for their children.

When Roy was ten years old, the love of his life moved next door.

In 1940 World War II was still nearly two years away and Harold Bruner, a Des Moines businessman, decided to pull up stakes and move his family to a California college town where his girls might refine themselves at the same time that they met prospective suitors. Miss Marguerite Bruner, the youngest of four Bruner girls, was far too young to enroll at Pomona College along with her sisters, but it didn't stop her from flirting with the boy next door.

She was just a year and a half younger than Roy. Her parents were well-off, well-educated and well-traveled. The Bruners took the girls on a tour of the globe before they settled down in Claremont. Her father graduated from Iowa's Drake University and had studied at Harvard Law School before going into his father-in-law's building supply business. And, though she never graduated, Marguerite's mother went to Drake and Wellesley College, before snagging her husband.

The Bruners swept into Claremont with worldly ways and a highbrow attitude and quickly became a fixture of the small town's society. Marguerite and her sisters came to know the same upper-middle-class California of sunshine, citrus and scholastics that the Millers did.

Marguerite was not nearly so driven as her future husband, though. She was a willowy girl with a high, giggly voice—so thin she could have been Olive Oyl in a school play. Roy and Marguerite went together through high school and college, finally marrying in an elaborate ceremony at Pomona College's Bridges Auditorium in 1952 during the summer following her graduation from Pomona and Roy's first year at Stanford. After a short stint of teaching near Palo Alto while Roy attended law school, she became the bubbly but patient 1950s housewife that she had always been expected to be. She and her three sisters all finished their undergraduate studies, married well and began raising families. They left breadwinning to their more-than-capable husbands and devoted themselves to cooking, shopping, child-rearing and mah-jongg games with the girls.

Outwardly, Marguerite appeared perfectly happy living in the shadow of her husband. She sang in the choir and taught Sunday school at the United Methodist Church on Colorado Boulevard while she and Roy lived in Pasadena.

After the move to Palos Verdes, Marguerite missed her subdued suburban hillside home, as well as the friends she and Roy had made at their church. They sampled services at some of the churches near their new home, but never fit in very well. Every Sunday that she and Roy could make it, the Millers continued to return to Pasadena.

To Marguerite, her church and her family were everything. Every one of her friends, in Pasadena and Palos Verdes, applauded her devotion to her sons. When her peers in the community decided to launch careers or put child-rearing on hold to pursue volunteer or docent work, Marguerite stubbornly stuck first and foremost to her obligations as a housewife and mother.

She adapted slowly but solidly to society on the "Hill," as the Palos Verdes Peninsula was known to the natives. She joined the Silver Spur Garden Club in Palos Verdes and became something of an expert in bedding flowers.

But even in her stretch of sylvan tranquillity, Marguerite Miller worried constantly about the creeping crime rate.

Lately, graffiti had begun to ooze into the suburbs. Gangs intent on easy money drove into the best neighborhoods, looking to pillage and burgle. Rape, robbery and the most senseless murders were no longer confined to the ghettos of South-Central and East L.A. as they had been in the sixties and seventies. A shooting here. A brazen daylight attack there. If it kept up, the violence and wholesale civic madness might eventually seep into every niche of the social fabric.

Except for a burglary they'd had at the house a couple of years earlier, Roy felt secure in Palos Verdes, even if Marguerite did not. Marguerite seemed to agonize over so much in her life: her safety, her religious convictions, her health.

Marguerite had become a health food devotee in the years since they had moved from Pasadena to Palos Verdes. She shopped for whole grains, shied away from fatty foods and preached the fortifying, revitalizing properties of a macrobiotic diet. There were times, after she'd been to one of her American Nutrition Society lectures, when she could drive Roy to distraction, running on about how the perfect diet could cure everything from athlete's foot to yeast infections. At five feet eight inches and less than one hundred pounds, she appeared to be less than the best living testimonial to the healthful effects of the diet she prescribed, but she did have boundless energy.

Her obsession with food seemed to make her happy, so Roy did what he usually did whenever Marguerite rubbed him the wrong way with one of her flights of fancy: he bit his tongue and smiled, showing the rough line of his disintegrating teeth.

Roy and Marguerite's sons were as tall and rawboned as their parents. Michael had come through a particularly rough adolescence to closely resemble a brooding version of his father: high cheekbones, deep-set eyes and a shock of wavy dark hair that smoothed easily into place without a comb. Jeff, on the other hand, more closely resembled his mother. He was as tall and handsome as the Millers got, with his wide brown eyes and sardonic, Mona Lisa smile.

Jeff was not a subject that either of the Millers liked to dwell upon. By 1983, Roy was no longer shattered, but it still hurt enough to silence him when he thought about it. Jeff's funeral was two years behind them. Roy, Marguerite and even Michael were getting on with their lives.

Roy stayed busy, usually from dawn to dusk, and beyond. There was enough patrician goodwill inbred in him to make Roy Miller want to dispense some of his blue-ribbon knowledge to those artistic and charitable organizations that could put it to the broadest and best use. Roy believed in keeping his mind occupied and his body moving. His career afforded him plenty of the former, and Los Angeles—which required an automobile trip to accomplish anything from a business luncheon to shoe repair—afforded him plenty of the latter.

He was proud of himself and his station in life, but Roy Miller was never a boastful man. He kept a low profile and quietly enjoyed his own personal realization of the American Dream. He and Marguerite had worked hard to overcome the obstacles they had encountered along their pathway to success. They were a good match. On this Thursday morning in March 1983, while he drove down from his home into Los Angeles, Roy Miller sentimentally thought of all the good things that had befallen him with Marguerite there at his side for these past thirty years.

Dr. Shapiro called Roy Miller at about a quarter to eleven.

It wasn't the first time that Michael hadn't made it to his standing Thursday appointment. Apparently Roy had placed too much faith in Michael's breakfast-making breakthrough.

If Roy knew Mike, he was probably holed up in his room playing his violin or listening to rock albums or fitfully brooding over his career plans. He hadn't held a job since he returned from New York City on his twentieth birthday in May 1982. He had dabbled with acting lessons for a couple of months in pursuit of an acting and modeling career.

So Michael was back home again and had been in counseling since last summer. Roy gave him about five dollars a day in spending money until he could get his life back together. Since June, Roy had also been paying to send Michael to weekly sessions with Sumner Shapiro at the psychiatrist's ranch office in Encino. For a while, Michael was going to see the Harvard-educated Shapiro every day.

Roy thought therapy seemed to help, and this particular March day had looked good at the outset. But Roy remembered a similar day the previous September, when he got a call at the office about his son trying to outrun the Palos Verdes Estates police. A patrol car clocked him streaking through a twenty-five-mile-per-hour zone at fifty in his little yellow Toyota. When Michael finally pulled over, his only explanation to the ticketing officer was that he was having problems. He was charged with evading arrest and reckless driving.

Michael pleaded guilty to reckless driving and the court let him off with a year's unsupervised probation and a $401 fine. That was proof enough that just one of Michael's bad days could equal a dozen good ones.

There were plenty of psychiatrists, psychologists, counselors and even channelers in and around Palos Verdes Estates to serve the troubled. Shapiro was fifty miles away, but he offered something special—at least Michael thought he did. When he first began with Dr. Shapiro, Michael's problems ranged all the way from delusional behavior to bed-wetting. Those kinds of problems could take months, possibly years, to solve. But there had been progress, Shapiro assured the Millers.

There would be no progress, however, if Michael didn't come to therapy. Dr. Shapiro said he had tried calling the house before he called Roy, but nobody answered. Marguerite was probably lunching with girlfriends from the garden club and Mike was no doubt hiding out in his room.

Roy still wasn't concerned. He didn't even call home right away. He had plenty to occupy himself without having to wring his hands over Michael's latest no-show. The President's 1982 tax return had to be finished up and filed within three weeks. Each year, the ritual had become a larger and larger media event. As soon as Roy had it done, the 1040 was rushed to the President and First Lady, who signed and dated it. Then copies were run off in the Executive Office Building and rushed next door on Pennsylvania Avenue to the Washington press corps before it even got into the hands of the Internal Revenue Service.

In addition to his two most famous ones, Miller had dozens of other rich and influential clients who frantically scrambled to locate those final precious credits, exemptions and deductions before midnight of April 15. It was not the best time of year for Roy to have to play watchdog in a game of hide-and-seek between Michael and his therapist.

Roy did try calling home himself a little after noon. There was no answer. He remembered Marguerite telling him that she had one of her nutrition meetings that evening, but he expected her to drop back by the house after lunch. He was beginning to become a little anxious about Michael, though. The boy played games once in a while, but it wasn't like him to stay missing for long.

At 3:30 P.M., after Roy returned from lunch, all alarms were off.

Katherine Murdock, Miller's secretary, entered his office with news that Michael had called. Michael was at his Aunt Marilyn's house in Santa Monica. Roy told Murdock to call his sister-in-law back and get Michael on the phone. He was secretly relieved that Michael hadn't gotten in an accident, but he couldn't show that at the moment. It was important to be stern when he let the boy know he was good and upset about his failure to keep another of Dr. Shapiro's expensive appointments.

Katherine returned a few moments later with the message from Marilyn Adkins that her nephew was asleep in his cousin's room and that Mrs. Adkins did not want to awaken him. The boy seemed exhausted, Marilyn had told her. Roy nodded and went on with his work.

He had a board meeting at Arcadia Methodist Hospital after work, but he tried calling Michael again around five. This time, Marilyn's husband, Paul, answered. Michael remained asleep in his cousin Bill's room, he told Roy. Roy told his brother-in-law not to bother the boy. He'd get in touch with him later in the evening.

Roy also called Dr. Shapiro again. The psychiatrist had good news: Michael was late, but he had showed up, after all. He told Roy that Michael had finally come by his office about two, before he went on to his aunt's house. It was far too late for his session, but the fact that he had shown up was an encouraging demonstration that Michael could take personal responsibility for his own actions. Shapiro told Roy that Michael had rescheduled his appointment for the following day, and Roy hung up, feeling much better.

That night, Roy left the hospital board meeting in Arcadia at 9:30, stopped for gas and then headed home.

Climbing back up the Hill in one's car after dark could be confusing if you didn't know the way. Roy had learned it so well after years of practice that he could have negotiated his way up blindfolded: right off of Hawthorne onto Palos Verdes Drive, straight up to Silver Spur and right again on Montemalaga to Via Visalia, on up to the top of the Hill.

The Miller home was in the middle of the block, but the lots were so large and the houses so sprawling that the nearest neighbors lived thirty yards away on either side. None of the house lights were on and the Miller family dog, Lance, was barking in the backyard. He hadn't been fed. Marguerite had apparently not yet returned from her nutrition meeting.

The extension phone in the garage was ringing as Roy drove in.

It was Kay Dunholter, one of Marguerite's friends, wondering what had happened to Mrs. Miller. The nutrition meeting had begun as scheduled, at 8 P.M., in a conference room at the First Methodist Church in Redondo Beach. It was a good talk. Marguerite would have enjoyed it, but she never showed up.

Roy hung up, closed the garage door and walked around the driveway to the front door. He began to wonder if his wife might have gone to visit friends back in Claremont during the day and just hadn't returned until later than she planned.

Earlier in the week, Michael had told his father that he had lost his house keys. The lost keys worried Marguerite more than they did Roy. When the house had been burglarized before, the burglars had jimmied the sliding glass doors that separated the master bedroom from the balcony over the garage. Sometimes she seemed downright neurotic about safety to Roy, begging him to always peer through the peephole in the front door before opening it to anyone.

But tonight the double bolt was safely locked when Roy got to the front door. He slipped his key in the lock and turned it. When the door swung wide, he stepped into the entryway. Something was not right.

A pair of smashed eyeglasses lay on an oriental throw rug. A broken red flashlight lay on the brick-pattern linoleum nearby.

"Marguerite!" Miller called.

He stepped inside where a light shone on the yellow shag carpeting in the living room. The small table lamp, which stood on a chest in the entryway, was activated by a timer, so it would have come on automatically at nightfall. The stereo played softly. A small pile of towels was on the floor. They appeared to have been used to wipe up something dark. Maybe shoe polish. Or chocolate. Or chicken blood. There was a large dark stain on the carpet and something else: a carved foot-long stick of heavy wood that Roy recognized as an Alaskan fishing club that had been in Marguerite's family for two generations.

Miller's eyes darted around the living room. Nothing else seemed out of place.

Then he glanced through the entryway at the door leading to the rear hallway. There were dark dreadful drops of liquid, drying on the linoleum. It was blood, but too dark and too plentiful to have come from any chicken.

No sound came from the rear of the house where the trail of coagulated blood seemed to lead. Roy Miller's long, haggard body hung suspended in time and space in the entryway. He knew the inside of this house as well as the intricate roadways that twisted over the face of the Palos Verdes Peninsula. But he did not move.

"Marguerite!" he cried one last frantic time before he backed tentatively out the front door. A mix of fear for his wife and fear of what might still lurk inside kept him from exploring further. He moved in a confused, awful haste up the darkened street to his nearest neighbor's home.

— 2

Marguerite Miller had always had a kind of maternal instinct for taking charge and helping those less fortunate than herself.

Mrs. Marvin Barab, who lived down the street and around the corner from the Millers, remembered Marguerite coming to her front door once and explaining in wide-eyed wonder the predicament of a Mexican man named Gilberto.

Marguerite had found him living in his car, she explained. Her hands and slender fingers fluttering like flushed doves, Mrs. Miller breathlessly told Mrs. Barab that she had struck up a conversation with the man after discovering him parked down the road from the Millers' house. She spoke Spanish, Mrs. Miller explained with a small measure of pride. It turned out that Gilberto was a gardener, so Marguerite invited him to do some planting and weeding around her house. He had done some fine work on the Millers' yard, she told Mrs. Barab in her anxious, high-pitched tremolo.

Could Gilberto, perhaps, do some yardwork for the Barabs? she wanted to know.

Why not? Mrs. Barab told her.

"We would use him occasionally and now he comes once a week," said Mrs. Barab years later. "Gilberto really is a very exceptional person. He'll do stuff in the house. He's trustworthy, responsible. Marguerite was right."

Thanks to her, said Mrs. Barab, Gilberto no longer lives in his car. In fact, he traded it in for a pickup and a power mower within a year or two. Like the residents of Palos Verdes, he had become a prosperous businessman. He had even hired his own people to work for him.

"He's got a regular route around here. I understand he owns a couple of houses in Tijuana. He's very successful."

Marguerite had the vision to see enterprise and energy in others. She saw it in her husband, after all. And she nurtured his career potential with the firm, consistent care that she had been trained since birth to heap upon all of the men in her life.

"She was hyper. She was different," said Gladys Duffill, whose husband was the Millers' contractor and handyman. "She called my husband whenever there was an emergency. They tied their dog to a hose bed once and the dog took off—a St. Bernard, I believe—and there was water shooting every which way. She called up frantic. She didn't know where to turn the water off."

Marguerite was both dreamy and exacting: as giggly and capricious as a schoolgirl, but a stern and obsessive taskmaster if family discipline was not maintained.

In certain respects, she was not unlike Roy's own mother. The former Ednabel Loofbourrow had read Kipling in college and had romantic literary pretensions dating all the way back to the Roaring Twenties. But as a teacher for a generation of Pomona Valley schoolchildren, she still spent years sternly administering classroom discipline and doling out arithmetic assignments to unruly junior high students. Like Marguerite, she went to church every Sunday. Like Marguerite, Ednabel raised two boys to manhood. And, like Marguerite, she wanted the very best for her sons.

After nearly fifteen years of living on the Hill, Marguerite was a familiar figure in Palos Verdes, even though most of her neighbors were little more than nodding acquaintances.

The women tended to know one another more than the men,

and the Millers' neighbors thought Marguerite had a good heart, even if she was something of a busybody. Some even characterized her as a flake. But a gentle flake. A kind and delicate and generous flake.

Marguerite was a passionate gardener who had done a little landscaping when the Millers lived in Pasadena. In Palos Verdes she became a fanatic. Marguerite grew vegetables for her family so that she could be certain that the broccoli or eggplant was chemical-free. Vegetable gardening might be considered déclassé in rich suburbs, but in Palos Verdes it represented the very height of enlightened eccentricity. She whiled away whole weeks fretting and fussing over ferns and bushes, ficus and begonias. She loved plants very nearly as much as she did human beings. They were pretty to look at, often delicious to eat and never spouted any back talk.

At a Palos Verdes nursery shop, shaded by a jacaranda tree, she would frequently appear midmornings, gazing for a time through the windows like a Dickensian waif. Then she would timidly enter and haunt the shelves, spending long minutes fussing over the plants and taking great note of how everything was growing. She spoke in whispers—at once reverential and yet insistent.

"She'd come in almost apologetically, but once she started talking, you couldn't shut her up," the store owner told a patron.

Once, when she had worked up enough nerve, Marguerite came to the counter and asked permission to plant flowers around the jacaranda tree outside. It looked lonely, she said. The owner had noted Marguerite's fine skin texture and exaggerated bashfulness and took her to be in her mid-twenties.

Marguerite was more than welcome to plant flowers around the jacaranda, the owner told her.

Marguerite smiled sweetly. Only then did the store owner notice that this frail, youngish woman before her was far older than she had first appeared. She had eyes sad enough to have seen a century. They were deep and weary, and seemed to the owner to be very nearly as lonely as the tree branches shedding purple blossoms outside her nursery door.

* * *

Marguerite was the youngest of four sisters and, in some ways, the most like her father.

"Harold was quite tall, at least six feet," recalled Jim Flagg, the Bruners' bookkeeper. "Three of his daughters, including Marguerite, were like him in that respect. His wife was not quite so tall, but she was more buxom."

In her later years, age hadn't improved Mrs. Bruner's figure or her disposition. She could be demanding and capricious. But Marie Buxton Bruner, the younger of two Iowa heiresses born just before the turn of the century, was a far different woman than she was in her youth.

Harold Bruner, on the other hand, remained much the same as he had as a young man: devoted, strong and traditional.

"Of course, to me, one of the best things you can say about a person is that he's a great family man, and Harold Bruner *was* a great family man," said his friend Mack Parks, a real estate broker who met the Bruners shortly after he came to Claremont in 1947. "He was devoted to his wife and four daughters and they were devoted to him."

Harold Bruner was an old-fashioned pillar of the community: 32nd Degree Mason, Kiwanis Club officer, Chamber of Commerce director, Shriner with the Za Ga Zig Temple and both deacon and historian of the local United Church of Christ Congregational.

He was the eldest son of nationally known zoologist, author and educator Henry Lane Bruner. Harold's mother died when he was four, but his father remarried and kept the boy on course toward an academic career. Professor Bruner taught at Iowa's Drake University while his son was an undergraduate.

His father drove Harold to succeed. He became a fraternity man: Alpha Tau Omega. He rose to the editorship of the *Delphic*, Drake's student newspaper, and was elected president of his senior class. In 1915 he graduated Phi Beta Kappa with a bachelor of science, majoring in social science and minoring in German and chemistry. The following year, he won a scholarship to Harvard Law School. But he would not become a professor like his father.

Marie, as she preferred to be called, also went to Drake and took courses in liberal arts, French, voice and piano before settling down to study English literature. When Harold went to Harvard, Marie transferred to Wellesley a few miles to the west. He was bent on success and financial independence. She was dedicated to a higher consciousness with a better class of people than one might normally find amid the cornfields and cattle droppings of Iowa.

Harold married Leona Marie Buxton in 1917 before serving a term in the army as a second lieutenant. After the service, he settled down to business for the next twenty years, working for his father-in-law.

David Henry Buxton founded Des Moines' Globe Machinery and Supply Company at a time when the Industrial Revolution was remaking the Midwest. Marie's father was a flamboyant sportsman who used Globe's profits to globe-trot. In 1912 he traveled around the world. Harold Bruner's father-in-law also paid frequent visits to Alaska, the western Atlantic, the Sea of Cortés, the California coast or anywhere else where the oceans were untouched and the deep-sea fishing splendid. As a member of the exclusive Tuna Club on Catalina Island, he hobnobbed with fellow sportsmen like western author Zane Grey, who held a string of sportfishing titles. Buxton himself caught a world-record number of tarpon on October 12, 1923, never to be matched again: twenty-six of the feisty Gulf of Mexico game fish in a single day.

After Buxton retired from his business in 1925, he took the unpaid job of president of the Drake University board of trustees. Like his father-in-law, Harold became a gentleman of independent means. Marie and Harold used their inheritance as capital for mortgage and commercial loans—a means of continuing to earn a very comfortable living—and joined the Audubon Society, lecturing on conservation, gardening and wildlife.

Like her parents, Marie insisted that the Bruners travel. While the depression wrought havoc on many American lives, the Bruners were flush with enough cash to afford their own trip around the world. They collected souvenirs on their visits abroad and displayed them around the house, often giving their guests the feeling that they had walked into a *National Geographic* museum: pottery, strands of turquoise and colored glass beads, bric-a-brac and oddities from around the world were always on exhibit to stimulate conversation. Here, a memento from an Asian wedding. There, odd-shaped swords and knives from faraway lands. And, there, a salmon-killing club from an Alaskan fishing village with a hand-carved profile of a toothsome pelican leering from each side.

"When I first came to Claremont, I remember being very impressed when Harold showed me a picture album of a trip they'd made up the Inside Passage to Alaska," said Mack Parks.

Outside of their penchant for exotic travel, the Bruners were strictly bourgeois. They raised their four daughters to address their parents with respect and to mind their table manners—especially when they were around Harold's business colleagues or one of the Bruners' frequent dinner guests.

"They were just a very fine family . . . a close-knit family. Some people might say too close-knit," said Harland Hogue, a religious studies professor at the Claremont Colleges, where he came to know the Bruners well during the forties and fifties.

"They hardly ever went anywhere without the whole family being involved. I think both Harold and Marie were very sincere, good people. They just believed in a very old-fashioned idea of a home. The father and mother called the tunes and the children obeyed. I don't say this without kindness because I respected them both and they both were friends. I went to their home many times for dinners. But that was sort of the family status quo: when you went there, the girls only spoke when they were spoken to. It was somewhat patriarchal. That was very evident."

"Claremont" was a serendipity word selected by Boston land developers because it seemed to mean clear mountain air and water. At the turn of the century, the town of Claremont consisted of a Victorian train station, an ornate hotel and a few smaller outbuildings. By 1940, when the Bruners arrived from Iowa, much of the railroad land that the Boston developers had hoped to subdivide into a fortune was transformed into Pomona College—the centerpiece of a 250-acre multicollege campus modeled after England's Oxford colleges. The shaded avenues are named for eastern Ivy League colleges, with Claremont City Hall sandwiched between Harvard and Yale streets. Unlike the commuter schools with which Southern California is most often identified, the Claremont Colleges are still characterized by broad lawns, treelined promenades, venerable stone lecture halls and old money.

Harold and Marie enrolled their eldest daughter, Betty, at Pomona College and sent the three younger girls to the Claremont public schools: Marilyn and Gretchen to Claremont High and young Marguerite to Sycamore Elementary.

The Bruners also cultivated the cream of Claremont's small-town society. By 1940, they were approaching middle age, but it was clear that they intended to partake of the good life. The Bruners were poised to enjoy an early semiretirement.

"They participated in the whole community," recalled Hogue. "Anything that happened at the college, they supported: music, art, lectures. Claremont has a big auditorium and the Los Angeles Symphony came out three or four times a year. The Bruners were always there."

Harold became a scholarly man about town. Marie evolved into something of a dilettante.

"They were both very forceful, aggressive people in the positive sense," recalled Hogue. "I mean, if you wanted somebody to chair a committee, you got on the phone and called them. . . . They were very stable, dependable, loyal . . . good citizens in the best sense. But they were dominating personalities. I say that just trying to be objective."

During the war, Harold took up the cause of civil defense, preaching a strong home front to bolster the boys in the Pacific. He and Marie also immersed themselves in their church, mixing

the teachings of the Claremont Congregationalists with the beliefs of the Kentucky-based charismatic movement called the
Disciples of Christ—an evangelical faith both Harold and Marie
inherited from their fathers. Harold joined the Monday Morning
Men's Group—an informal gathering of Christian men like
himself.

"You can't talk about the Bruners without talking about religion," said Hogue. "That's part of the picture. They were very
active and devoted to this. They were very ardent members of
the Disciples of Christ."

The fundamentalist sect, founded in 1832 by a pair of dissident
Scottish Presbyterians and a Kentucky Baptist, matched Mor-
monism and Christian Science as one of the most widely followed
new Christian denominations to emerge from nineteenth-century America. Disciples of Christ preached a return to the absolute letter of the New Testament. The sect's fundamentalism
became so profound by the turn of the century that the Disciples
divided into warring camps over issues such as support of missionaries and the installation of organs in churches. Hard-line conservative members of the church maintained that the New
Testament never mentions anything about church organs or missionary societies. Therefore, the hard-liners argued, the Disciples of Christ should have no organs in their churches and should
not support missionaries.

But the Bruners followed a more liberal, if charismatic, brand
of worship.

"Harold was of the era when young people were very, very
religious," said his secretary, Laura Dennison. "It was a different
kind of fervor, almost a missionary zeal.

"And Marie spoke in tongues. She had buttons around that
house that said things like, 'Please forgive me: God's not finished
with me yet.' He was this very intelligent person and she was a
quasi-mystic."

They believed in a return to fundamentalism and the miraculous aspects of early Christianity, though Harold was not smug
about his religion. Few men in town had a more liberal open-

door policy. During holidays, the Bruner house was often the most festive on the block. They dressed in costume at Halloween, bought new dresses for the girls at Easter and hung the flag on the Fourth of July.

The family lived in a beautiful home on the west side of Claremont three blocks from the campus. Within a few years, the Bruners' gala Christmas parties had become so popular that they often attracted a hundred guests or more.

"I think, looking back on it, Claremont was an interesting place to live because you had the academic group and you had the business group and you had the retirees as a group," said Hogue. "And sometimes the groups remained rather separate and did not mingle too well. Some of the businesspeople were a little too interested in commerce and some of the academic people were a little stuffy.

"But the Bruners were friends with all three groups. They had lots of friends in the college and business community. Harold was very wealthy and a handsome man. Both the Bruners were. Both of them tall, striking-looking people. Mrs. Bruner could speak as clearly, forcefully and vigorously as her husband," Hogue continued.

That's how she came to be an annual lecturer in his world religions course at all-female Scripps College. His students studied the religions of India during the first semester each year: Hinduism, Buddhism, Jainism, Zoroastrianism.

"But when we came to Zoroastrianism, there were not too many things in the library about it, even though they were a very influential group. I remembered the Bruners saying that, in their world travels, they had been in Bombay and had somehow received an invitation to a very wealthy [Parsi] family wedding. I had heard them talk about this very beautiful wedding, so I asked her to come to the class.

"So every year she came and told about this wedding. She was very intelligent and described in detail how the bride and groom were dressed and gave us a marvelous picture. She was very eloquent. She had that ability."

Marie also spoke to high school and civic organizations about her family's world travels. As part of their entry into the social life of their new community, Marie joined a sorority called the PEO Sisterhood while Harold joined the University Club—an all-male mix of academics, businessmen, clergy and professionals. With a median age of sixty-seven, members tended to be retired members of the Claremont Colleges establishment.

When the question of allowing women to join the University Club came up, as it would periodically, Harold was among those who regularly opposed it. According to Bruner's account of the club's infrequent debates, it "was discussed with the gallantry, the penetrating acumen and the judicial fairness characteristic of the academic masculine mind."

He was a genteel traditionalist in an era that encouraged such behavior. As for Bruner's girls, they might have fit as easily into the plot of Jane Austen's *Pride and Prejudice* as Bruner himself.

"The Bruner girls wore their hair up in braids like their mother and always seemed to dress in a distinctly Scandinavian way," recalled classmate B. J. Barnes. "They were a presence."

A restrained presence, however.

"They were all lovely, well mannered, intelligent and outgoing when they were away from their parents," said Hogue.

When their parents were nearby, "they took their silent place unless you asked them a question," Hogue added.

Betty Marie, born in 1920, was the oldest and looked the most like her mother. At Pomona College, while her sisters were still in high school, she found John Crowell: a geology major whose professor father held a doctorate and whose academic prospects seemed way beyond the parochial reach of the Claremont Colleges. While Crowell finished out World War II as an army air force captain, he and Betty became engaged. In 1946 she became the first of the Bruner girls to marry.

Marilyn, the second oldest, was not so quick to the altar. She had her father's intellectual determination and her mother's aristocratic poise. As tall and willowy as her younger sisters, she turned out to be the least likely of the four Bruner girls to give up her career for a man. When she graduated from Claremont in 1942, after the Bruners had only been California residents for two years, Marilyn dominated her graduating class at Claremont High. She was elected Girls' League president, secured a lead role in the senior play, won the DAR citizenship award and earned straight As to boot.

She was serious, competitive and socially conscious. Marilyn earned a degree in sociology and psychology at Pomona College and tried to put it to use in a career. She became a professional YMCA director—first in nearby Pomona and later in the Los Angeles suburb of Alhambra. She was the last of the Bruner girls to marry, waiting until she was nearly thirty. She didn't move to Santa Monica to start a family with her new husband, Paul Adkins, until the mid-1950s.

Gretchen was the family knockout with winsome eyes, creamy complexion, a dancer's posture and a short, blond mane of Rheingold hair that she styled into waves or kept tucked into a French twist. She carefully followed in Marilyn's footsteps through high school. Like her older sister, she presided over Girls' League, starred in the senior play and made the honor roll.

But once out of high school, she followed the path blazed by her oldest sister, Betty. A year after earning her bachelor's degree from Pomona College, Gretchen became the wife of doctoral candidate Calvin Catterall. In 1950 they wed in Pomona's Bridges Auditorium, where Betty had married John Crowell four years earlier.

Harold's master plan for marrying off his daughters worked best of all with his youngest, though he couldn't have known it when he and Marie first moved in next door to the Miller family.

Roy George and Ednabel Miller were not nearly so auspicious a couple as the Bruners. They were both native Californians: Ednabel, the daughter of a Methodist minister from nearby Garden Grove, and Roy, the son of the first Ford dealer in the Pomona Valley.

They met as undergraduates at Pomona College in the early

1920s and led quiet middle-class lives together for the rest of the century, never moving from the neat stone and wood house at the corner of Berkeley and Eleventh streets that they had built for themselves in 1935.

At the close of World War I, Roy had done his stint in the army, just like Harold Bruner. Unlike the well-traveled Bruner, Roy served close to home: twenty-five miles east of Claremont, with the Army Air Force Medical Corps at March Field in Riverside, California. He went to business school after he was discharged in 1919 and later drove a stagecoach between Mount Baldy and the town of Upland. When he entered Pomona College, the earnest, stern-faced young economics major was a few years older than most of his classmates.

"The college has recognized Roy George Miller as one of its most loyal members," wrote the editor in Pomona College's 1924 *Metate* yearbook. "Holding membership with the YMCA cabinet as vice-president, with Lyceum [a debating club] and with the Sigma Tau fraternity, of which he has been president, he has further shown his interest by entering class baseball, belonging to the varsity squad as a sophomore."

Roy was as laconic as his first son and namesake. He was a serious man of few words, weighed carefully and well before they were uttered. He was invited to deliver the annual Lincoln Day address to the La Verne Lions Club for years, in part because he resembled the sixteenth President without the stovepipe hat and chin whiskers. Roy believed in hard work, conservative business practices and Christian principles.

Chubby-cheeked Ednabel, who loved the great outdoors and remained a Camp Fire girl through her undergraduate years in college, aimed for a career in teaching. She joined the campus literary society, the Math Club and the Astronomical Club, and wore the fashions of the day, bobbing her hair like Clara Bow so that she resembled a cleft-chinned "It Girl."

They married in 1925, but didn't have their first son, Roy David, until four years later. By that time, Ednabel was a junior high math teacher in Pomona and her husband had secured his position as assistant manager of the La Verne Fruit Exchange.

The elder Roy Miller was one of a handful of executives who made the deals with East Coast buyers for the trainloads of oranges, grapefruit and lemons produced in the groves around Claremont. Cheap land, cheap Mexican labor and cheap transportation, brought on by cutthroat competition between the Southern Pacific and Santa Fe railroads, made the navel orange and lemon business a $3-million-a-year operation for the growers and packinghouse owners around Claremont, even in the middle of the Great Depression.

By the mid-1930s, Roy had also become a founding member of the La Verne Lions Club and Ednabel had accepted a position on the Claremont Public School Council, where she eventually was elected president. In the meantime, they became parents for a second time: Roy David's younger brother, Marvin Dale Miller, was born in 1932.

"They were a regular salt-of-the-earth family," observed Don Wheeler, son of a pioneer Claremont family. "There's not much more you can say about them."

The Millers were determined that their children would fare better than they had. Like the Bruners' daughters, the Millers' sons would be encouraged to go to college, find a suitable mate and settle down. Roy David would become a lawyer, and his younger brother would become a clinical pathologist.

Almost from the day the Bruners moved in next door, Roy David took a fancy to the youngest of Harold and Marie Bruner's girls.

Marguerite was nine. Roy was ten. For social standards of Claremont during the 1940s, neither was perfect. While a war-bred machismo was the posture of most of the boys at the time, Roy remained brainy and gentle. The girls might be swooning over Frank Sinatra, Bing Crosby or any man in a uniform, but Marguerite swooned only over the boy next door.

Roy grew up with a fierce appreciation of religion, the outdoors and music, and so did Marguerite. Roy played the cello. Marguerite played violin. Roy was a Boy Scout. Marguerite hiked the Claremont foothills with her sisters. Both of them tall and skinny, they were made for each other.

Roy and Marguerite saw each other every day, including Sundays. Like the Bruners, the Millers attended Claremont's only real Protestant church: the big stone Claremont Community Church on Harrison Avenue in the center of town. From the outset of what turned out to be their long courtship, Roy and Marguerite sang together. They sang in school. They sang in church. By the time they were in Claremont High, they were singing to each other.

Roy asked her to the prom and Marguerite asked him to the Sadie Hawkins dance. Neither of them was pinup material, but they didn't need to be. As acquaintances would come to understand instantly in later years, Roy and Marguerite had a tender relationship based on a deep, mutual understanding of each other's frailties that literally dated back to childhood. They never really considered marrying anyone else.

With her flyaway sandy-blond hair, wide-set eyes and extreme slenderness, Marguerite would never rival Gretchen for her beauty or Marilyn for her proud poise. Her chances of landing a doctoral candidate with her feminine charms alone were as slender as her body.

But then Roy was no doctoral candidate when Harold and Marie first met him. He was a skinny, lantern-jawed son of a citrus seller. In addition to proving himself to his own demanding parents, Roy now had the added burden of proving himself to the Bruners.

Though he never distinguished himself as much of a hitter or fielder, Roy played varsity baseball three years in a row for the Claremont High Wolfpack. He ran in the track team's lightweight relay team and took up tennis, as much to please his tennis-playing sweetheart as to add another sports emblem to his letterman's jacket.

He played his cello for the school talent shows and even tried his hand at stage acting when the drama coach needed an actor to portray a kindly victim for the melodramatic 1940s murder mystery *Through the Night.*

But Roy's real success lay in academics. He joined and remained a member of the Scholarship Society all the way through high school. Whereas his classmates would describe themselves in the 1947 Claremont High yearbook with adjectives such as "individualistic," "frank," "shy" or "humorous," Roy described himself with two nouns: "statistics" and "cello." In a way, it was both accurate and prophetic. His razor-sharp statistical mind would carry him to the top ranks of tax lawyers, but his love of music would preserve his soul.

Marguerite's self-styled graduation description was equally prophetic, if persistently puzzling. Beside her picture in the 1948 yearbook was a list of her musical and athletic (hockey, tennis, Pep Club) accomplishments, along with a series of three words commemorating her six years at Claremont High and Junior High: "violin," "Roy" and "hearse." What she may have meant by equating her love of music and young Mr. Miller with a funeral carriage remains a riddle lost with time.

In the spring of 1952 Marguerite graduated from Pomona College and announced her betrothal to Roy. The couple went to Harland Hogue to ask him to marry them.

"Some couples are relatively easy to counsel. Others are a little more difficult. They're more restrained. I just remember that Roy Miller was not as outgoing as some potential grooms are. Nothing against him, though. He was quiet. She did the talking," remembered Hogue.

Roy also took a number two position at their wedding. He had already been away from Claremont for a year, and his return from Stanford to claim his bride was a step back in time for him. In contrast, Marguerite was effervescent, newly graduated and radiant.

Some 350 guests turned out for the wedding of Miss Marguerite Joan Bruner to Mr. Roy David Miller. Once again, Harold gave away one of his daughters in venerable old Bridges Auditorium, where the Los Angeles Symphony came to play several times each year. The aisles were decked out in pink gladiolus, pink candles and pink nosegays and white taffeta, satin and lace.

"Because a lot of the Scripps students had no pastor of their own or they were away from home or they wanted to be married there on campus, I just had dozens and dozens of weddings, most of which were happy affairs," said Hogue. "But this was very happy. And, of course, the Bruners were so highly thought of that many people came out for this wedding."

Marguerite wore pearls, veil, Chantilly lace and a white bouffant dress, trailed by a white train over white satin. Her bouquet was a single white orchid surrounded by feathered coral carnations and white, waxy, sweet-scented stephanotis blossoms. Following a gala reception at the Bruners' home, the couple left for three weeks in Colorado and Northern California before settling in Los Altos in the fall to begin Roy's second year at Stanford Law.

Marie Bruner may have been robust in her youth, but by the time her youngest daughter married Roy Miller and moved to Northern California, she had begun to fall into ill health. After all the girls had left home, it was her husband who increasingly ruled the roost and influenced the lives of both his daughters and his grandchildren.

"Mrs. Bruner had some very serious illnesses before she died," recalled Harland Hogue. "She traveled to the East for treatment and was under medical care for some time. I don't think there was anything psychological so far as I knew. Of course, we all know very little about other people, it seems."

As Marie Bruner's health failed, Harold sold their home next door to the Millers and moved about a mile away to a 2,600-square-foot custom-built home in the Mount Baldy foothills, with central air-conditioning, a greenhouse, pool and deck. The Bruners still entertained, but their home was no longer the salon where Claremont's tripartite society of academics, retirees and citrus growers came together. Instead of throwing lavish block parties, they concentrated on being grandparents. Most of the grandchildren paid regular visits and often attended church with Harold and Marie, when she was able. Despite her cancer, Marie passed on her love for music and miracles. Harold taught them to love books . . . especially the Bible.

One thing that Marguerite's mother remained throughout her declining years was a cultured Christian blue blood and a believer in the American Dream. The Bruners' position was hard-won, not bestowed by birth. Both Leona Marie and her husband had inculcated noblesse oblige in their daughters and even their grandchildren, demanding a strong sense of family pride, love of success and an abiding respect for Christian mysticism.

Claremont's orange industry began a long, slow fade in the fifties and sixties. After World War II, the influx of postwar families into Southern California made the orchards far more valuable for subdivisions than agriculture. As farmers sold off orchard after orchard, and citrus trees were uprooted and burned to make way for bungalows, the fortunes of the La Verne Fruit Exchange plunged. Roy Miller's parents watched helplessly as their livelihood withered and died.

In 1960 the last packinghouse in La Verne shut down and so did the Exchange. Roy George Miller retired, his career having spanned the citrus era in the Pomona Valley.

The Miller boys had made the right career decisions. Their father's profession was now part of history, at least in Southern California. But the world would always need top-notch doctors and honest, hardworking lawyers. Marvin became a leading member of the medical staff of West Allis Medical Center in a well-to-do suburb of Milwaukee. His brother, Roy, joined the most prestigious law firm in Los Angeles.

The La Verne Lions Club that the boys' father helped to found in 1928 was one of the last bastions of the old citrus industry, but it also faded. Before Roy George became too deaf and feeble to attend his service club luncheons, his son Roy occasionally went with him to meetings whenever he could get away from his law practice. That, too, eventually came to an end.

"There are only about a dozen members left in the Lions Club," said Gaylan Smith. "It is the end of an era. Roy [George] Miller was the last manager of the La Verne Fruit Exchange, but he stopped coming to meetings years ago too."

On March 8, 1993, Roy George Miller died at his Claremont home, Ednabel at his side. He was ninety-five.

When Marie Buxton Bruner died in August 1979, she was eighty-four years old. In her will, she left $5,000 to the Christian youth group Teen Challenge in Cucamonga. She also left clear and proper instructions that $10,000 was to be spent on a family pictorial history, depicting the Bruners' world travels. Each of her ten grandchildren, including the two sons that had been born to Roy Miller and her youngest daughter, Marguerite, were to receive copies of the family history.

Harold Bruner turned out to be his wife's executor, at least for a short while. He carried on another fifteen months and two days after Marie passed away. He busied himself writing histories of both the United Church of Christ Congregational and the University Club. He also began making arrangements to establish a camping scholarship in Marie's memory for the younger members of the Bruners' church.

But he never finished his work.

Harold collapsed of heart failure in church just before morning services on the last Sunday morning in November 1980. His daughters and his grandchildren—especially Roy and Marguerite's sons, Jeff and Michael—were heartbroken.

He left an estate worth $311,000. As scrupulous in death as he was in life, Harold Bruner's estate demanded a premium refund of $103.80 from the American Association of Retired Persons when the organization canceled his health insurance. The Automobile Club of Southern California also returned $12.31 in prorated 1980 dues and *TV Guide* refunded his subscription. Even the IRS refunded $1,121.

Harold named his eldest daughter, Betty, executor of his estate. His daughter Gretchen got his 1975 Mercedes 280 sedan and each of the ten grandchildren received $1,000 from the Bruner estate.

On August 2, 1981, nineteen-year-old Michael David Miller signed the receipt for his $1,000 share of his grandparents' estate.

His older brother, Jeffrey, never got his. By the time his share of the Bruners' estate was ready, he had been dead for six months.

— 3

The Miller boys grew up in a very different California than Roy Miller, his younger brother, Marvin, or any of the Bruner sisters had.

Jeffrey was born in 1957 shortly after the Millers returned to California from Oklahoma. Michael was born four and a half years later, in 1962. They were California natives, like their father, but the Southern California they inherited was measured in big-city angst, not small-town dreams.

By the late 1950s, when the Millers first became parents, the brand-new San Bernardino Freeway ripped through the Pomona Valley, replacing the old Southern Pacific *Superchief*. Six lanes of traffic thundered past the quiet coffee shops and tree-shaded avenues of the college town where Roy and Marguerite Miller grew up.

It was a rough-and-tumble future that young lawyer Roy Miller had prepared to meet head-on, but his bride feared this brave new world at times. She hid from it and prayed on Sundays for dispensation whenever it got beyond her control. She fought the environmentally toxic urban encroachment by staying healthy.

She hiked and exercised and ate a natural macrobiotic diet and encouraged her husband to follow suit.

Before settling down to start a family, Marguerite and Roy had temporarily escaped the hurly-burly of postwar Los Angeles by relocating to Stanford. Cradled in its own valley at the base of the San Francisco Peninsula foothills, the university afforded the same cultural opportunities they had both enjoyed at Pomona College: concerts, plays, lectures. Palo Alto even resembled Claremont with its modest small-town business district of coffeehouses and bookstores, surrounded by broad, shady residential avenues and two-story, turn-of-the-century Victorian houses.

Marguerite could afford to enjoy this new place, but Roy had his work cut out for him just getting through Stanford Law School. The class two years ahead of him would yield two Supreme Court justices. Several members of his own class would go on to become federal judges. The competition was so intense, even during the fifties, that one-third of the first-year law class flunked out after passing the stiff admission criteria.

While her husband finished his last two years, Marguerite taught elementary school in the Ravenswood district east of Palo Alto. They delayed starting their family until they were ready. Theirs was a well-planned union, with Marguerite carefully plotting their lives together. It would be the perfect family.

After Roy graduated from Stanford in 1954, the young couple spent some time at Fort Sill, Oklahoma, while Roy served out his army time. When he returned to Los Angeles, he found that passing through the Stanford gauntlet virtually guaranteed entree into the legal profession. His future wasn't easy, but it was assured.

"Law was still a profession in those days," said J. Keith Mann, one of Roy's law professors. "It is no longer. It has become a bottom-line routine and the first thing you do is kill the associates by overworking them and squeezing them so that they'll leave."

As a Gibson, Dunn and Crutcher associate in the late fifties, Roy might have had a heavy workload, but there was very little squeezing. He was on his way. Marguerite was finally ready to have children.

The contrasts between the two Miller boys were sharp and unmistakable from the very beginning. Jeffrey was curious and gregarious—the one more likely to hang out with the guys after school or search for drowned earthworms in the gutter puddles up the street after a downpour. Michael was shy. He spent more of his childhood peeking out at the world from behind his mother's full skirts.

Marguerite fussed over him, racing to his crib each time he cried. She nursed him until he was seven months old. He seemed to constantly need her attention and she always came running. The bond between Michael and his mother was tight and close.

Then she got pregnant a third time. The pregnancy was unexpected and troubled almost from the start. Marguerite spent most of her time in the bathroom or in bed and did not always come when Michael cried at night. She had to stop breast-feeding him too. She miscarried at four and a half months and remained in bed a few weeks longer, recuperating.

The Millers never had another child.

Marguerite regarded her children as her most precious responsibility and wanted to protect Jeffrey and Michael from the hazards of a fast-changing world. She began her work by controlling their diet. Jeffrey was steered away from candy, even during trick-or-treat time on Halloween. Michael was macrobiotic, even before he was born.

Marguerite converted all those around her to a diet of whole grains, raw vegetables and fresh fruit. She practiced what she preached, especially while she was pregnant, eating no refined sugars and limiting animal fats. From the moment they were born, she consistently kept her boys away from candies, crackers, cookies and cake—any of those snacks that came to be known by the euphemism "junk food." She understood the effects of cholesterol long before most of her neighbors had ever heard the term used by their doctors.

Only acquaintances not close to the Millers were spared Marguerite's lectures. She was not above a mild scold when she saw other parents' children devouring chocolate bars or ice cream cones.

"They were the first family I ever knew that knew what granola and alfalfa sprouts were," remembered one of the boys' earliest baby-sitters from the mid-sixties.

The Millers' first home after Roy went to work in Los Angeles was on a hillside in Pasadena, two blocks north of Sierra Madre Methodist Church and two blocks south of Don Benito Elementary School. From the beginning of their lives together, Roy and Marguerite instilled in their sons the twin values of religion and education. If one put one's heart into learning and one's faith in God, they reasoned, one's future was assured.

Their new home was a large tract house in a new subdivision, but there was little shrubbery along the treeless street. It was very unlike what Roy and Marguerite were used to back in Claremont, but it was a far cry from the dismal military housing in Oklahoma or the spartan student apartments that they endured while Roy was in law school. Besides, the bare yard gave Marguerite a free rein in planning her lavish garden.

Up and down the block, young white, upwardly mobile families like their own were moving in. Muriel and Ed Eley lived next door.

"She seemed like she was a good mother," said Muriel. "The only thing I could see was that she was a little strict with the kids as far as their diet was concerned. She was really into healthy diet: no sugar and stuff like that."

Though Marguerite was picky about the food her family ate, she wasn't much of a disciplinarian. Among enlightened parents, "planned permissiveness" was the catchphrase of the day, and the Millers prided themselves on being enlightened.

An older girl who lived across the street and used to stay with the boys while Roy and Marguerite were at church remembered how unruly Jeff and Michael could be at times—especially Michael, who exhibited all the characteristics of a hyperkinetic youngster: short attention span, giggling fits, flashes of temper that faded as quickly as they erupted. When Marguerite enrolled him in nursery school, he was asked to leave after a few weeks because of disruptive behavior.

"He was kicked out of nursery school and they said that he was just too aggressive and threatened kids with a truck over their heads in the sand pile," Marguerite remembered many years later. "We took him to a child guidance clinic they recommended in Pasadena and the head of it took his case, but there was very little improvement and little communication between the therapist and myself. Mike did not seem to like the man either. He was a man in his early forties, I suppose, and shuffled when he walked and I often wondered just what he did with Mike and if there was anything disturbing."

After that, Michael spent a lot of time playing by himself.

"He didn't seem to do much climbing on the bars and jungle gym as Jeff had," said Marguerite.

Marguerite seemed unusually solicitous no matter how badly her sons acted.

"We had a sliding glass door next to our garage that led into the den and the kitchen," remembered Muriel Eley. "Once, after the Millers had just moved in, Marguerite was over talking to me and one of the boys was holding on to her skirt. All of a sudden, he picks up a rock while we were talking and throws it at the sliding glass door!

"He didn't break it, but he did nick the door. Instead of swatting him or raising her voice or finding out why he did it, she just bent down and smiled at him and said, 'Now, you know you shouldn't do that,' in this tiny, soft-spoken voice. I couldn't believe she would just let him get away with it."

Despite the rocky beginning, both Miller boys quickly made up to the Eleys, especially when Muriel Eley and her daughter were baking. Before she knew about Marguerite's taboo on sugar, Mrs. Eley invited both boys over for fresh cookies and milk, only to hear about it later when Marguerite stormed to her front door. She stopped short of accusing the Eleys of poisoning her family, but her manner did seem both alarmist and a little condescending to Muriel.

"She had a lot of nerve," said Muriel Eley. "We hired some contractors once to do some remodeling work on our house. A few days into the work, my husband saw Mrs. Miller out in front talking to one of the men. The next thing we knew, they were gone and the work we had them doing had been left behind, only half-done. It turned out that she had convinced them to drop what they were doing at our house so that they could come over to her house and do some remodeling work for her."

In another instance, the Eleys had a small electrical fire in their home that got out of hand, causing a lot of smoke and some minor fire damage. The Eleys put it out, but not before calling for help. Before the fire department showed up, the Millers arrived at the front door for a tour of the damage, with Marguerite leading the way.

"They invited themselves in and traipsed all through the house, inspecting everything," said Mrs. Eley. "She wasn't mean about it. She could be very sweet. She just took over. She had a lot of nerve."

Marguerite attended every PTA meeting, every teacher-student conference, every recital, while they lived in Pasadena. She encouraged the boys to join the Glee Club and sing at Sunday school on weekends. Every Tuesday, she took them to choir practice. By junior high, Jeffrey had joined a school singing group. When he was only four, Michael started regular violin lessons as a participant in the fashionable Japanese Suzuki method of learning music. Marguerite never let either boy skip practice.

Roy was not nearly so omnipresent a parent. He spent more and more time at the office, socializing with clients before and after work. He was not an absentee father, though. During Little League games and soccer matches, Roy was there to cheer his boys on. Their teammates remember Roy officiating at some of the soccer games and wielding a bat now and again, the way his own father had done during his college days in the 1920s. When his sons joined the Boy Scouts, Roy became an adult leader, just as his own father had when he and Marvin were Scouts.

Jeff made Eagle Scout, but then Jeff excelled in almost everything he tried. He never auditioned for a chorale group without succeeding. He was ferocious on the soccer field. When he took up tennis and skiing, he became an expert. His mother bragged about him incessantly.

Michael was a different story. To begin with, he wet the bed.

Bed-wetting among preschoolers wasn't uncommon, physicians advised Marguerite. One in ten boys had trouble through the age of five and some youngsters continued to have accidents through their eighth or ninth birthday. But even the Millers became concerned when Michael continued to lose nocturnal bladder control regularly, all the way into junior high. Tests revealed no physiological problem, so Marguerite took the boy to a series of psychological specialists, all without results.

He remained hyper too, like a kid who had just snuck two Cokes and a Hershey bar on an empty stomach. Beginning in kindergarten, his quarrels with other children often ended with Michael landing a kick to their ribs or sinking his teeth into a classmate's arm. Teachers complained that they had to hover near him constantly.

The string of psychologists and physicians that Marguerite took him to recommended some kind of psychoactive medication, such as Ritalin or amphetamine. For reasons that the doctors were unable to explain, such prescription stimulants had just the opposite effect on hyperkinetic youngsters. A wild child on Ritalin could concentrate, improve his grades, even take a leadership role in his class.

Marguerite rejected drugs out of hand. Nutrition was the answer. Instead of getting angry when Michael's teachers called with the latest horror story, Marguerite gave her son a good scolding and redoubled her efforts to regulate his diet.

The school district had him tested in the second grade. To the Millers' pleasant surprise, the results showed that Michael was above the national average in intellectual potential. He had an I.Q. of 118.

But there were problems. The term "dyslexia" was not widely used or understood in the late sixties, but that was partly what appeared to afflict Michael. Quite simply, the test showed that, as bright as Michael was, the boy did not always register in his brain what he saw with his eyes. He seemed to read well enough, understanding as well as recognizing words and sentences, but he had trouble relating newly learned facts to those things that he already knew and understood.

In third grade, chiefly because of the test results, the Millers agreed to have Michael transferred to a learning disability class.

"He was always the hyper kid causing a ruckus in the orchestra," said Beth Pearson, who met Michael in fifth grade, just after his family had moved from Pasadena to Palos Verdes. "He was hyper even in elementary school. He didn't do well with grades and everyone always teased him. I always felt so sorry for him. He was always very intense, but not very focused. You definitely knew there was something different about him.

"He was a very good violin player, though, and he got teased for that. But he stuck with it. I admired that."

Playing the violin was a triumph in ways beyond overcoming social rejection. It was something that he could be very good at—even better than Jeff.

Michael had always been awkward—a product of gangly genes inherited from his parents. But unlike his brother's long-limbed angularity, Michael's muscle coordination didn't smooth into sleek athleticism with the years.

By the time the family moved to Palos Verdes in 1969, Michael was growing painfully aware with each passing year that Jeff was a winner who never seemed to disappoint his mother, actually measured up to his father's high standards of achievement on occasion and was one of the bright young people in the community.

Michael, on the other hand, was a geek.

The schools drew the Millers to the Hill in Palos Verdes as much as the sea breeze, the spectacular views or the proximity of Roy's professional peer group did.

"Palos Verdes is a sheltered environment. There is no sense of being part of L.A. It was kind of its own little island," said Jeff

Dollinger, a contemporary of both Jeff and Michael Miller. "It was a great place to be raised, although it contributed to my naïveté."

Unlike the Pasadena public schools, which had already begun to experience an influx of minorities, Palos Verdes remained predominantly white throughout the 1970s. It was the home of successful professionals whose children were driven, goal-oriented students. Teachers loved to teach and students loved—or pretended to love—to learn. Property taxes were high there, but the quality of education that those taxes subsidized during the seventies was at an all-time high.

"Ninety-seven percent of the kids at Palos Verdes High went on to higher education," said Connie McIntyre, who taught music to both Miller boys when they first arrived in Palos Verdes. "The mantra was: you *will* be successful . . . you *will* go on to other things."

The Palos Verdes school Jeff first attended was a venerable old intermediate school, built in 1926, overlooking Malaga Cove on the north side of the Peninsula.

"It was right next to the ocean with an open-field playground," said Keith Watson, the Malaga Cove principal at the time. "Architecturally it was Spanish-European. It was an ideal setting, with high academic achievement levels and very supportive parents."

It was a school without visible drugs or gangs or fights. When the school staged its annual open house, parents were advised to come early if they wanted a parking place. Christmas programs were grand songfests with standing room only. On the Fourth of July the school district sponsored a gala ice cream social. When the eighth-grade class graduated to high school, the auditorium was packed with more relatives than many college commencements.

"It was very folksy," said McIntyre. "I started there in 1967, left and came back. It was just a wonderful place to teach. No one rocked the boat and you had the ideal situation with eager students and a lot of involved parents. Sometimes, maybe overly involved."

Among the legion of concerned mothers, Marguerite was particularly vigilant: always poking into classrooms, calling up teachers to monitor her children's progress, volunteering for PTA duty. Always involved.

Roy came off more as a reluctant, or distracted, crusader.

"I do remember that the mom was always at our concerts. The dad came to concerts too and picked the kids up from rehearsal. He was always there, it seemed, but was not real talkative. She was very gabby, though. You'd meet Mrs. Miller at the bakery and she'd spend the longest time bragging about her college-bound son," McIntyre said.

The college-bound son she was talking about was Jeff. Michael's grades were as erratic as his temper. It was a constant worry to the Millers whether he would get into college at all. In the sixth grade in Palos Verdes, when he was retested for intelligence, he scored 85—a thirty-three-point drop from his score in second grade.

Jeff was smarter, faster, stronger and better-looking.

"In high school, Jeff was sort of gangly and slender, but he grew into himself. His physique filled out and his voice got deeper," said his classmate and close friend Phil Hogan.

Michael came to worship his older brother. Jeff served up the typical hazing older brothers do, pointing out his kid brother's shortcomings and "pounding" Michael when he got out of line. But he took care of him too, defending him against the slings and arrows of the most cruel rivals known to man or boy: other junior high students.

"Both of them were kind of like those type of kids who don't always get along with others all of the time, but get along together," McIntyre recalled.

They were Millers. They were different. They stuck together.

But as Jeff grew older, his perspective inevitably expanded. He made new friends in Palos Verdes, both male and female, and even Marguerite's strong, overly protective presence couldn't prevent him from growing up and becoming popular.

Michael was a different story.

"Mike was a very lonely person," said Don Brough, who became his counselor in high school. "I used to see him walking around town by himself. He liked the girls, I think, but he was such a pest.

He would tease them, pull their pigtails, and that was about as close as he could get."

In some ways, Michael was so envious of Jeff that he actually wanted to *become* his older brother. By design of age and genes, the older, wiser Jeff attracted girls while Michael repulsed them. Michael was always more frail, like his mother, while Jeff seemed to take after the old man. In the eighth grade, Michael began eating special foods loaded with protein in an attempt to appear more masculine. He also went on an exercise binge, eventually buying a set of barbells he kept on a weight stand next to the bed in his room. For all his androgynous frailty, he never lacked aggressiveness.

"He exhibited a certain belligerence, even in junior high," recalled one of his fellow orchestra members who got into a shoving match with him before a concert. "He pushed me into a bunch of chairs and I've had a bad back ever since. Michael was just a little bit stronger than I thought he was. That incident is probably why we never became very good friends."

That same classmate recalled another incident a year or two later in high school, when it was raining particularly hard and water was cascading off the school building roofs. Michael convinced several others to join him in pulling a younger boy under the torrent in order to get him wet. In the process of soaking him, the youngsters broke the boy's wrist. Michael was quick to point out when the finger of blame was being pointed that he didn't break it by himself. But he was the instigator of the prank.

Nor were these isolated incidents. Michael tussled with classmates often in junior high.

"I can't even remember the specific incident that caused the fight, but I had a confrontation with him at my locker once during junior high," said Roman Pena, another of Michael's Palos Verdes peers. "I raised my arm. He raised his arm. Next thing I knew, he broke my glasses."

Puberty was unkind to Michael—even more unkind than the metamorphosis tends to be with most people. He had already started to develop acne by junior high. It would get worse in high school. His pimpled, pitted complexion only increased his awkwardness and ostracism. Nevertheless, he continued to win respect with his music.

"Mike was a talented violin player, but very high-strung and moody," said Kurt Albershardt, whose own limited expertise with the violin put him in the back of the orchestra while Michael sat in the first chair. This pomposity struck a sour note among his peers. "The way he carried himself and the whole presence about his being . . . I don't want to say he was imperious, but he treated everyone like peasants. He didn't relate to other people," said Albershardt. "He deemed them unworthy of talking to him."

In the orchestra room, he was particularly vexing about his superior position as first chair. When anyone excused themselves during rehearsal and tried to scoot past Michael, he refused to budge. Kurt made the mistake of setting his violin on Michael's chair once. Michael ceremoniously picked it off the seat and threw it to the floor, breaking it.

"No violinist with any sense would throw it on the ground. Some violins cost a half million dollars," said Albershardt.

"I was one to yell at the kids," said Palos Verdes High music instructor Gary McRoberts. "I would throw keys at them and sometimes I'd pick chairs up and throw them at them. Mike was a talker—a quiet talker, but unnerving. We would have four-hour rehearsals and I'd expect everyone to be there listening. We worked very, very hard and I couldn't have people acting like little kids. He would go *psst!* to someone sitting nearby. I'd lead him out of the room and never let him back in."

McRoberts set a demanding pace for his singers.

"They rehearsed an hour a day during class and I made them rehearse during lunch—an hour at lunch," said McRoberts. "Tuesdays, we'd meet at somebody's house. The year we went to Europe, we did 170 concerts in 178 days of school and the kids still managed to be on athletic teams and keep up their academics."

Choirmaster McRoberts was not nearly so harsh a taskmaster as he leads people to believe. More than a decade after he left Palos

Verdes High, many of his students remember him with fond rever-
ence as being one of their best instructors: a hip yet demanding
perfectionist who was also easy to talk to about subjects that their
own parents couldn't or wouldn't understand.

He felt obliged to discipline Michael Miller at times, but he
listened to him too.

"Michael was one of five boys in their freshman year who went to
the music store to buy a little something for Mr. Mac," McRoberts
remembered with a wry grin.

The gift they bought for him was a record album containing the
infamous "Seven Dirty Words" monologue in which comedian
George Carlin makes light of mainstream America's horror at such
frank Anglo-Saxonisms as "fuck," "shit," "cunt," "dick" and
"motherfucker." At the time the five sniggering Palos Verdes High
freshmen bought the tape, the U.S. Supreme Court had just ruled
that those seven dirty words were so explicit they could not be
uttered over radio or television.

"Their parents, of course, wouldn't let them listen to that at
home," said McRoberts. "So they bought it and said, 'This is for
you. Can we listen to it?' "

Teachers like McRoberts understood that teens rarely feel comfortable chatting about sex, drugs or other taboos with older relatives, whether they be parents or grandparents. Often that
reluctance to talk extends into other sensitive areas of their lives,
cutting them off from adults altogether. That was especially true
in the Miller clan, where the strong religious beliefs of both the
Bruners and their Claremont neighbors, Ednabel and Roy Miller,
loomed large in the marriage of Marguerite and Roy David.

McRoberts heard confessions and concerns to which most parents were oblivious.

"A lot of students weren't getting their answers at home, so they
found out other ways. One of the ways was to hang around teachers
and ask questions. Michael was kind of that way," said McRoberts.

Michael's contemptuous attitude at Malaga Cove had mellowed
somewhat by high school. If anything, the gawky young man that
Gary McRoberts knew was less the jeering bully he had been in

junior high than he was the pale shadow of his older brother. Despite his endomorphic resemblance to Jeff, Michael remained emotionally immature all the way through high school.

"I have a five-year-old who wants to do everything his older sister does," said McRoberts. "I think Michael felt that way with a lot of teachers. We had to be careful of saying things like, 'Well, Jeff did this. Why can't you do this?' The right answer should have been, 'Well, I'm not Jeff, I'm Mike.' "

But if Michael ever made such a protest, few of his teachers were listening. He suffered the comparisons in silence.

"I had to make it clear for him just to be who he was. And if he didn't make all the groups that Jeff made, that was okay. I'm not sure he ever fully understood. Thinking back on it, he was always looking and searching and he was alone a lot," McRoberts recalled.

Michael graduated the year after Gary McRoberts left Palos Verdes High, but the first Miller that McRoberts encountered when he came to work there was Jeff. McRoberts sympathized with Michael. Jeff was a hard act to follow.

Jeff Miller wore his sandy-blond hair in a neat surfer shag, longish at the back and hanging ever so slightly over each ear. His sad blue eyes were set wide apart and a barely noticeable overbite gave the delicate bone structure he'd inherited from his mother the appearance of strength, especially around his squarish jaw.

He was six-foot-three and weighed about 175 pounds all the way through high school, but he never let his lean frame keep him from becoming an athlete. He played all four years at Palos Verdes High on the tennis team. He also played soccer as a junior and made annual treks to Mammoth Mountain with the Ski Club.

Jeff was a great student too, having been one of only a handful in the highly competitive high school to receive a commendation from the National Merit Scholarship Association upon graduation.

Throughout his high school years, Jeff never abandoned the music his mother taught him, winning a new and better seat each school year. First, he contributed his thickening baritone to McRoberts' A Cappella group for freshmen; then Madrigals, the next group up the ladder, when he became a sophomore. By his

junior year, Jeff had auditioned for and been accepted in Chorale—
the top singing group on campus. He also joined the Sun Machine,
a song and dance group that specialized in difficult harmonies that
ranged all the way from doo-wop and Dixie to Brubeck and Bach.

When compared to the inner-city school where McRoberts first
taught as a feckless young choir instructor fresh out of college,
Palos Verdes High School seemed to be a teacher's Mecca.

"I was at Dorsey High in '69, '70, and '71. Personally, I had no
problems with the kids, but [one] teacher wore a gun in a holster
to class," he said.

At Dorsey, down on the flatlands in South-Central Los Angeles,
McRoberts had students who had been arrested for dozens of felon-
ies: armed robbery, burglary, assault . . .

"We actually had a couple of guys in class who were out on
parole," he said.

By contrast, he discovered that being tardy twice in a row to
class was treated as a felony at Palos Verdes. Truancy was the
equivalent of a capital crime.

It was no surprise to McRoberts that there was no communication between Palos Verdes and the rest of Los Angeles. There was
simply no common ground. When McRoberts crossed Pacific Coast
Highway from Torrance and climbed into the Peninsula foothills,
it was like crossing a border. In the rearview mirror he saw shoe-
box apartment buildings, 7-Elevens, drive-in movies and treeless
block after treeless block of stucco houses with slab foundations.
Up ahead were eucalyptus-lined concourses that ran past quarter-
acre horse ranches, members-only tennis clubs, cliff-edge mansions
and Jacuzzi lifestyles.

"I had a friend who lived in a guesthouse, removed from his
parents' house, in the old part of Palos Verdes, beyond Malaga
Cove," recalled Doug Kaback, one of Michael's classmates and a
member of McRoberts' Chorale. "This friend was fourteen or fifteen
at the time and he had his own house that you had to go through
a little wooded area to get to. His own house!

"On the other side of the hill from us was Torrance. We hated
Torrance. Can you see how kids who have their own *house* at

fifteen would come to look down on a place like Torrance? It was classic middle-class America and we didn't want to be associated with it."

At Palos Verdes, McRoberts' annual department budget for choral and musical performances alone was over $50,000, a sharp contrast to the $50 he'd been allotted at Dorsey. He was able to take his singers on performance field trips all over the country; to host choral extravaganzas that would have made Johannes Brahms beam; and to stage Broadway musicals that rivaled some of Southern California's best professional civic light opera.

The year he arrived, the school put on a version of *Hello Dolly!* in which Jeff Miller had a small role. It was a production that would have received a standing ovation from Barbra Streisand *and* Carol Channing. It helped that no expense was spared in the costumes, lighting and set design. But the young singers and actors were more than a cut above other high school players too.

"The only equal we had was Beverly Hills High," said McRoberts' fellow music teacher Chip Hipkins. "All these kids had had singing and dancing lessons since they were in diapers. They were semiprofessionals even in high school. We tackled plays like *The Crucible*; musicals like *Man of La Mancha*. And they were *not* like any high school productions I'd ever seen before. Or since."

In such an atmosphere, it was easy to forget that the adult performances were being carried off by teenagers, many of whom had been pushed into a sophistication way beyond their years. It didn't take long for McRoberts to learn that the pressure of sustained happy faces among the children of the very rich could be deadly.

"The first year I was there, there was a thirteen-year-old who fell off one of the cliffs," recalled McRoberts. "He was a freshman. He's sitting in his living room one day and he just gets up and leaves the room. He ran and ran and ran and ran, right off a 250-foot cliff outside his house.

"I felt real bad afterwards. I find out later he's been in therapy for quite a while. A thirteen-year-old. I used to talk to the kid. He seemed fine."

That first tragedy snapped open his eyelids. The happy-go-lucky teens McRoberts chaperoned on singing field trips to jazz festivals in Reno and Monterey and as far away as Montreux in Switzerland, no longer seemed like the Brady Bunch.

"There was one girl who came to Palos Verdes in her senior year and she was so stoned, she didn't know where she was," he remembered. "She lived with her mother, and her father felt so guilty for not being there that he gave her money and never asked what she used it for. She would walk around stoned in class. One day I just said, 'Get her out of here.'

"I talked to her a few days later and said, 'If you ever come on this campus again like that, you're going to jail or getting help.'

"She said, 'I wasn't doing anything.'

"I said, 'Laurie, we all sat here and watched you drool all over yourself. You were an absolute idiot.'

"She said, 'I didn't do anything. You're making it up. I don't do those things.'

"I said, 'Laurie, if you do it again, I'm going to *get* you and that's the bottom line.'

"Four years later, she was dead."

There was a minimum of one such student tragedy each of the six years he spent at Palos Verdes, according to McRoberts. Usually, it was a teen who had learned how to mask pain over a period of years. Their teachers were their parents and guardians: adults who were masters at the put-on-a-good-face routine. Because they were brighter and far more sophisticated than the poor minority students at Dorsey, who tended to wear their hearts on their sleeves, these rich and troubled students succeeded in going unnoticed—even to teachers like Gary McRoberts.

"You know, the unfortunate thing is we don't always identify them," he said. "And we're a little hesitant as teachers also, I think, to go up and say: I think there's a problem here and we should look into it. Because what if you're wrong? Are you going to get sued for slander or something like that?"

After he left Palos Verdes to teach at a junior college in Orange County, McRoberts took years of photo albums from his music field trips with him. Jeff Miller is featured in most of the albums, alternately decked out in a tuxedo or clowning for the camera along with the rest of McRoberts' troops, wearing T-shirts that read, "We're bitchin' cuz we're from P.V."

"I knew these kids as well as anyone, but I didn't know them either. Not really. No one does," said McRoberts as he pored over the photo albums. He has tried to keep track of their progress over the years. Few have become what they thought they would.

"This kid was a great guitar player and went into computers," said McRoberts, pointing to a frizzy-haired Bob Dylan look-alike in a jaundiced snapshot. "He still plays once in a while.

"This gal right here—June was her name—she used to argue for hours with this girl, Lisa. June was an atheist and into bodybuilding. She called herself 'Thunder Thighs.' I understand after high school she found some rich guy after she worked at Cordon Bleu's restaurant as a chef or something.

"Here's another guy who became a chef, up in San Francisco," he continued, pointing to a moon-faced youth with a mop of black, early-Beatles hair. "This one here, Tony, he's an actor in Hollywood. This guy's father was the vice president of Exxon. He works in theater tech. He was an Eagle Scout, like Jeff."

The photo album featured a trip that they had taken in 1975 to Northern California and Reno, said McRoberts. It was the year Jeff graduated from high school and Michael graduated from junior high.

On that trip, the troupe of about two dozen Chorale members stopped their bus the first afternoon for a snack in the Central Valley town of Three Rocks. They all piled out and went into a roadside diner, where everyone ordered up ice cream sundaes. As he spooned the vanilla into his mouth, Jeff told one of his friends that it was the first time he had ever tasted ice cream. At home, he said, he was never allowed to eat it.

Both Jeff and Michael always carried two suitcases with them when they went on field trips, said McRoberts. One contained clothes and toiletries. The other contained food that their mother had packed for them.

"He'd [Jeff] get upset with Mom," said McRoberts as he flipped through the photo album. "There was no display of any violence. He never went into a fit of rage. But he did talk about it."

McRoberts had heard scores of teenage boys before and after Jeff Miller grumbling about their mothers' hovering attentions, but not like Jeff. Marguerite controlled him and his younger brother like a couple of Ken dolls. They didn't like the control, but at the same time they cared deeply for their mother.

Caught by the camera laughing and horsing around with his peers, Jeff looked as though he hadn't a care in the world during the Chorale field trip. But none of them did.

Pointing to a photo of a grinning fellow in an impromptu street-corner singing scene, McRoberts said, "This guy's gone to halfway houses and everything else. He was fine until after high school. Then he got strung out on heroin. This guy's a doctor, or trying to be. This is his little sister. Their father was a football coach. I think Jeff was into football too."

McRoberts' finger stopped on a photo of a forlorn figure he identified only as "Kathy." Except for her eyes, she looked like a homecoming princess bundled up against some cold winter wind. Her smile was frozen and her cheeks were high, but there was just the hint of worry or sorrow—or both, perhaps—beneath those eyes.

She was a real trouper who sang with the group all through high school, just like Jeff, McRoberts explained. She liked boys and she liked parties. She was quite talented—even wrote songs for the group, he said. She and McRoberts had philosophized often about life and love and all of those related subjects that tend to be the grist of late-night coffee-shop conversations: Is there a God? Why are we here? Why is evil allowed to coexist with good?

Kathy was bright, talented, pretty . . . a typical P.V. teen with a golden future laid out before her, according to McRoberts. Or so it seemed.

It wasn't until afterward that he learned she had been in psychiatric counseling for over two years, that their conversations may have carried far more weight than he could ever possibly have imagined and that she may have been an early victim of incest.

"She went to a ballet one night," said McRoberts. "She came home, wrote a song for the girls' ensemble, doused herself with gasoline and lit a match. She was seventeen."

4

During the 1970s, Roy Miller's law firm catapulted to international authority and prestige, with branches in New York, Seattle, Denver, Washington and Dallas and foreign bureaus in London, Paris, Tokyo, Riyadh and Hong Kong. By mid-decade, Gibson, Dunn and Crutcher—formed in 1903 with the merger of Bicknell, Gibson and Trask and Dunn and Crutcher—routinely described itself in superlatives: biggest, most prestigious, most diverse, most powerful.

With over two hundred lawyers billing as high as $200 an hour an average of nearly two thousand hours each year, Gibson, Dunn and Crutcher had money, prospects and a client list that read like the Fortune 500: Pfizer Inc., Rockwell International, Times Mirror, Bank of America—even the U.S. Postal Service and the government of Saudi Arabia turned to Miller's partners for legal advice.

Among his colleagues, Roy Miller counted former Assistant Secretary of the Treasury Gerald Parsky, former Securities and Exchange Commissioner Francis Wheat and nationally known antitrust expert Julian Von Kalinowski. The firm's litigation department gained a fierce reputation as a small army of about eighty hard-nosed trial lawyers who rarely settled and spent their clients' resources freely in order to drown opponents in paper. Its corporate and business law department was equally ferocious, supervising some of the biggest stock offerings, mergers and corporate takeovers in U.S. history.

Roy himself was one of twenty-nine lawyers in the tax/probate department. Taxation was not as glamorous as trial work or negotiating multimillion-dollar corporate raids, but it had its moments. When billionaire recluse Howard Hughes died of kidney failure in 1976, for example, Gibson, Dunn and Crutcher was consulted in the handling of probate. When L.A.'s corporate elite needed shelter from the IRS, Gibson, Dunn and Crutcher structured trusts and tax shelters that helped build personal fortunes.

Miller now found himself working in a department headed by Gulf Oil Corporation's tax attorney, Norman Barker, and Times Mirror board member (and husband of *Los Angeles Times* heiress Camilla Chandler) F. Daniel Frost. As tax lawyers, they operated at the very heart of American power: creating and holding on to capital.

Roy developed a reputation as a shrewd if conservative tax slasher, who operated with impeccable honesty but still managed to skew the numbers in his clients' favor. He won praise for his tax wizardry, but he was not destined to endure his entire career parked behind a desk with his sleeves rolled up and a calculator in hand, banging out numbers over somebody else's Form 1040. After nearly twenty years with the firm, his quiet, determined manner had gained for him the respect and trust of senior partner William French Smith.

Smith was a no-nonsense blue-blood conservative who believed in business because America *was* business. He was a Harvard Law graduate and a member of the exclusive California Club. He also held memberships in the ancient, secretive Bohemian Grove conclave elite and, on the East Coast, maintained membership in the General Society of Mayflower Descendants and Sons of the American Revolution.

Smith was, more importantly, a founding member of Governor Ronald Reagan's "kitchen cabinet." He was among the very first to urge Reagan to run for President. As early as 1966, Smith helped chart the road map that would lead Reagan to 1600 Pennsylvania Avenue.

He kept a low profile but had strong opinions about coddling society's miscreants. Smith had no patience for student protesters, welfare cheats, draft dodgers, bleeding hearts, criminals or malingerers who pretended to be mentally ill.

While Reagan was still in his first term as governor, Smith supported the future President's plans to shut down many of California's mental hospitals on grounds that community treatment of psychotics was preferable to "warehousing" them in expensive asylums. At the same time, Smith pushed for more money to punish lawbreakers, not rehabilitate them.

"When the citizen-governor tried to reduce the cost of social services and to close down some of the hospital 'warehouses' that were then home for the state's large mentally ill population, he was depicted as the enemy of the people," wrote the *Washington Post*'s Lou Cannon in his 1991 history of the Reagan presidency, *The Role of a Lifetime*.

"Reagan, in fact, was on to something," he continued. "He had become governor during a time when tranquilizers and other new methods of treatment were encouraging use of community treatment programs in place of huge, inefficient hospitals that were little more than prisons for the mentally ill. While this had the potential for reducing the state budget it did not quite fit the script of 'squeeze, cut and trim.' Community treatment would also prove expensive, although this was not then well understood. Certainly, Reagan did not understand it. He liked the idea of shutting down the hospital warehouses, both on humanitarian and fiscal grounds, but he did not know enough to make the case for community treatment. Put another way, he lacked the knowledge to change the script. When the subject arose at a March 15, 1967, meeting of the governor's cabinet, Reagan's participation reflected the limits of his Hollywood experience, not the advantages of having been an actor.

" 'Do you know how hard it is to mispronounce "psychiatric"

once you know how to pronounce it right?' he said irrelevantly during a key meeting on the mental-hospital budget cuts. 'I had to do it in *Kings Row* and at first I couldn't do it. It's like deliberately singing a flat note.' "

Like William French Smith, Roy Miller was a shrewd conservative who worked quietly but effectively for his clients' best interests. The senior Gibson, Dunn and Crutcher partner took notice. When Smith began helping his old friend Governor Reagan seriously attempt to move from California to Washington in the late 1970s, Roy Miller was groomed to take over Smith's job. If Reagan moved to the White House and Smith went with him as Attorney General, the mantle of personal attorney to the former governor of California would fall to Miller.

During this fast-paced, heady period in Roy Miller's career, his wife was moving at a more timorous speed. Marguerite missed Pasadena—especially her church. The family attempted to find a new religious home, notably at the nondenominational Neighborhood Church of Palos Verdes, but Marguerite never felt comfortable there. To some degree, her new network of nutrition-enlightened comrades on the Hill provided some comfort in the face of her family's loose spiritual roots.

"She was one of those people you call every day," said Sally Alonzo, one of Marguerite's first friends in Palos Verdes. "You'd call Marguerite if you wanted to know how long you could keep potatoes in the refrigerator or how long you could keep meat before it went bad."

Marguerite found comfort in chatting with other wives and mothers who believed the old maxim "You are what you eat." Here were friends with whom she could commiserate when Jeff or Michael wasn't responding correctly to diet or biofeedback or her suggestions about their futures.

"I didn't have that great a marriage, and part of my relationship with the Millers was looking to their family as a role model," said Sally. "I had my two daughters. The Millers had their two sons. They looked so happy."

To outsiders, they appeared occasionally stiff and physically gangly, but the entire family—Mom, Pop and the kids—seemed as much on an even keel as any 1950s family living their lives mimicking a situation comedy. But the appearances of warm stability did seem to crack at times.

"She was wonderful, but Marguerite was one of *those* type of people, if you know what I mean: so powerful, but in a quiet, soft-spoken way," said Sally. "When I'd be over there, she would be in the kitchen cooking or helping with homework with one of the boys, and you'd hear her saying: 'Well, that's great but what about if we do it *this* way?' It was very subtle, but you could see it in their faces. They were not good enough."

Marguerite held herself to the same standard of perfection that she maintained for her family, forever launching self-improvement campaigns. In Palos Verdes she found more room in which to perfect her green thumb than she had in Pasadena. The Millers' yard was five times the size of the hillside subdivision lot where they bought their first home. The sunny summer exposure and cool winter fog that rolled in off the Pacific fostered an environment suited for a host of different flowers and vegetables.

Marguerite joined the Silver Spur Garden Club, whose members had the time and energy to develop deep interests in a particular type of flower or shrub the way that horse or cat breeders zero in on Appaloosas or Siamese. The Silver Spur boasted begonia, zinnia and fuchsia specialists, among others. Marguerite found herself at home with her passionate peers.

Her sons' passions flourished on the Hill too. Despite an attachment to Pasadena very nearly as strong as his mother's, Michael seemed to adjust. He still had an unpredictable temper and occasionally had a bed-wetting accident, but he fared better in school. Jeff, during his four years at Palos Verdes High, grew into a successful, popular young man.

Especially to Tracy Conrad.

They met through music class, found common ground in art and literature and cemented their relationship on the tennis court. They were both racquet experts. They were also talented at another game.

From *Romeo and Juliet* to "Teen Angel," adults always seem to have a blind spot when it comes to adolescent passion, dismissing moony eyes, meeting at each other's lockers and hand-holding as ephemeral puppy love. So it was with Jeff and Tracy.

"They met when they were sophomores and by the time they were juniors, they were sleeping together, which was more unusual for that time," said Phil Hogan. "Now I think most kids do sleep together in high school. Not then, though. He was very happy with her and she was very beautiful."

To the adults in their lives, nothing appeared unusual.

"Jeff was popular, but not all that popular," said Gary McRoberts, who recalled no particularly serious chemistry between Jeff and any of his coed friends in McRoberts' close-knit choral groups during high school. "The strange thing was that the boys liked the girls, but they had no idea about social skills. Kids didn't really date. They went out as groups."

High school was comprised of cliques, and each clique swapped partners as easily as square dancers, according to Doug Holker, who ran with the jock clique on campus. But seldom did clique members venture outside their group to date. To the Palos Verdes High School Student, "group dating" was a drift-in, drift-out phenomenon with little in the way of teen commitment that characterized the "going steady" philosophy of an earlier generation.

"All the guys had their group of friends, and their girlfriends would come in and go out, depending on who they were seeing," said Holker.

"I thought it was healthier, but maybe it wasn't," said McRoberts. "They'd go out as friends, not as couples. The only time you'd see them as dates was at the prom or the winter formal. Maybe it was a reaction to the sexual revolution of the sixties. Maybe they were afraid."

Or maybe, like Jeff's parents and his other teachers, McRoberts underestimated the depth of feeling among his happy-go-lucky students. Marguerite sensed something more in the Jeff-Tracy combination, though. According to Phil Hogan, Roy accepted Tracy—

as he accepted most of Jeff's friends—but Marguerite never did get along with her. Tracy herself still refuses to talk about Jeff or her relationship with the Millers.

By his senior year, Jeff had become a star. His small part in *Hello Dolly!* as a sophomore had blossomed into one of the leads when it came time to do the senior musical. He played Will Parker in *Oklahoma!*, cornponing his way across the stage in the hick role, wearing chaps and a ten-gallon hat.

"I ain't gonna stop talkin' pretty to you 'til you give me a kiss," says lovesick Will to Ado Annie, played by classmate Peggy Lynch, in a haystack scene.

As a moony cowpoke, half-clowning and half-wooing his prim lady love, the onstage Jeff was far removed from his normal intensity. Offstage, the wish to succeed that his parents had instilled in him helped drive a wedge between him and Tracy.

"Part of the reason Jeff and Tracy broke up was that she was into art and he was into acting. She was really good and when he became the main man in the musical, he felt the pressure to hang out more with the groupies," said Hogan.

When Jeff and Tracy became seniors, Danese Cocke became the other woman. Like Jeff, Danese loved dancing and drama. She was also a member of Sun Machine. Tracy drifted out of the picture.

Holker, who had been dating Danese until the end of their junior year, saw Jeff as "nothing great." Among the girls, though, Miller had developed a reputation as a volatile, yet sensitive intellectual with a terrific backhand and an ironic sense of humor. On top of it all, he had deep blue eyes and a bashful boyish smile that, again, the adults in his life rarely saw.

"Jeff was very serious and never smiled, but he was really no trouble at all during high school," said his counselor, Richard Selway, who wrote Jeff's recommendation on his application for admission to Dartmouth.

Jeff was trouble to Doug Holker, though. When Jeff got his girlfriend, Holker was mortified. But Jeff and Danese fell into the "group dating" category that teachers and parents liked to see, and it didn't last. By graduation, Doug and Danese were back together and Jeff was off to Dartmouth.

Even though he had moved on, Jeff never lost touch with Tracy.

"Breaking up with Tracy was a major crisis in his life," said Phil Hogan. "She started seeing someone else while he was at Dartmouth."

Dartmouth was Ivy League, but quite a different Ivy League from the other old-money eastern colleges that grew up during this century alongside urban centers. The cosmopolitan atmosphere of Harvard Square or Columbia on New York's Upper West Side is completely missing from Hanover, New Hampshire.

The training ground of Daniel Webster, Nelson Rockefeller, Dr. Seuss and C. Everett Koop stands in stately repose next to the Connecticut River—untouched by industry, politics, revolution or urban decay. Dartmouth remains the bucolic home of maple syrup and covered bridges.

"I loved the personality of the college. I liked the feel out there," said Steven Koehler, one of Jeff's roommates at Giles Hall during his freshman year. "The changing seasons, the isolated feeling . . . but in a good way. It made the college feel like a very close place, because it was the only thing in town."

Dartmouth loves its traditions. Each autumn, students build a homecoming bonfire of railroad ties, crisscrossed nearly two stories high on the grassy mall in front of the Dartmouth bell tower. In the winter they build a huge snow sculpture on the same spot during their cider-swilling, bone-chilling Dartmouth Winter Carnival. During warm weather, students stretch out on blankets in the Dartmouth cemetery a half-block from the library, studying Chaucer and Kant while lying beneath hardwood trees on two-hundred-year-old graves. Dartmouth Crew members can be seen in the spring, sculling up the Connecticut River in long boats, looking like a scene from a nineteenth-century Currier & Ives etching.

In 1975 Dartmouth was as isolated from urban chaos as Palos

Verdes was from the rest of Los Angeles. As Watergate and the Vietnam War were both winding to a close, many of Jeff's Palos Verdes classmates were coming down from the Hill for the first time to California colleges where campus activism still flourished. But the Millers shied away from rebellion. Dartmouth was the school that Jeff and his parents selected to further his education.

He played freshman tennis at Dartmouth but switched to crew when he became a sophomore. Jeff stuck close to campus both years, except for the fall of 1976, when he went to Europe for three months to study French at the Sorbonne as part of Dartmouth's Language Study Abroad program. He developed an ear for the language and sprinkled his English with *"Je ne sais quoi," "J'espère"* and other gallicisms for months after the experience.

"He was pretty outgoing," said Koehler. "He was a tall fellow— pretty athletic. Always leaving sweaty socks under a chair and stuff. He was, I guess, pretty intense, but I don't remember him getting angry or anything."

Jeff also sang in a barbershop quartet during his sophomore year after he returned from Paris. Despite the conservative behind-the-scenes bent that he had learned from his father, he also participated in campus politics as a member of his class council.

He pledged Kappa Kappa Kappa, but never lived in its ramshackle two-story headquarters along Frat Row, preferring the dorms. In later years, long after Jeff graduated, the "Tri-Kaps" developed a reputation as a home to neoconservative students and changed its name to a different set of Greek letters so that it wouldn't be confused with the other KKK. But in the 1970s there were more altruistic eggheads than rowdy jocks in Kappa Kappa Kappa.

"Tri-Kap was not the fraternity of the hard-core animal-house types," said Jeff's fraternity brother Bruce Smollar. Kappa Kappa Kappa became better known for supporting campus cleanups and blood drives than toga parties.

"We were gentlemanly, even wimpy," he continued. "Even in that gang, Jeff wouldn't be among the noisy ones. If we played a round of beer pong, he'd chug with the best of us, but he was the kind of guy who'd rather discuss the meaning of the world than drink a beer."

Jeff lost interest quickly in fraternity life. Phil Hogan, who was studying geology at Princeton three states away, phoned a few times while they were both sophomores. At the time, Jeff told him he was going to follow in the footsteps of one of his uncles and become a geologist. There was pressure from home to become a professional—perhaps a lawyer, like his father. Marguerite demanded perfection. Roy was not as exacting, but he also wanted his sons to succeed. At what they were to succeed was up to them, but Roy demanded success.

In the summer between Jeffrey's sophomore and junior years, Roy took Marguerite and Michael with him to visit Jeffrey in New Hampshire. The sophomore summer family visit was a Dartmouth tradition reminiscent of mountain church retreats. Jeff was used to the ritual. The Millers had participated in them fairly regularly since joining the Methodist Church in Pasadena when the boys were still babies. Instead of a Christian campground in the San Bernardino Mountains, their Dartmouth retreat was to be the rustic Ravine Lodge in the Green Hills near Moosilauke.

"I remember being very struck by his family," said Daniela Weiser-Varon, who was a year behind Jeff at Dartmouth. "These are such weird little things to remember, but I thought his mother was just very nitpicky. I remember her as laughing all the time. A very high kind of laugh. Someone whose face is always in kind of a smile, but it's a bit artificial."

During sophomore visitation, Dartmouth hired students who needed a summer job to cook, clean and make up beds at the lodge. Weiser-Varon was assistant cook that particular summer and it was her misfortune to learn firsthand about Marguerite's growing obsession with food.

"His mother was just really irritating to me," she said. "She was constantly asking for things. The way the lodge is run in the summer, it is very laid-back. It's the kind of place where everybody gets one breakfast, one lunch and one dinner. Everyone gets the same thing and you eat family style.

"There were a fair amount of people up there that summer, but she was always coming into the kitchen asking me to cook something different or something special. Always."

Marguerite's manner was amiable but insistent. She may have understood the meaning of the word "no," but controlled her conversations in such a sweet way that the other party didn't dare invoke any negatives. From the very first time she and Daniela spoke, the younger woman felt like a servant rather than an undergrad tackling a summer job. She came to dread Marguerite's frequent treks to the kitchen.

"If breakfast was pancakes, she would come and ask for boiled eggs. She'd say, 'You know, my son cannot eat pancakes. Can you make him some eggs?'

"I'd say, 'Well, we don't usually, you know . . .'

"But there was something about her that I just thought: if it means so much to her, I'll make her some eggs.

"I'd say, 'What would you like?' and she'd want soft-boiled eggs. Well, if we were going to cook eggs, we'd cook lots of scrambled eggs for everyone. Soft-boiled eggs is not something you make when you're cooking for a hundred people. But she came in and asked me to make these eggs and I did. And then she literally told me how many seconds they had to cook!"

When Daniela emerged from the kitchen with the perfectly timed eggs, followed closely by a hovering Marguerite, the Miller boys were already eating. Pancakes.

"When I went out and served them the eggs, one of them—I think it was Michael—already had like this big plateful of pancakes and bacon stacked up six inches high and was eating them with great relish. She didn't like that at all."

Michael was a high school freshman at the time, already over six feet tall and starting to fill out like his older brother. Weiser-Varon was shocked when Marguerite scolded him. He glowered at her, reluctantly put down his fork and ate soft-boiled eggs as he was told.

"I mean she may have only been there for two days, but she somehow managed to get under my skin a little bit," said Weiser-Varon. "I was very nice to her, but I remember being really struck by the fact that here were these two young men—one of them a Dartmouth sophomore and the other just a few years younger. I mean, teenage guys, right? But it was like they were two little toddlers, the way she interacted with them."

Back at Palos Verdes High, whatever advantage Michael had had over most of his peers in junior high because he was taller quickly vanished. They caught up to his height and began to develop into young men who could no longer be bullied. Michael could not fight the family genes.

"The first time I ever saw the family was at the Neighborhood Church here in Palos Verdes," said Donald Brough, Michael's guidance counselor at Palos Verdes High. "They looked like someone just let them out of a detention camp. The father was particularly thin. You would have thought they all had terminal cancer."

It was his own extreme inherited thinness that first interested Michael in the possibilities of wonder diets. Michael had begun pursuing a solution to it in junior high, reading muscle magazines and following the video advice of Jack LaLanne, *Body Buddies* and early morning televised aerobics classes. He ate lots of meat and then he ate no meat. He drank milk and then he avoided all dairy products. Then he saw Rheo Blair on television.

Rheo H. Blair, who billed himself as "Nutritionist to the Stars," operated a combination salon/spa at his home near Wilshire and Western, just a short drive east of the Miracle Mile. He had gained fame feeding vitamin supplements and protein powder to the likes of Charlton Heston, Lawrence Welk, Glenn Ford, Regis Philbin, Jay North, Liberace, Jon Hall and Bob Cummings, among others. The results, according to Blair's clients, were nothing short of astonishing.

Philbin even made the pompadoured dietician a regular on his popular Los Angeles morning television program. Blair told the morning audience of KABC-TV's A.M. *Los Angeles* remarkable "before" and "after" stories: marvels that often included sworn affidavits from proud parents who had given up all hope for their scrawny pubescent sons. One such printed testimonial that Marguerite and Michael read after seeing Blair on TV was the story of sixteen-year-old Chuck Welling. The brochure asked the arresting rhetorical question "What Miracle Saved Chuck's Life?"

"As Chuck's father, I want to express my gratitude for the ABC show that enabled us to learn about Rheo H. Blair," read the affidavit. The "before" photos accompanying the sworn statement showed a thin, spindly-armed, swaybacked boy with a grim frown, unwashed hair, glazed eyes, turkey neck and skin dotted with acne.

His resemblance to Michael Miller, who was also sixteen at the time, was quite close. And the resemblance didn't just end at the way Chuck appeared in his "before" photo. He also had a personality to match Michael's.

"When we first saw Rheo on the A.M. *Los Angeles* show, Chuck was wasting away," wrote his father. "We had made every effort to get the best possible medical and psychiatric care and we had just come to the conclusion that the only way to help Chuck was to place him in an institution. Rheo was the first person who diagnosed Chuck correctly and we did not hesitate to let him take Chuck under his care.

"Now, three months later, I can testify that this is the first time in sixteen years I have enjoyed my son's company! I was speechless when I first saw Chuck. I was so elated over his rebirth that I had trouble sleeping that night."

Indeed, the "after" photos depicted an adolescent hunk with a clear complexion, broad shoulders and a confident smile. A letter Chuck's mother wrote to Philbin and his cohost, Sarah Purcell, after her son went through a ninety-day regimen under Rheo Blair's supervision was even more revealing—and convincing to concerned and empathetic mothers like Marguerite Miller—than the affidavit that Chuck's father had turned over to the Nutritionist to the Stars:

Dear Regis, Sarah and the ABC staff:

Yesterday as I waited in the Ambassador Hotel to see Chuck for the first time in around 90 days, I recalled the torturous times we had been through because of his violent temper tantrums. He was just wasting away, getting thinner by the day. He almost looked like death itself. He had a respiratory problem and used two to three large boxes of Kleenex a week. Emotionally he was in serious trouble. It was difficult for him to be pleasant and nice for any length of time. Chuck simply could not maintain his school work, his concentration was very poor and his energy level was worse. The challenge was too much.

Chuck would fly into rages, smashing anything in sight. My house will testify to that. We did not know whether to send him to a correctional institution or not. We gave this boy every nutritional advantage possible, plus therapy sessions with a psychiatrist. His friends even got a taste of his feelings if they were not careful. The only thing that soothed his feelings was his love for good music and his ability to play the organ.

When I turned my head and saw Chuck walking down the main aisle of this hotel, I was speechless! I was overwhelmed! Here was a young fellow that looked like a Grecian god. He had grown almost an inch taller, his stance was strong and direct, his shoulders were broad and manly, his chest very well built and his limbs were well developed.

Chuck's face, so happy and content! The expression coming through his eyes saintly or maybe angelic! He was good-natured the entire day. The hollow areas of his face had filled out nicely. The texture of his skin was fine and smooth. He had a ruddy, healthy glow!

This was my son? This living breathing vision of perfection standing before me? I could hardly contain myself. It's unbelievable! I felt like crying with happiness. I looked at this new person all afternoon. I could not get enough. Twice a stranger came up to me and expressed how she would like to hug Chuck because his expression was so loving and sweet.

All this is the direct result of super-nutrition and the excellent care given Chuck by nutritionist Rheo Blair. Rheo has re-created my child, giving him a better than average chance that he never had before. Now he will go on to make a successful, happy life for himself.

The way he was going, there was no possible chance for a normal future. My hope for Chuck and for his success in life is now filled with assurance and confidence. That night I had trouble sleeping. The excitement and exhilaration of the day would not turn off. This is nothing less than a miracle. I thank the Lord in heaven for this answer to my prayers.

I will always be grateful because you people provided the time for Rheo Blair to star on your show. Otherwise I would never have known about this wonderful program of rehabilitation. . . .

Before he was ever Rheo Blair, Nutritionist to the Stars, the wavy-haired athlete with the deep voice and Muscle Beach physique was Irvin Johnson: a frustrated Chicago lounge singer and pianist who turned his attention to bodybuilding after he failed to earn a living with his voice.

He was the younger and more feeble of two New Jersey brothers whose parents had encouraged them to enter show business. Norman Johnson played horns while Irvin sang and played piano along the New Jersey roadhouse circuit of the thirties and forties. It was the same place Frank Sinatra got his start and, had World War II not intervened and had Irvin's health held out, Norman still believes the Johnsons might also have had a shot at the big time.

But Norman went into the military. Irvin wasn't physically acceptable for the draft. When he was nine years old, he lost a kidney in a freak accident—a secret he maintained throughout his adult life. As he grew older, his health deteriorated. He described his own condition as anemic. Nothing he did—fasting, vegetarianism, even the Charles Atlas muscle-building course—seemed to help. Then, in his early twenties, he stumbled on a book called *The Miracles of Milk*, which advocated drinking a glass of milk every half hour as a way to better health. Johnson drank six quarts a day every day and began to feel terrific.

When he went to New York to follow in the footsteps of his idol, movie crooner Nelson Eddy, he carried a satchel of milk with him everywhere he went. At auditions, he got the nickname "the Singing Milkman." Johnson learned to play the piano, drink a glass of milk and do Nelson Eddy impressions.

While in New York, he improved on his milk diet with every supplement ever sold in a health food store: B-complex elixirs, mineral waters, rice polish, brewer's yeast, garlic tablets, calcium, protein.

He increased his body weight from 144 to 175 pounds and started working out at the gym.

The Borden Company got wind of the Singing Milkman and hired him to beef up an already muscular young model, Bucky Le Fevre, as part of the company's milk product promotion. The idea was to train Le Fevre so that he could match one of the feats of Hercules: lifting a young bull every day as it grows to its full adult weight. Using Johnson's milk and supplement regimen, Le Fevre pressed Borden's bull until it was over six hundred pounds.

But Johnson remained far more interested in becoming Nelson Eddy than Vic Tanny. He moved to Chicago to study with a renowned voice coach. To earn a living while he indulged his show biz pretensions, he fell back on hustling good health. He bought a gym and started training young men who wanted to become Mr. Olympia, Mr. America or Mr. Body Beautiful. By the time his voice was ready for Hollywood, Irvin Johnson had toned the torsos of more than a hundred bodybuilding title holders.

Irvin Johnson also became Rheo Hughes Blair. It was a name suggested to him by a Pasadena numerologist who predicted that converting his first name to "Rheo," the Greek word for "change," would also change his luck. The new name did help make him a star of sorts. After several years of trying to become the Nelson Eddy of the 1960s, Johnson resigned himself instead to being Rheo Blair, Nutritional Scientist.

By the time the Millers heard the Blair testimonials, Johnson owned a by-appointment-only nutrition palace in Hollywood that had come to be known as the Blair House, and his high-protein diets had become even more unconventional: fertilized hen's eggs, certified raw milk and cheese, organically grown hormone-free beef.

Marguerite had also seen him on television and read about his claims of being able to turn weaklings into weight lifters. What interested her just as keenly as the bodybuilding was Blair's claims that proper nutrition soothed hyperkinetic lives dominated by mood swings.

She called and introduced herself.

The interior of the two-story Cape Cod-style home she first took Michael to visit resembled a sound stage for some late 1930s operatic drama of the Jeanette MacDonald/Nelson Eddy variety. Red, white and blue draperies covered the windows, and the only dark object in an otherwise pure white living room—from carpet to ceiling—was a Baldwin grand piano.

Blair, who only consulted his clients one-on-one so that he could tailor his nutrition course to each person's specific needs, would personally lead prospects from the living room on a tour of the therapy center he'd set up in his home, beginning with the dining room.

Hanging from the ceiling was a set of chrome-plated bars, placed about one yard apart, all the way across the room. Once clients were enrolled in the program, Blair had them hang from the bars and, later, swing their way across the room Tarzan style as a form of exercise.

Along the dining room walls, Blair had a gallery of "before" and "after" photos of his clients.

The "befores" were either lumpy figures who resembled out-of-shape sumo wrestlers or paper-thin youngsters with curved spines, bad complexions and spindly limbs, not unlike Michael Miller. The "afters" were spectacular reincarnations: the same young men sporting biceps, triceps and pectorals that would make any trainer proud.

Blair also had a screening room where he regularly hosted Nelson Eddy parties for friends and fellow Eddy enthusiasts, exhibiting his collection of rare sixteen-millimeter prints of *Naughty Marietta, San Francisco* and the rest of the Eddy-MacDonald movie library. Homophobic comments comparing Eddy and MacDonald to "the Singing Capon and the Iron Butterfly" were grounds for instant expulsion from Blair House.

The kitchen included a couple of Taylor ice cream shake machines, used to concoct his Blair drinks, usually comprised of cream, fresh fruit such as strawberries or bananas, coconut and his custom combinations of vitamins, minerals and protein powder.

Blair's pièce de résistance was his indoor spa. Before hot tubs and Jacuzzis ever became a fixture of the California lifestyle, Blair built a deep communal tub amid a series of standard-size baths that he had set up in one room of his house. High-pressure jets were built into the plumbing, and the water in each tub was maintained at a different temperature—all the way from tepid to scalding.

His clients stripped and moved from tub to tub, raising and lowering their body temperature at the same time that the water jets stimulated their skin. According to Blair, the process promoted better blood circulation—a prerequisite to carrying the nutrients of the shakes he had blended in his kitchen to each of the trillion cells in his clients' bodies. The ceiling and walls of his spa were tiled with mirrors so that his naked clients could watch themselves turn ashen to pink. His state-of-the-art Macintosh stereo system piped in semiclassical music and show tunes to help them relax.

In one publicity shot that his TV fans never saw, Blair helped a buxom blonde step daintily from tub to tub so that the concentrated minerals imported from Hot Springs, Arkansas, and the underwater aloe vera brushes imported from West Germany could stroke her naked skin into even finer rejuvenated form than it already was. In the photo, Blair showed sexual detachment, holding the outstretched hand of the comely nude, but to teenage boys like Michael Miller, the vision of that flaxen-haired beauty with her million-dollar smile and spa-hardened nipples was Blair's best sales tool.

Michael signed up immediately for the Rheo Blair treatment and Marguerite couldn't have been more pleased. At Blair's insistence, he became a protein addict. Turning over his health problems to Rheo Blair didn't solve all his problems, though. He still wet the bed at times, prompting Marguerite to cart him to hypnotherapists. Whenever he went into a tantrum, breaking dishes in the kitchen or kicking the walls in his bedroom, she made him discuss his problems with the Reverend Lance Martin at their church or one of his school counselors.

"She was one of those typical PTA mothers: popping in and out of the school, sticking her head into my office," said guidance counselor Don Brough. "She was a pest. She'd walk around the halls, talking about schizophrenia, always on her soapbox about nutrition. She had a very high-pitched childlike voice—not an adult voice at all. High and sweet and childlike."

Marguerite badgered her son with that same sweet voice. But though she might have taken charge of his physical, spiritual, medical, musical and mental nourishment, Michael had to figure out girls by himself.

Michael didn't have a steady like Jeff, but once in a while after he became an upperclassman, he dated a freshman or sophomore. Girls never went out with him more than once, but nobody ever accused him of being gay—something that would have been the mark of Cain for any young man growing up on the Hill. He was just . . . different.

"I always felt really sorry for Mike," said classmate Beth Pearson. "He always tried so hard, but everyone teased him so he teased back. He was in the teasing mode with girls, picking fights and the like because he couldn't relate to them."

Michael walked, talked and ate his own way, often to the point of being downright offensive.

"At the time it didn't mean diddly, but he used to eat tuna straight out of a can in class," said classmate James Dunphey. "He told me he did it because he had heavy acne. Some witch doctor said this was good for his skin. I remember that most vividly because, God, it stunk."

He tried his hand at tennis, but didn't have the concentration, speed or stamina to match Jeff on the courts. Marguerite enrolled him in adaptive physical education, which was normally for handicapped students or students afflicted with some sort of chronic physical problem.

Like Jeff, he tried to shine in Chorale. Unlike Jeff, he did not comprehend the subtleties of social acceptance in the unforgiving crucible of high school.

"He used to volunteer for things other people knew better not to volunteer for, like solos," remembered John Aristei, another classmate. "He had a high nasally voice and he wound up being the scapegoat of a lot of jokes in Chorale. People would imitate his voice. It was all meant in jest, but it probably didn't help him at all."

"He was the brunt of a lot of jokes, but he took them all so well," Dunphey continued. "Like the runt of a group. He'd bear the brunt of it, but he always had a pretty good attitude."

When the teasing at school became too much, Michael escaped into his room at home. There, he had the Who. "He had every album they ever recorded," said Aristei.

Among them was the rock opera *Quadrophenia*—a dark, grim musical. The mind of the tortured protagonist of *Quadrophenia* is split into four personalities, giving the album its title.

And Michael played it over and over in his room after school, memorizing the question asked in the overture: "Can you see the real me, preacher . . . doctor . . . mother?"

During his junior year at college, Jeff's life began to change. He was a junior class leader during Dartmouth's annual freshman trip into the wilderness outside of Hanover. He hiked with the younger students and joined in campfire discussions about the geology of New Hampshire. It was like a step back in time to his Boy Scout days, when the stars twinkled overhead and he got to clear his mind of everything but shale and granite.

The future weighed heavily on Jeff's mind that summer. His fraternity brothers and other Dartmouth acquaintances already talked about taking the Graduate Record Exam or the Law School Aptitude Test, and where they hoped to study law or attend graduate school. While most of his peers knew exactly where they were going, Jeff hadn't even declared his undergraduate major.

Competition to get into the best schools, including Stanford, Law, would be intense. Things had changed in the quarter century since Roy went there. Instead of weeding out a third of the first-year law students by attrition, Stanford and the other prestige law schools in the United States did the weeding before anyone got in. The best schools had developed a screening process weighted heavily on extracurricular activities as well as grade point averages and test scores. Less than ten percent of the applicants made it in and those that did get in usually stuck it out all three years.

Jeff wasn't sure he wanted to be a lawyer, but it was one of his choices. And one way to get a leg up on the competition was to participate for a semester in a Dartmouth-sponsored legal internship. Through Dartmouth's Amos Tucker Foundation, Jeff applied to a pro bono legal-aid operation run by priests at the inner-city Patrick House for drug and alcohol abusers in Jersey City, New Jersey, just one subway stop from Manhattan.

"It wasn't always the altruistic kind of kid who wanted to do this," said Honey Frisher, Dartmouth's liaison with Jersey City's Patrick House program. "The internship was off campus, close to the big city, close to Broadway and great theater and music, and it was still very much a way into law school. In fact, the students who came to work in the legal clinic, instead of the methadone treatment center or the inner-city schools, were usually the ones who had the least interest in doing any real social service."

Jeff won his legal internship, and after the 1977 Christmas holidays, he was all set to spend four months in Jersey City. Edward Rowland, who remained his close friend through college, was also going down to Jersey City on the Tucker internship and offered to be Jeff's roommate. At Thanksgiving, he invited Jeff home to turkey dinner with his family.

During dinner, Edward's mother registered an uneasy impression of the handsome young Californian. He was polite and he was friendly, but she saw a very insecure young man. Jeff expressed great pride in his father, speaking often at the dinner table about the dizzying heights to which Roy Miller had risen in Southern California legal and political circles. But Jeff himself seemed haunted by feelings that he didn't quite measure up to Roy's level of success. Or that he ever could.

"I didn't see any of that, but my mother did," Rowland said.

Jeff also spoke about his younger brother between mouthfuls of cranberry sauce, pumpkin pie . . . and ice cream.

Michael wrote and called him often about his chronic troubles back home, Jeff said. Michael was different, he told the Rowlands. He went from one extreme to the other. He earned as many As as he did Fs—often in the same semester. He was impulsive. He was restless. He didn't fit in . . . didn't have it together. But he was trying, Jeff said. Michael was trying.

5

Jeff and Edward left for Jersey City after Christmas. Honey Frisher, a veteran of dealing with pampered undergrads, was ready for them.

"We got twelve students a semester. The first thing I'd do was send them out to look at the neighborhood," she said. "I asked them to draw me a map of every store, every home: 'What's at No. 542 on such and such a street? Where's the nearest school?' It forced them to get out and see where they were."

The Statue of Liberty stands just a few hundred yards away from Jersey City, her back turned toward the poor and working-class neighborhoods. The predominantly black population resided in row houses and institutional tenements abandoned by an Irish and Italian working middle class a generation earlier. The whites who did remain in Jersey City were generally cops, judges, priests or social workers who commuted to and from their jobs during the day, but rarely remained there after nightfall.

By January 1978, when Jeff Miller and Ed Rowland drove up the hill on the south side of town to an old rooming house adjacent to St. Patrick's Church, Jersey City was at its nadir.

The streets were still treelined, children occasionally skipped rope in the schoolyards and fine old depression-era movie palaces still screened late-run movies, but any other resemblance to suburban tranquillity had been erased. Graffiti seemed to mark every stationary object from hospitals to fire hydrants. Dead cars rusted in front yards and along curbs, their tires slashed and headlights crushed. Abandoned brick storefronts in the once-thriving business district at the top of the hill now housed vagrants and vermin.

Shops that weren't boarded up had bars on the windows. Grocery stores carried a scant inventory of random staples. The only consumer item available in quantity, if not quality, was dispensed on virtually every street corner along with heating spoons, rubber constriction bands and hypodermic needles.

Frisher had a ringside seat for the whole transformation. A Jersey City native, she grew up, left and went to college during the heady 1960s, but she pledged to try to come back and reverse the situation. As a social worker, she took up residence in a terrible hometown neighborhood and lived with its accompanying frustration. Father Ed Kearney, one of the local priests at St. Patrick's, urged her to take the job as coordinator of the Dartmouth program. It was a way of recruiting new foot soldiers in the battle, he said.

She was skeptical.

"Dartmouth is this other world with lofty ideals and philosophizing, where you've got a lot of students from some white suburb in Connecticut whose daddy was senior vice president of something or other," she said. "They've never known what it means to be without hope.

"So they come to Jersey City for a few weeks and take a look around and go: 'Oh *wow!*' Then when they go out into the real world after they graduate, it gives them the ammunition to form any stereotype they want. You know, they could say, 'I was in Jersey City and I *know* what poverty means.' "

But, to her pleasant surprise, not all of the poor little rich kids she feared she would have to baby-sit were as callow or as cynical as she first believed. Some started out that way, but by the time they finished up their four months of social work boot camp, they had changed: many of them profoundly and conclusively.

"If you could get them out on the street, it didn't take long for them to start figuring things out for themselves," said Frisher. "They found the places where runners collect numbers and where different drugs are sold. They found the candy stores where lots of people wander in and out but there never seemed to be any sales.

"They met the kids who don't have any chance of being anything or doing anything. I made them go out and shop. It became their home. They started asking questions: How come they don't pick up our garbage when they're supposed to? How come the street sweeper hasn't been here in three weeks?

"Then I'd send them into the schools or whatever their designated programs were. Once a week, we had a seminar. I'd bring in a speaker: a judge, counselors, teachers. Judges talked about the breakdown of the legal system. That's when even the smug ones started asking: You mean the legal system *I'm* going into, like Mommy's and Daddy's?

"Following the seminars, we'd go back to Patrick House [the drug and alcohol rehabilitation clinic associated with the internship] and talk about these things. Cops and drugs and government programs and taxing and funding and politics and how they all interrelated to create a place like Jersey City. Most of these kids were from Republican families who grew up in country club neighborhoods. Their reaction was:

" 'Wow! This is *not* what Daddy told me! This little kid down the street has no hope, no future. If I could teach him to read, he could get into Dartmouth! If I could get this guy off drugs and out of jail, I could help him get a job!'

"They started looking at life in an entirely different way. By the time they left, they had become totally emotionally involved. Usually, they became a part of what was going on here. The people in Jersey City didn't become them; they became the people in Jersey City."

From Frisher's point of view, there could not have been a better candidate for Jersey City shock therapy than Jeff Miller.

"Jeffrey was a pretty intense person and always very serious," said Thomas Gettinger, one of a dozen Dartmouth students who participated in the Tucker internship along with Miller. "You really couldn't say that he was humorous or easygoing. Not a very happy-go-lucky kind of guy."

At the time, however, he struck Gettinger as being exceptionally self-confident.

To Ron Radding, the Jersey City lawyer Jeff worked for during his internship, he was "a very nice fellow, very pleasant. . . . He was intense, though, especially on the tennis court. I used to team up with him against my two partners, who are much better than me. Having Jeff as my partner just about brought me up to their level."

Radding's Patrick House legal clinic consisted of three full-time attorneys including Radding, and interns like Jeff who acted as their investigators. It was a tight group committed to nuts-and-bolts justice for the disenfranchised. They acted as both civil and criminal advocates for Jersey City's alcoholics, ex-cons, children, rapists, handicapped, battered seniors, strung-out single mothers and starving junkies—anyone who could not afford to hire their own attorney.

In Radding's estimation, the tall, sandy-haired Californian with the mean overhand smash had the right personality for a legal career. In dealing with a distraught or angry client, Jeff acted detached but never disinterested—behavior that seemed more acquired than instinctive. If he were about to react to a situation emotionally, he made almost a visible effort to keep himself in check, clenching his jaw to keep from bursting out.

He loved working cases, of which there was never a shortage. Dozens of people lined up outside the doors of the Patrick House legal clinic every week, looking for help. Most of them were survivors, often less than innocent themselves. Clean-cut Dartmouth undergrads like Jeff found themselves offered everything from primo marijuana to sex acts in exchange for a little help with The Man.

"I remember one case where these two women accused our client of forcing them to have oral sex," said Radding. "As it turned out, they had both just been released from mental institutions and both women made plays for our client and for us. When I sent Jeff out to interview them, they offered to let him sodomize them! Our client was acquitted."

He was no fool when he arrived in Jersey City, but Jeff did strike some of the old hands like Frisher and Radding, and even some of his fellow interns, as naïve. He spoke often of reaching out to the black community and made a routine of going to church most Sundays in the neighborhood. As the weeks passed and he became familiar with the despair of poverty, he burrowed in and worked harder and longer hours.

Within two years of Jeff's internship, the federal money stopped. A new conservative contingent from California moved into the White House in 1980 with some tough attitudes about rehabilitation programs and wholesale handouts. Even some moderate Democrats on Capitol Hill had had enough of big budgets for social programs with slow-start results. They were given a new name to match those disaffected Democratic voters who helped eject Jimmy Carter from the presidency: "Reagan Democrats."

"We stopped the program in 1980," said Radding. "We were federally funded and when the feds said no more money, the state followed suit. The only thing left after the money stopped was a trailer that was set up to supply methadone to addicts."

For Jeff Miller, Patrick House was a time for him to think on his own terms, apart from school and parents. "I remember Jeff hanging out in the living room a lot," said Daniela Weiser-Varon, recalling the rambling two-story rooming house where the Dartmouth students lived, across an alley from St. Patrick's Church rectory. Under the charge of the Dartmouth students, it became more of a dorm than a rooming house, but without on-campus restrictions. Girlfriends and boyfriends who came to visit often slept over, amateur musicians sat out on the stoop plucking their guitars well into the night, and after-dinner discussions frequently turned into all-night drink-and-debate sessions.

"We had this big living room where we always talked when we were up late," said Weiser-Varon. "My sense of Jeff was that he was really looking for something and he didn't know what it was. But I guess many of us were searching during that time of our lives."

Four priests lived next door. At the beginning of every term, they invited the students over for dinner. The idea was to welcome the interns and give them moral support, but the dinner was also meant to destroy priestly stereotypes and offer a friendly dose of how men of the cloth act in the real world.

"We would be talking after dinner and then Father Sheehan, the Irish priest, would look around the table and he'd pick a girl with the most Irish Catholic-looking face," said Weiser-Varon. "Of course, he picked me. There was this moment of quietness and then he put his fist out and said: 'So, missy, what was it you wanted to know about celibacy?' Apparently he did this every time a new group of students came, but I didn't know that."

The priests of St. Patrick's were as streetwise and cynical as Honey Frisher. They rarely wore robes, collars or any other vestments. One of them smoked cigars and was building himself a getaway home at the beach. Another wore Bermuda shorts whenever the temperature climbed over seventy. They were politically active and often crafty in their methods. Two of them became attorneys and went on to found their own Jersey City law firm.

"These priests were great. They were warm and they were very used to having young people living next door," said Weiser-Varon. "When our showers broke down, we went over and took showers in the rectory. That sort of thing. There was this stream of girls with curlers in their hair and towels wrapped around them, walking over to the rectory. Jeff spent a fair amount of time over there."

The priest he spent most of his time visiting was the least radical—at least on the surface.

"Ed Cordero was generally the most intellectual. All the rest were on the verge of being excommunicated," deadpanned Honey Frisher.

A short, stocky Filipino Jesuit who wore glasses and spoke in soft, moderated tones, Father Cordero passionately advocated the Catholic doctrine of Aquinas and Augustine. He wore his collar more often than the others, yet he was not bent on converting the interns. He let those who were interested come to him. He heard confessions either as a sacrament or late at night during bull sessions in the front parlor of the rectory.

Jeff and Father Cordero's relationship made perfect sense to Ed Rowland. Jeff went from short-tempered to morose and back again as the weeks passed in Jersey City. The only time his roller-coaster mood seemed to even out was after his late-night encounters with the Jesuit next door.

"He was forever self-examining and judged himself extremely hard," said Rowland. "He was especially hard on himself when it came to women and what he thought an ideal relationship was. He judged other people just the opposite. Jeff was always willing to believe the good in people and give them second chances."

The two students talked occasionally after putting in long hours on their respective internship jobs. Sometimes they took the subway under the Hudson River and caught a movie or listened to some jazz in Manhattan. It was during those outings that Jeff revealed a failed romance he'd had with a young French woman while he was overseas with the Language Study Abroad program. While they were in Jersey City, he made a halfhearted play for a nurse who worked in the Patrick House drug and alcohol rehab unit, but that didn't work either.

"Jeffrey had a real problem with women," said Rowland. "He was very intimidated by the idea of actually getting involved."

He was not alone. Weiser-Varon remembered one of Honey Frisher's postseminar bull sessions that somehow segued from social issues into the uncharted territory of sexual relations. In a few moments, nervous twitters turned to an informal poll on sexual taboos.

"We started asking questions like, 'Would you sleep with someone who's done this or would you sleep with someone who had done that?' " said Weiser-Varon. "Now, I don't remember who it was, but some guy—it wasn't Jeffrey—asked the women, 'Would you sleep with a guy if you knew he had slept with a man?'

"Several of the guys were really shocked by the question, but the women were a lot looser. I don't mean sexually; just more open.

We kind of tossed it around and said, 'Well, gee . . . it would kind of depend. Did he sleep with the other guy more than once? Is he really gay?' And then this guy who asked the question said, very calmly: 'Because I *have* had a sexual experience with a guy.' He was one of the men who had a girlfriend at the time and I just remember that the women were saying things like, 'Oh, that's kind of interesting.'

"But the men got very, very quiet."

When he returned to Dartmouth from his Jersey City internship, Jeff began participating in a personal growth group. In some ways, theology and the study of personal convictions fit his reflective personality. In other ways, it left him questioning everything about his life at once.

Bruce Smollar scoffed at the Jersey City internship as "one of those bleeding-heart liberal programs where people go to do good things for a while and risk their lives.

"It could be really brutal," he continued. "The people who did that were usually leftover 1960s types and I never figured Jeff to be one of them. I guess it was an eye-opening experience. Maybe he should have kept his eyes closed."

Later that same year, Ed Rowland flew to California to visit Jeff on his home turf and got to size up the Miller family. He only dropped in long enough to introduce himself, but saw what appeared to him to be a very typical family: a brooding kid brother, a slightly tense but pleasant mother and a stiff, workaholic father.

"Michael was aloof, but his mother was very friendly," Rowland remembered.

It was uncanny to Edward that his mother had guessed so right about Roy Miller after only one sit-down dinner with Jeff. The elder Miller was quiet, logical, amiable, but just as aloof in his own way as Michael. To Rowland, Jeff seemed to hold his father in ambivalent awe: he wanted to be just like him at the same time that he wanted to be utterly different.

When they got back to Dartmouth, Jeff declared his major as religion.

"He was introspective and mentally restless," said Dartmouth religion professor Charles Stinson. "He would think things through, make up his mind and then change it."

Jeffrey was pleasant, personable and very bright, but not very practical, according to Stinson. The California beach boy who came to Dartmouth had developed into an ascetic with haunted blue eyes in a relatively short period of time.

"He looked like a Norman Rockwell painting: an All-American-looking boy who looked like he would be very mellow," Stinson said. "But when you talked to him, you realized he had this intensity. He was very moody and was constantly wrestling with many issues."

During his final year at Dartmouth, Jeffrey became enamored of process theology, which attempted to explain God in terms of nuclear physics and a flowing view of reality. As first defined by Alfred North Whitehead in the early part of the century, process theologians saw God as a split personality: the Creator who never wavered from his moral and physical laws and also the abstract Creator who was nonetheless constantly influenced by the world and human beings.

Jeffrey's plunge into religious studies hadn't made him a monk. He met an attractive black coed on campus who began actively pursuing him, but he wouldn't allow himself to let the relationship get beyond flirting. When he talked about her with friends, it was in a self-flagellation frame of mind: maybe he didn't want to date her because he was a racist.

Except for a single music class, his schedule consisted of nothing but religion classes during the 1978–79 school year. He studied Chinese religion, New Testament and modern theories of Christ. He took courses in Luther and the Protestant Reformation, Religious Language and Belief and Introduction to Religion and Ethics. One of the last two classes he took at Dartmouth was called Sexuality, Society, and Religion and was described in the catalog as "an examination of judgments made by classical and contemporary religious moralists on some of the problems occasioned by human sexuality . . . Special problem areas to be considered include premarital and extra-marital sex, homosexuality, contraception, abortion, population growth and genetic engineering."

During his senior year, he road-tripped with Edward Rowland to visit divinity schools. The two of them dropped in at both Princeton and Yale to check into requirements for graduate theology degrees and to get a feel for the professors who taught there.

"At that time, Jeff seemed really lost," recalled Rowland. "He was searching for something that would be just his."

While they were on the road, the pair stopped back in Jersey City to visit their old haunts. Jeff spent time with Father Cordero and dropped in on Ron Radding, who remarked on Jeff's increased introversion the same way Rowland had.

"He didn't seem the same, but I thought he was just tired from the trip," he said.

"Some people were depressed the semester after Jersey City," said Weiser-Varon. "You know, you go through this very intense situation and in some cases you feel that you're really making a difference and you're having an impact and you're needed. Then you come back to Dartmouth and it is such a different world. It's very hard to readjust. I'm not surprised that he changed majors."

Jeff had grown even more quiet, more guarded. Some old friends kiddingly accused him of paranoia.

"He was very watchful," said Weiser-Varon. "You know, he had an intent way of looking at people, but not in any menacing way. He wasn't antisocial. He wasn't weird. There was a quality to his quietness. It was someone who was deliberately quiet. Quiet and watchful."

In the 1979 Dartmouth yearbook, the editors paid tribute to three of Jeff's classmates who had died during their years in Hanover. Their names were stripped in block letters across a brooding black-and-white photo of a setting sun as it dipped beneath the tree line of a low New Hampshire ridge in the wilds east of the Connecticut River. Beneath the block-letter names was an elegy:

"And the granite of New Hampshire keeps a record of their fame."

Jeff's senior portrait was several pages away, among the living.

Jeff graduated and moved back to California. He and his parents quarreled often about his future, though his father went to bat for him in getting him admitted as a theology graduate student at the Claremont Graduate School of Theology.

Before he was admitted, Jeff visited Claremont regularly, but it was in order to speak with his grandparents about his fears and faith. The pentecostal mysticism that the Bruners embraced had begun to take on a new sheen for him, following Jeff's analytical studies back at Dartmouth. Harold and Marie's insistence on biblical literalism became the staple of any conversation he had. He looked with renewed interest at faith healers, shamans and the laying on of hands.

His physical appearance began to change at about the same time. His tennis player's handshake, so firm and certain in high school, became a limp grip. His shoulders slumped and his forehead creased with premature worry lines while his eyes seemed to sink deeper into his skull. He walked with a stooped gait.

Roy and Marguerite reluctantly accepted their son's passion for theology. But before Jeff enrolled at Claremont, his worsening physical and emotional condition got the better of him. He lapsed into rages, especially over questions of faith. He also felt guilty about fantasies he had started to have: sexual fantasies, he confided to his closest friends. Sexual fantasies involving Father Ed Cordero.

He met Pastor Ralph Moore in August, two months after his graduation from Dartmouth. It was also the same month that his Grandmother Marie died suddenly—not directly of the cancer she had fought over a period of years with everything from drugs and diet to prayer, but of internal hemorrhaging.

"He was walking on the street one day and was talking to himself," said Moore, the founder of Hope Chapel. "We met him all broken up. We gave him a rationale. We gave him something—call it a superstition if you want—that 'I can function. I don't have to be perfect.' "

Hope Chapel, a fundamentalist "street" mission, operated out of an old bowling alley in Hermosa Beach, a half dozen miles down the Hill from the Millers' home and light-years away from the Christianity Jeff and Michael had been brought up to believe in.

Unlike the century-old stately stone First United Methodist Church on East Colorado Boulevard in the heart of old Pasadena, Hope Chapel had a short history and a radically different philosophy. It took no special training to interpret the Bible. Everybody was a minister, everybody was a disciple, and neither robes nor suit and tie were required to get in the front door. Moore and his followers even created a Hope Chapel Ministry Institute to train members in lay ministry, offering a Certificate of Christian Studies to anyone who completed twelve courses.

But members didn't have to have a certificate to preach. Moore operated his ministry like a tent meeting, which was almost how it began. He and thirteen others formed Hope Chapel in 1971, often reading from the Bible on the beach to teens playing volleyball or trying to get a tan. A small abandoned church a few blocks from the beach became Hope's first permanent home. They moved to the Manhattan Beach Community Center and finally to the dilapidated Bay-Vue Bowling Center on Pacific Coast Highway as the congregation outgrew each location.

Dripping surf trunks or Harley-Davidson zipper jackets were just as acceptable at a Hope Chapel service as the spit and polish that Marguerite Miller had always insisted her boys apply before they went to their Pasadena church each Sunday. Hope Chapel's affiliation was the Foursquare Church, founded fifty years earlier by the legendary Los Angeles evangelist Aimee Semple McPherson.

But Moore preached his own version of the Foursquare Gospel: an open-door policy, a verse-by-verse application of the Bible to everyday problems and a personal responsibility on the part of all Hope Chapel members to hit the streets and bring in new members. Hope developed techniques for preaching in parking lots, prisons, ski resorts, aerobics classes—anyplace where people gathered and might listen for a few moments to Hope Chapel's version of the Word of God.

Jeff fit in immediately. He became the kind of zealot who could lead reluctant pamphleteers into a McDonald's restaurant and preach the gospel while lunching naysayers used the tracts they handed out as napkins or makeshift ashtrays. He wasn't discouraged. He held his head high and marched onward, pausing to spout a verse or two from his Bible if anyone showed the least interest in the Gospel according to Miller.

He not only became involved in Hope Chapel's Bible studies and Sunday services; Jeff showed a sensitivity and brilliance that Moore had rarely seen among the ragtag youth who comprised the bulk of Hope Chapel's on-again, off-again parish.

"When he was normal, he was really something," said Moore. "He was really impacting people's lives."

When he became "born again," Jeff gave up process theology as well as the other theological theories he had studied back at Dartmouth. He wrote Professor Stinson telling him as much. Included with his letter was a twelve-page Christian tract published by the Campus Crusade for Christ, called "Have you Heard of the Four Spiritual Laws?"

Jeff took these laws to heart:

1. God *loves* you, and offers a wonderful *plan* for your life.

2. Man is *sinful* and *separated* from God. Therefore, he cannot know and experience God's love and plan for his life.

3. Jesus Christ is God's *only* provision for man's sin. Through Him you can know and experience God's love and plan for your life.

4. We must individually *receive* Jesus Christ as savior and lord: then we can know and experience God's love and plan for our lives.

The pamphlet, similar to the kind handed out to passersby on Hollywood Boulevard or Times Square, "clearly defines what the Christian faith is all about: something which nine religion courses and 21 years in church did not do for me," Jeff wrote his former professor.

In addition to the tract, Jeff enclosed a copy of an evangelical book with his letter—a 128-page paperback titled *More Than a Carpenter*, by Josh McDowell.

"I would like to share a small book with you which I have enjoyed very much," Jeff wrote. "It presents very convincing historical arguments for Christianity. Perhaps it could be used as a supplementary text for your Christology course. Please let me know your reaction to the book."

Professor Stinson and Jeff's family were not the only ones stunned by Jeff's abrupt retreat into Christian fundamentalism. High school chums who met him on the street, at the beach or in the Palos Verdes shopping center couldn't believe it.

"He was never that religious before in high school," said Phil Hogan. "When his parents forced him to go to Pasadena every Sunday, he hated it. He preferred going to a local church or not at all. I think he would have much rather been like my brother and I. Our parents sent us to the Unitarian Church until we were about thirteen. After that, we went surfing Sunday mornings instead."

Roy Miller would have preferred that Jeff attend First Methodist in Pasadena, but he wasn't about to pressure him. As his son became more moody, alternately displaying a temper and sadness that he had not seen before, Roy remained reluctantly supportive.

"He was a prince of a man," said Pastor Moore. "He must have experienced a lot of pain at home. Mr. Miller was very levelheaded, concerned—a tolerant man. He would have been happy to see Jeff do anything."

Marguerite had quite a different opinion. According to Moore, she based her faith on "a poetic sense of justice in the universe." In that way, she was different from Harold and Marie Bruner. Jeff's newfound evangelism was not as understated as her own father's and it left her cold.

"I think she felt that, if Jeff would just go back to being the way he was before—a good student—the world would be his," said Moore.

Instead of using his Dartmouth degree to launch a career, however, Jeff took a job clerking at a Christian bookstore near the beach.

By Christmas 1979, Jeff was obsessed with the ongoing battle between Christ and the Antichrist. When his cousin Carin from Ohio spoke with him, it seemed as though that was all that he wanted to talk about.

He continued to attend church in Pasadena with his parents from time to time, but he had trouble keeping his born-again ardor in check during the conservative Methodist services.

During a Christian conference in the San Bernardino Mountains, moderated by First Methodist's pastor, the Reverend George Mann, Jeff broke away from his family in the audience and made his way to the dais, shouting to the startled assembly the good news that Christ was coming again. Mann sent Jeffrey back to his seat, but not without a mortifying shock wave rippling through the audience—and the Miller family.

Even Ralph Moore worried about Jeff. Displaying a passion for evangelism was one thing; publicly embarrassing a responsible clergyman and lifelong family confidant like the Reverend Mann was quite another.

"He got all goofed up," Moore said sadly.

It was during that same period that Jeff got back together with Tracy Conrad. They were both searching for some meaning in what they would do with their lives, according to both Phil Hogan and the Reverend Moore. They had that much in common. Instead of picking up where they left off in high school, however, they discovered they had become two very different people.

Tracy was cynical like most young adults. She was neither an anarchist nor a nihilist, but she did question everything, especially religion. Jeff's born-again passion didn't wash with her and he couldn't convince her the way he could Hope Chapel's street kids and down-and-out dopers. She launched into a diatribe against simplistic Christianity that left Jeff defenseless.

He read to her from the opening verses of St. Paul's letters to the Corinthians—the so-called love chapter of the New Testament—according to Moore.

"If you don't have love, you don't have anything," he told her, holding his hands up to shield himself from her words.

"What if God doesn't exist?" she asked.

Jeff returned to Hope Chapel following his debate with Tracy. He sat down with Pastor Moore and repeated Tracy's question over and over while he rocked back and forth with his arms wrapped around his thinning rib cage: "What if God doesn't exist?"

"He turned into a basket case," said Moore.

The Millers weren't blind to Jeff's personality changes and sent him to psychologists as they had done for Michael. When that didn't help, Marguerite thought she could deal with the problem through food.

One of her nutrition advisors, dietician Carlton Fredericks, maintained that proper nutrition could help and might even cure schizophrenia—a mental disorder she had come to believe might be afflicting her son.

"In perhaps half of the schizophrenic population, cerebral allergy and hypoglycemia are present," Fredericks wrote. "No schizophrenic can be considered adequately investigated and treated if there has been no check to determine if diet is contributing in any way to the problem."

Fredericks claimed that amino acids offered help to some schizophrenics, as did megavitamin therapy supplemented with niacinamide, pyridoxin, Vitamin E and even hydrochloric acid.

"The cure rate in schizophrenia is magnificently high," Fredericks wrote. Waiting too long to change a potential schizophrenic's diet was risky, though.

"Long-term schizophrenics are less likely to respond, although some do," he wrote.

But Jeff was beyond control. During an argument over religion, Jeff wrapped his fingers around his mother's throat and tried to strangle her. In another incident, he kicked out a window. Marguerite called Hope Chapel in a panic. Two of Jeff's disciples showed up and spoke soothingly to him, but wound up escorting him to the mental ward of a hospital.

One evening after the beginning of the year, Ralph Moore got a call from Jeff. He was in the hospital again—a psychiatric hospital.

"I am going into a catatonic state," he told the pastor.

"Are you sitting or standing?" Moore asked.

"Sitting."

"Stand up!" Moore ordered.

"Why are you making me stand up?" Jeff wanted to know.

"Because I want you to know that you are in control."

Jeff hadn't always been the model patient, but he told Moore he was cooperating with the hospital staff this time. He did confess that he was still "playing games" at times, like lapsing into catatonia.

"He was more in control than he wanted to acknowledge," said Moore.

⟳ SONS

In Sophocles' tragedy, Oedipus punishes himself by putting out his eyes. Even though he had no way of recognizing Laius as his father; even though Laius had tried to kill his infant son and was responsible for this lack of recognition; even though Laius was the one who provoked Oedipus' anger when their paths crossed; even though Oedipus did not desire Jocasta but became her husband thanks to his cleverness in solving the sphinx's riddle, thus rescuing Thebes; and even though Jocasta, his mother, could have recognized her son by his swollen feet—to this very day no one seems to have objected to the fact that Oedipus was assigned all the blame.

ALICE MILLER
Thou Shalt Not Be Aware:
Psychoanalysis & Society's
Betrayal of the Child

6

Rheo Blair carefully screened his clients through astrology and numerology. Following each TV appearance, as many as eight hundred people phoned him for appointments, but Blair turned most of them down. Those he preferred for his program had to have the right name.

He matched names with numerology charts that attributed a different quality to each letter of the alphabet. His "Science of Characteristics" attached human traits to certain letters. "R" stood for exactness; "S" meant strength; "D" indicated daring, etc.

" 'M' meant you could be a bum or a genius," said his physical therapist and longtime assistant, Richard Backlund.

The chief characteristic Blair looked for was an open mind. Michael Miller, an analytical Gemini, passed muster. So did Jeffrey, the harmony-loving Libra who dropped in at Rheo's when he was home visiting from Dartmouth. But Marguerite Miller, the intuitive Pisces who viewed the world as a cold and cruel place, never did.

"Their mother told them never to lust after women," said Backlund. "She filled their heads up with this mumbo jumbo crap that even *thinking* about fucking was the same thing as doing it. Don't

IN THE BEST OF FAMILIES

even look at women, she told them. Can you imagine? Saying that to a teenage boy when all his hormones are raging?"

Blair himself regarded sex as pleasurable procreation and nothing more, making his clash with Marguerite all but inevitable. Even though a tall statuesque blonde accompanied the Nutritionist to the Stars everywhere in public, rumors stalked Blair for years that he was gay or bisexual. Backlund concluded that Blair simply didn't care. Because he had almost died of physical maladies as a youth, food was far more crucial to him than sex.

One of the first things that Backlund recalled Michael asking him was to set him up with one of the leggy starlets who regularly showed up for a dip in Rheo's Jacuzzi. Backlund ultimately turned Michael down for fear that Mrs. Miller would have a fit if she discovered any extracurricular activities at Blair House.

"I remember once I accidentally put the bite on her at a health food convention," said Backlund. "I had a beer in my hand, I was feeling good and she looked just like my girlfriend's mother. I came up behind her, put my arms around her and gave her a big hug. She turned around and I saw it wasn't my girlfriend's mother at all. I'd met Mrs. Miller once before. I apologized. She was a pretty woman and I told her so. She got all giggly. She wasn't a bad person; just real rigid about this lust thing."

She was equally rigid about nutrition theories. Marguerite never ordered her sons to stop seeing Blair, but she did object to what they were eating. Rheo's laissez-faire attitudes toward sex may have been troubling, but Marguerite's big concern was the meat that her sons were putting into their bodies.

"She was very interested in vegetarianism at the time," Blair told one interviewer. "She wouldn't get angry at Mike. She would get disappointed. She'd say, 'Meat kills people, Michael. How can you do this?'"

Blair's diet appeared to be doing just the opposite. In a single summer, Michael gained twenty-six pounds, developed his arms, chest and a set of shoulders, and rid himself of most of his pimples. Roy Miller seemed far more appreciative of the Blair protein program than his wife. He watched with pride as Michael developed into a strong young man, and Roy paid for it all, on time and without complaint, according to Backlund.

"Rheo was terrible with money," said Backlund. "He borrowed from everyone and let his IOUs pile up, even though he had scads of cash to pay up. He borrowed thousands from *me* and didn't pay me back for years and I worked for him! He just forgot."

Blair made a habit of sticking checks in a drawer for months and sometimes forgetting to cash them at all. Backlund remembered coming across two such uncashed checks months after the Miller boys stopped coming to Blair House. The checks were for $2,500 apiece and bore Roy Miller's signature. To his knowledge, Backlund said years later, they were stale-dated, never cashed and finally torn up and tossed in the trash.

Rheo Blair had succeeded with Michael. And still Marguerite interfered, almost as if she were jealous of Blair's success. At times, she even traced her family's decline to the day Michael began seeing Rheo Blair. Until then, both of her sons sat down to meals around the dining room table, stuck to the homework routine she had set up for them and joined in family outings without much protest. Michael, in particular, was manageable and malleable.

But after a time in Rheo's care, Marguerite began to complain that Michael seemed obsessed with his body, to the detriment of other creative pursuits and amusements. He was no longer even interested in his violin or acting practice.

After Rheo, both her boys seemed aloof. And worse, they strayed from their diets. Marguerite had to become a food policeman. She wrung her hands anxiously and clucked her tongue when she caught Michael wolfing down whole rolls of liverwurst. If Backlund snuck the boy out of Blair House for a steak and lobster dinner in Beverly Hills after a workout, Marguerite would find out about it and Michael would pay for going against her wishes with stern looks and hurt, high-pitched rebukes for weeks afterward.

Through her reading and health seminars, Marguerite found a suitable replacement for Blair in Dr. Paavo Airola, and it was his regimen that she wanted the boys to follow.

Airola's 638-page holistic masterwork, *Everywoman's Book*, was published in 1979 and became Marguerite's nutrition Bible. His book's dedication might well have been addressed directly to Marguerite's own long-held image of herself: the Christian wife, mother, helpmeet and woman.

> I dedicate this book to every woman who has the foresight and the wisdom to accept with joy and honor her glorious, divinely-designed role of womanhood, and, realizing that the future of mankind and the fate of civilization rests in her hands, exemplifies womanhood, with all its richness, in every facet of her life—as a wife, mother, student or in whatever her chosen profession or field of endeavor may be.

Airola was a Finnish painter who immigrated first to Canada following World War II and later to Phoenix, Arizona, where he set up an artist's studio. His great passion, however, was the pursuit of perfect body chemistry through food. He published a dozen other health and nutrition books before writing *Everywoman's Book*. His how-to manuals covered everything from Swedish beauty secrets to preventing hair loss to staying slim through drinking juice and fasting. He revealed "worldwide secrets of staying young" and developed cookbooks for hypoglycemics and cancer victims.

Airola was big on raw fruits and vegetables. While he didn't flatly forbid his followers to eat meat, Airola made it clear that his "Optimum Diet" consisted only of seeds, nuts, grains, vegetables and fruits. A high-animal-protein diet was "a very dangerous course to follow," he warned. Too much protein could lead to heart disease, cancer, hardening of the arteries, osteoporosis, premature aging, diabetes and arthritis, he said.

"A high protein diet can cause severe deficiencies of B-6, magnesium, calcium and niacin," Airola wrote. "Mental illness and schizophrenia are often caused by a niacin deficiency and have been recently successfully treated with high doses of niacin."

Airola also had the cultural standing that Rheo Blair did not. Besides having a listing in *Who's Who in American Art*, Airola was a fellow with the International Institute of Arts and Letters and a member of the Royal Canadian Academy of Fine Arts. His watercolors and oils hung in galleries from Stockholm to Toronto. He had academic credibility as well. He was president of the International Academy of Biological Medicine, the International Naturopathic Association and Dr. Albert Schweitzer's International Society for Research on Civilization Disease and Environment.

His crowning seal of approval, however, was his invitation to lecture on his nutrition theories at Stanford University's Medical School. Marguerite was an instant convert.

Airola also had a theory that garlic could lower blood pressure, filter toxins from the blood, act as an antibiotic and prevent indigestion. Marguerite followed the tenets of Airola's book *The Miracle of Garlic* by prodding Michael and the rest of her family to regularly consume cloves of it or, at the very least, take daily doses of garlic tablets. Garlic didn't make Michael especially popular with his waning roster of friends, but it did please his mother.

Even if there had been no Paavo Airola, Rheo could not have tolerated Michael much longer. Marguerite's increasing penchant for total vegetarianism had become a constant irritant to Rheo, but Michael's own attitude was even worse. The boy might have a Gemini's openness, but Rheo was tired of bucking his tiny attention span and chronic self-indulgence.

"Michael was a terrible procrastinator—about the worst I've ever seen," said Blair. "We'd give him a protein drink and a bunch of vitamins and five hours later he'd still be looking at them. He could not concentrate and he could not sit still. . . . We had to call his parents and tell them to take him home. He was too hard to work with. He had no self-discipline at all."

Though he was canceled as a regular client, Michael continued to return to Blair House to seek medical advice. Blair was no physician, but he did work with one in particular. He recommended that Michael see Dr. James J. Julian.

Dr. Julian anglicized his name when he came to California. Back in his hometown of Williamsport, Pennsylvania, before he graduated from the Philadelphia College of Osteopathic Physicians and Surgeons in 1954, he was James Joseph Giuliani. But when he moved to Southern California the following year with his mother and sisters, he became James Julian, Doctor of Osteopathy. In 1962, after the state of California began to recognize osteopaths as physicians, he went to the California College of Medicine in Orange County and became an M.D.

He specialized in preventive medicine, nutrition and a treatment for obesity called bariatrics. By 1970, he had incorporated and bought his own medical building at the intersection of Cahuenga and Hollywood boulevards, which became the James Julian Holistic Health and Weight Loss Center. During the 1980s, he opened offices in Ventura County and North Hollywood and began putting out a regular alternative-health-care newsletter under the acronym CAN: Consumer Advocate Newsletter. Dr. Julian and Rheo Blair established a profitable symbiotic relationship.

When skeptical parents asked the inevitable questions about the medical implications of Rheo's wonder diets, he sent them to Dr. Julian. For his part, Julian endorsed Blair's methods in advertisements, brochures and over radio and television.

"Had I not witnessed firsthand the dramatic improvements taking place in the Blair students, ranging in age from two to ninety-two, I would not have believed the impressive results achieved with this man's system of body care," Julian effused in one such testimonial.

"This emotional, mental and physical transformation is the most profound I have ever observed!" he gushed in another.

Like Blair, Dr. Julian professed to believe in nutrition and vitamins instead of drugs or surgery.

Dr. Julian was a New Age physician before the dawn of the New Age. He jumped on Nobel Laureate Linus Pauling's bandwagon when the University of California physicist popularized preventive or "orthomolecular" medicine with his claim that massive doses of vitamin C could cure colds and a host of other ills. The soft-spoken but intense Dr. Julian also counseled his patients to meditate, study life extension techniques and take megavitamin shots. He was an early champion of the controversial intravenous blood-cleaning process known as "chelation therapy" as a safer and cheaper solution to hardening of the arteries than heart transplants or bypass surgery.

Dr. Julian also favored hypnotherapy and subliminal behavior modification as a means to better mental and physical health. True subliminalists believed that audiotapes, used while a patient was both awake and asleep, could overcome bad habits, control appetite, regulate the autonomic nervous system or enhance self-esteem.

"Rheo used to say you could go to fifteen doctors and they'd give you fifteen different reasons why you're sick," said Backlund. "Rheo said it was one thing: digestion. We're all walking chemistry factories. What you eat affects everything you do. It can even make you schizo. Rheo changed a lot of kids who came in schizo. With nutrition, he could build them up at least three-quarters of the way so they weren't hearing voices and all that crap. The last quarter of the way was up to them."

While Marguerite Miller had gotten Michael out of Blair House, he did continue his visits to Dr. Julian.

When Michael graduated from high school and Jeff graduated from Dartmouth, a renaissance in health care got under way in Southern California. The holistic movement that began in the early seventies came into full bloom. Books by nutrition gurus like Adelle Davis and Nathan Pritikin were climbing the best-seller lists, health food bars and exercise spas popped up in every neighborhood, and top TV talk show hosts welcomed medical miracle workers onto their shows.

Dr. Julian's moment was at hand. He lectured, did radio talk shows and published nutrition guides. He even hosted a pilot for a holistic television series called *Ask Dr. Julian*.

While billing Julian as "the holistic doctor to the stars for the past twenty-five years," and featuring such subjects as "the treatments and methods involved in age retardation, life extension and rejuvenation," *Ask Dr. Julian* did not crack the network or syndication markets. But it did give Julian the profile he needed to take his "ounce of prevention" message to Merv Griffin's audience when he was invited on the show.

He told Merv's audience that true health and fitness in the United States was hampered, not helped, by a monolithic bureaucratic regulatory structure and a ruling medical elite. The Food and Drug Administration, in collusion with the American Medical Association and major pharmaceutical companies, kept miracles away from the American people, he said.

Merv's studio audience applauded enthusiastically, especially a thin, high-strung middle-aged wife and mother from Palos Verdes who had first come to know about Dr. Julian through her son's association with Rheo H. Blair.

After the show, Marguerite insisted on meeting Dr. Julian, and not only did she like what Dr. Julian had to say, she also liked what she saw: a handsome holistic physician who had brought his widowed mother and unmarried sister to the show.

Michael was "a quiet, unassuming, bright young man," recalled Helen Giuliani, Dr. Julian's sister. "He started coming in specifically for nutritional treatment. He came with his mother. She believed in vitamin C and all of that."

Michael seemed to be mirroring the same personality disintegration that had afflicted Jeffrey since his return to Southern California—something that could not be blamed simply on food. There was an unhealthy empathy between the brothers. Whatever Jeffrey did, Michael wanted to do too. Just how deep that empathy ran was not readily obvious to either parent or to the typical mental health professional that Marguerite had been taking them to. Even after the dread word "schizophrenia" began creeping into the conversations that Marguerite had with her elder son's physicians and counselors, she held on to the stubborn belief that the correct combination of fruits, faith, vegetables and exercise could turn things around.

After Jeffrey turned to religious fundamentalism, Dr. Julian did what he could to pull Michael out of his funk by boosting his vitamin and mineral levels. Ultimately, when Jeffrey began to flash fury without warning, it became clear that both boys needed more than vitamins and a meatless diet. The Millers began visits for Jeff and Michael to a different kind of counseling clinic located near Dr. Julian's headquarters.

The American Institute of Hypnosis offered a dynamic new type of therapy, grounded in hypnotism, the power of suggestion and B. F. Skinner's principles of behavioral modification. It called for repetitive conditioning: listening to a taped message over and over and over, sometimes for hours—even days—on end. Proponents praised the process as groundbreaking. Critics called it brainwashing.

"I dealt with the patient on a face-to-face basis, doing the hypnotherapy," explained Robert Matirko, the only state-licensed marriage, family and child counselor on staff. "Then what I would do is use the tapes and psychotherapy. Then I would help with the understanding dynamics of the personality plus the reinforcement dynamics. For people to change, it's like exercising: you have to do it over and over again before it sinks in in the reprogramming of the individual into new patterns. . . .

"I would give a running progress report on that patient. In other words, 'needed further treatment in this area,' 'resistant in that area' and so forth."

During those troubled times in 1979 and 1980, the institute started treating both Miller boys. Jeff began undergoing therapy there following his 1979 graduation from Dartmouth. Michael planned to go away to college in Northern California in the fall of 1980, but he, too, started getting regular counseling at the center while he was at home. His grades were poor and it looked like he might not get into a decent college if they didn't pick up.

In October 1979 Dr. Julian wrote a formal letter and prescription to the institute, recommending that Michael begin a weekly program of hypnosis to help him relax, develop personal motivation and change bad habits.

The American Institute of Hypnosis was more than a counseling clinic, though. It was a venerable Hollywood holistic institution that had been around since the early 1960s, run by a charismatic psychologist who publicly boasted that he was the namesake of the equally charismatic turn-of-the-century populist politician William Jennings Bryan—even though they had different middle names.

But by the time Jeff and Michael Miller became patients, the American Institute of Hypnosis was under new management.

Two years before either of the Miller boys set foot inside the American Institute of Hypnosis, its founder passed away. On March 4, 1977, hypnotherapy pioneer Dr. William J. Bryan, Jr., dropped dead of a heart attack in a Las Vegas hotel after delivering the first of three days' worth of lectures on the therapeutic wonders of hypnosis.

"He was a tremendous lecturer—a very dramatic teacher and very humorous too," said Dr. Mary Cretens, a public health physician from Michigan. "He said most people's problems went way back. He could regress people back to their babyhood and help solve their problems."

Dr. Cretens was one of hundreds of doctors, health professionals and laypeople who had heard about or seen Dr. Bryan's hypnosis demonstrations and willingly paid $275 to enroll in one of his three-day courses.

"He used to say that the patient would tell you in the first three sentences what his problem was and how to solve it," said hypnotist Frank Dana. "He got his clues from their language."

One story Dr. Bryan told during his lectures was that of the Irish husband and father of ten who came to him because he was "relatively" impotent. During the initial interview, the father told Bryan he could get an erection, but that he was "nonproductive" while having sex.

Dr. Bryan deduced from the man's story that he equated sex with procreation, as many doctrinaire Roman Catholics do, and when he put him under hypnosis, he simply told him that he didn't have to impregnate his wife every time he made love to her. With that, the man's impotency was cured.

Such stories were the bread and butter of Dr. Bryan's lectures. He was an able teacher and counselor, but he was an even better showman, according to Dana. That was one reason he gave his seminars in Las Vegas. There was the added attraction of gambling, showgirls and lounge acts in addition to advancing a medical professional's postgraduate training. The whole trip qualified as a tax write-off.

Bryan hired strippers to perform at his seminars, pointing out that embarrassment at the nudity was a direct result of preconditioning that might be altered through hypnosis. As another example, Bryan would call a man and woman to the dais and hand them each a foil-covered object. The man was given a milk-chocolate reproduction of a vagina and the woman, a penis. While they stood awkwardly before the seminar group, Bryan lectured them both on how they had been preconditioned to attach too much significance to the chocolate replica of the sexual organs they held in their hands. With that, he plucked up both the penis and the vagina and gobbled them down with gusto.

Dr. Bryan was a dynamic, self-described Renaissance man who incorporated his institute in Nevada, even though he ran it from the heart of Hollywood. He was well aware that the counseling techniques he had developed were a gold mine. He took himself and his calling quite seriously, but he lived well too. As an overweight but robust man of forty-nine, he gained a national reputation in the 1960s as the person who finally solved the case of the Boston Strangler by getting the murderer, Albert DeSalvo, to confess while under hypnosis.

"In my opinion, Dr. Bryan was a true genius," said his longtime executive administrator and secretary, Annette Rowland. "Along with his M.D. degree, he also had a J.D., a Ph.D., two honorary L.L.D.'s and was a reverend deacon of the Old Roman Catholic church. He was the author of three books [two on law and one on religion] as well as the founder and editor of the *Journal of the American Institute of Hypnosis*, which had been in continuous publication since 1960 until his death. In addition he also was the founder of, and principal lecturer of, the American Institute of Hypnosis, which subsequently became the American Institute of Hypnosis, Inc., specializing in the teaching of hypnosis to physicians, dentists, attorneys, psychologists, nurses."

Bryan showed no sign of illness at all when he opened the seminar on that Friday morning in 1977 with a lecture on the miraculous results of ranging through a patient's subconscious.

Shortly before, he had divorced Olga Bryan, his wife of twenty-three years, and married his young assistant, Savilla Higgins. Hardly older than Dr. Bryan's own two daughters, Miss Higgins was his aide-de-camp on the lecture circuit for only a short while before he began showering her with gifts. He was on his way to the Las Vegas airport to pick up a diamond bracelet for her when his heart gave out, according to Dr. Cretens.

With Dr. Bryan's sudden death, his empire collapsed, and it appeared as though nobody would get their money back. The following autumn, Savilla Bryan sold off Dr. Bryan's practice: his taped lectures, his books, his equipment. Then she put the institute up for sale.

Among Dr. Bryan's students was one who saw profit potential. He was Larry Gamsky, a former door-to-door stainless-steel-cookware salesman who had moved his family of four from Chicago to warmer climes in the late 1950s in order to cash in on the American Dream. By the time he enrolled in Dr. Bryan's hypnotherapy course in 1960 and started dabbling in hypnotism himself, Gamsky was absolutely certain that he had found that dream.

He remained a member of Dr. Bryan's circle off and on for the next seventeen years, eventually rising to the post of Bryan's office administrator. Along the way, he aspired to become a counselor himself. He helped Bryan devise an automated hypnotizing system that allowed the psychiatrist to put up to a half dozen patients into trances at one time through a series of prerecorded hypnotic tapes. They franchised the automated system and sold sixty-nine of them throughout the United States to physicians, psychologists and other would-be hypnotherapists.

"Hypnosis is like the old cliché about using a gun," said Frank Dana. "It isn't dangerous until you put it in the hands of someone who fires it."

In California, hypnotherapy wasn't even regulated by the state the way that psychologists, physicians and marriage, family and child counselors all were. In fact, anyone could learn and practice hypnosis.

By the fall of 1977, six months after Dr. Bryan's death, Gamsky had convinced a Denver physician who had also taken Dr. Bryan's hypnotherapy course to join him and a third entrepreneur in purchasing the American Institute of Hypnosis. Dr. Harry Dan Kuska, Larry Gamsky and Frank Mingarella became the new proprietors and hypnotherapists-in-residence at 7188 Sunset Boulevard.

For his share of the collateral, Kuska put up $5,000 and his license to practice medicine. His own practice was in Denver, but he applied for and received certification from the Board of Medical Quality Assurance—the gauntlet out-of-state physicians must pass through before they can practice in California. He bought a condominium in the San Fernando Valley with plans of establishing a second home in California. His license went up on the institute wall, and at one point, in early 1979, he was angling for a teaching position at Union College in San Francisco so that he could affiliate the college with the American Institute of Hypnosis and give it added authority.

But Dr. Kuska rarely visited Los Angeles. On the other hand, Mingarella and Gamsky were at the institute almost all of the time. They had been involved off and on in businesses together for several years, once forming a real estate partnership in 1973 with Frank Dana.

Dana, whose real name was Frank Frankolino, was a diminutive real estate broker who hired Gamsky as one of his salesmen in 1972. He met Mingarella the same year through Gamsky and they joined together to form MDG Investments, a real estate speculation company. After that venture failed, all three men went their different ways.

But they remained united by a fascination with hypnotherapy. Gamsky formed his own health care management firm and continued to work with Dr. Bryan. Dana also began dabbling in hypnosis while he pursued his acting career. Mingarella, who had made and lost a small fortune as marketing director for a health management organization, joined Gamsky's management firm.

When the opportunity to take over Dr. Bryan's practice came along, Gamsky and Mingarella were quite ready for another shot at fame and fortune. Both men were middle-aged divorcés who had tried several different get-rich schemes over the years, but with little success. Soon after the pair took over the institute in late 1977, Gamsky gave up his 1973 Mazda for a late-model car and Mingarella sold his 1976 Subaru so he could lease a brand-new Lincoln Mark IV from a Beverly Hills auto dealer.

Mingarella and Gamsky even found a way to actually become doctors. They enrolled in Newport University, a pay-as-you-go college in Orange County that offered degrees in counseling for reasonable rates and very little investment of time. Doctorates were awarded as much for life experience as for academic work. With a few thousand dollars in tuition plus some reading and writing assignments, they could legitimately call themselves "doctor."

Dr. Gamsky got his counseling degree first, in the fall of 1978. Dr. Mingarella paid his $2,250 in tuition and quickly followed suit. They both had business cards that read "professional seminars, medical hypnoanalysis and hypnotherapy."

Dr. Gamsky even made a brief national television appearance shortly after they began running the institute, when a camera crew from a new ABC television program called *20/20* showed up one day outside the clinic. In a segment about hypnotists, the camera crew photographed Gamsky in the institute lobby, speaking about the plus points of hypnotherapy. At one point, the camera focused in on Gamsky's degree, hanging on the wall behind him. Gamsky's TV debut was incidental in the context of the entire *20/20* segment, but the potential for attracting new clients made even a brief on-camera appearance worthwhile. Gamsky was well aware of the power of the media in spreading the hypnotic word. By the time he and his partner had taken over the institute and had run it for a year, Gamsky had made over 125 radio and TV appearances.

Frank Mingarella was equally busy with publicity. "Frank was trying to increase getting clients [by] getting on talk shows and doing PR work," recalled Frank Dana, who hired on as one of their hypnotherapists. "He got . . . a radio station promoting the American Institute of Hypnosis. His function was to create as much business for the institute as possible. The actual running of the institute was [left to] the head therapist, which was Larry Gamsky."

There were other medical doctors who worked at the institute for short periods, but Kuska was "our head doctor," said Dana. "And, if there were any questions, we could always reach him in Denver," he said.

Everyone involved seemed to have an ulterior motive, usually revolving around show business. "Mr. Mingarella and myself were going to promote a TV series called *The Mind Explorers*, based on the files and case histories of the American Institute of Hypnosis," said Dana. "And so I put together a formula and an outline and we registered that with the Screen Writers Guild." But *The Mind Explorers* didn't get far. Instead, Dana found himself joining in the day-to-day chores of the institute.

"I became kind of an assistant to Mr. Mingarella and his functionings," he said. "Also I did a lot of public relations work—a lot of research on the American Institute of Hypnosis and its functions. Later on, Mr. Gamsky was the administrator and there came a point when he stepped down from that position and became a therapist and I became the administrator.

"What happened was the employees at the front desk all quit en masse and so I had to put on another hat and start answering phones, booking people, putting them in rooms—there was no one else there but myself. And so that's when Mr. Gamsky decided to practice and made me the administrator."

The new administrator, as well as other members of the staff, wondered whether or not it was ethical for the institute to treat patients without having a doctor around. Once, Dana asked Gamsky, "Is it necessary for an M.D. to be on the premises? I see Dr. Kuska's license there."

Gamsky dismissed his concern. "That's sufficient enough. He doesn't have to be here. His license is on the wall," Dana remembered him answering.

But working without medical supervision did get dicey at times. Dana remembered the institute's counselors using more than tapes and hypnosis on their patients.

"Larry Gamsky was working with a Dr. Martino and they were using what is called laughing gas, but the medical term is nitrous oxide, I think it is. And I brought that to the attention of Frank Mingarella that, 'Hey, you know, what's the qualification of using that?' And he immediately went in and they got rid of that particular substance."

Dr. Kuska may not have been present, but he did keep the place afloat while it continued to swim in red ink. He cosigned on two loans to keep the doors open while it got back on its feet following the death of Dr. Bryan. One loan was for $7,000 and a second one was for $50,000.

When Gamsky asked him to cosign on a third loan in the fall of 1978, he said no. The institute still had to make good on the loans he'd already signed for.

"I was pretty well out of it by the time I started to get disillusioned that the money they said they were going to raise was not going to happen and I was not willing to put another penny in it," said Kuska.

Gamsky and Mingarella might have been Dr. Kuska's friends and fellow believers in Dr. Bryan's pioneering hypnotherapy techniques, but when Gamsky and Mingarella failed to keep up the payments on the loans, it was Dr. Kuska that one of the creditors tracked down for their money. When he refused to pay, the creditor repossessed Mrs. Kuska's Mercedes-Benz.

Dr. Kuska assumed that the institute continued to bleed red ink because of the profligacy and mismanagement of Gamsky and Mingarella. He was partially correct. The institute accepted Medi-Cal and privately insured clients, but filing forms was an administrative headache neither Gamsky nor Mingarella wanted to deal with. They apparently preferred clients like the Millers—and there were several—who were desperate and affluent enough that they were willing to pay thousands up front without waiting for their insurance companies to reimburse.

The checks Roy and Marguerite Miller signed to put their sons through the institute's program were being cashed. But where did the money go?

Unfortunately, being three states away most of the time, Dr. Kuska knew very little about the influence, smooth sales pitch and hungry wallet of hypnotist, cult deprogrammer and ex–bail bondsman Richard B. Martino.

— 7

One weekend in the autumn of 1979, Dr. Martino and Dr. Mingarella met Roy and Marguerite Miller at the front door of the American Institute of Hypnosis.

The attending psychiatrist who had been treating Jeffrey accompanied the Millers. So did Jeffrey. The psychiatrist spouted dire pronouncements about violence and catatonic states and the possibility of institutional commitment if Jeff did not improve. Jeff's institute workup on its standardized twelve-page patient history charted a young man out of control.

He had acted out once too often. There were still bruises around Marguerite's delicate neck where her son had tried strangling her. The Millers had been extraordinarily tolerant. They had tried the accepted routes: counseling and temporary commitment to a traditional mental ward. This was Jeff's last chance.

Dr. Julian and the therapist he had recommended, Dr. Martino, had already told the Millers about the excellent results that could be achieved at the institute. Now, with Jeff's latest outburst, if the marathon hypnotherapy at the institute could not turn him around within seventy-two hours, he would be committed to a mental hospital for his own safety and for the safety of those around him.

117

Jeffrey Miller stood before the institute staff, shackled hand and foot on this particular Friday afternoon. His clothes were disheveled and he wore a dazed, angry expression on his face, and acted as if he were drugged. When it became clear to him what he was doing there, however, Jeff went wild. His voice was shrill as he cursed and invoked God.

Mingarella and Martino each grabbed one of his arms. Jeff spat and swore like John the Baptist and rattled his restraints, resisting like a man headed for a death sentence.

"He was really, really strong," remembered one of his therapists.

But he was no match for a pair of 250-pound men motivated by the rewards success would rake in. Martino waited until they had him in a back room, out of his parents' sight, before he slapped Jeffrey hard across the face. When an assistant pointed out that there seemed hardly any need to hit a man who could not fight back, the lumbering Martino advised the assistant to mind his own business.

Out in the lobby, Roy and Marguerite paid their fees and left. Martino promised the Millers that the treatment might be arduous and expensive, but it would be effective. They thanked him and called him "doctor."

Richard Martino was many things, but doctor was not one of them. In actuality, Martino was a portly bail bondsman from Coral Gables who for most of his adult life had done anything that led to easy money. Back when Dr. Bryan was still alive and lecturing in Las Vegas, Martino first figured out that Bryan's brand of hypnosis, applied to the angry children of affluent and very desperate parents, could add up to a lot of money. Simply put, rich parents who could not control their own teenagers would pay dearly for a hypnotist to control them for them.

Before he came to California in the late seventies, Martino had developed a sideline to his bail bond business in Florida. It was the age of cults, when Pied Pipers like the Reverends Jim Jones and Sun Myung Moon were siphoning young people away from their families. A whole new profession—"deprogramming"—was in its early stages of development and Martino—that is, "Dr." Richard B. Martino—was at the forefront.

Martino had the girth, guile and expertise for tracking down bail jumpers. He had once worked as a security guard, so he knew how to deal with authority. A certificate from one of Dr. Bryan's hypnosis seminars was all he needed to add cachet and "doctor" to his curriculum vitae.

In California, Martino transformed himself, first setting up shop at his home in the Hollywood Hills as well as Dr. Julian's two-story professional building. Martino was now in the business of reprogramming wayward youth. Billing himself as "America's first cult deprogrammer," specializing in "hypnocriminology" and "psychodetoxification," he held himself out as the best and final solution to a parent's teenage nightmare. He charged plenty, but he promised results.

Several months after he'd established his practice and after he moved his offices two blocks south of Dr. Julian's Holistic Health and Weight Loss Center, Martino gave his clinic a name: the Institute of Behavioral Science.

There appeared to be no formal association between Martino's Institute of Behavioral Science, Julian's medical operation and the American Institute's host of hypnotherapists. They coexisted in a competitive environment of referrals and reciprocal treatments in the heart of Hollywood. But among the rich and desperate, referrals and word-of-mouth advertising always seemed to work best. In the therapy business, competition for clients could be cutthroat, but at another level—especially on a hard case—there could be cooperation too.

Jeff Miller was a hard case. In fact, Jeff Miller's marathon therapy was the first time that administrator Frank Dana could recall that Martino, Julian and the American Institute of Hypnosis all came together to work on a single client.

For the next seventy-two hours, the therapists worked in six-hour shifts, alternately screaming at and coddling their wild-eyed charge like demon-chasing exorcists. Instead of offering prayers and wafting incense, though, they worked on building his self-esteem. Instead of pounding the devil out of his soul, they tried shaking him free of his inhibitions, phobias and obsessions. Their language was that of pop psychology, but their actions remained those of Pentecostal shamans.

Jeff was strapped into a chair and lectured. He couldn't eat without permission. He spat at his captors. He couldn't go to the rest room without an escort. He spat at them again. Earphones were slapped on his writhing head so that he could hear Gamsky's taped messages, over and over and over, urging him to snap out of it. Dr. Julian remained on call throughout with a syringe to inject him with megavitamin doses.

Martino's therapeutic style was laissez-faire: use whatever means necessary to force the patient into normal behavior, including threats, sodium pentothal, coaxing, nitrous oxide, even harsh physical violence. Larry Gamsky, the morose, short-fused chieftain of the crew who represented the institute, relied on hypnotic trances and more endless taped messages. Julian continued to be a strong believer in vitamins, minerals and body chemistry.

During his seventy-two hours at the institute, Jeff received generous doses of all three approaches to mental health crisis intervention.

In nonmarathon sessions, Robert Matirko, the only state-certified marriage, family and child counselor on the institute's staff, described typical therapy: "I would do face-to-face: what we call psychotherapy [or] counseling: discussing their problems, conflict . . . leading up to any other things that may be affecting their personal family function. Also I did the hypnosis—face-to-face again. And then we had a tape system there which I used for support and for the patient to gain further insight into his problems.

"Bryan created the tapes from what I knew," Matirko continued. "Subsequently, Larry Gamsky filled in and did tapes as well to improve and upgrade the tape system."

The institute's tape sound system was Gamsky's brainchild. He wired listening stations all over the building so that up to six clients could be subjected to the tapes at any one time. From a master control station, a therapist could then regulate which of the hundreds of taped messages the clients listened to and the number of repetitions they got to "reprogram" their thought processes.

Gamsky himself spoke on many of the tapes, reading in his nasal monotone from scripts he wrote himself.

"Just remain completely, completely relaxed, as your whole mind, body and psyche concentrates completely and totally upon these suggestions," he would intone.

Once the patient was under, the tape instructed him or her to cooperate and enjoy his therapy.

"You will be aware that your personality is changing because of the therapy," droned Gamsky's voice. "Your mind, your body and your psyche will cooperate. You will be fascinated by the change. Your personality will accept the change and incorporate the change within its system. You will be delighted with the change. You will cooperate with the change. You will be aware that the therapy caused the change. You will feel tremendously proud that you were able to do this. . . ."

Matirko was originally from Pennsylvania but practiced for several years in South Africa. While he was there, he saw Dr. Bryan's hypnosis demonstration during one of the psychologist's world lecture tours. In February 1979, when Gamsky offered him $375 a week to work for Dr. Bryan's reinvigorated institute, Matirko took it.

Gamsky's therapy was not radical or unique in theory. It was only in practice, when each individual therapist's diagnosis took its own turn, that things sometimes got out of hand.

A "primary behavior disorder and conduct disturbance" was one of the more common labels the counselors at the American Institute of Hypnosis applied to their patients. Jeffrey Miller fell into that category.

"Yeah, it would be where usually a young person or adolescent gets into trouble or difficulty, where the behavior or his acting out is the primary problem and he becomes, like, a conduct disturbance," said Matirko. "It's his conduct you're looking at, how he is functioning. It's not quite antisocial, but almost borders on it. It's that type of thing."

Spoiled, angry teens who wanted everything their way, right away, were this type of institute client. "They want immediate gratification, and what you try to do is try to get them to control their emotional overreactions to their environment," said Matirko.

Martino often treated such overreactions with the back of his hand, provided the patient could not slap back. "We had some tapes on temper control and others which border on controlling impulses and things of that sort," Matirko recalled. Teenage boys tended to have the temper problems, he said. In addition to the tapes, Matirko also taught self-hypnosis so that angry clients could relax and cope better under stress.

When there were underlying conflicts, Matirko regressed patients in a hypnotic state back to adolescence or childhood, searching for those conflicts so they could be removed or reprogrammed.

That's what the therapists did with Jeffrey, but they were unprepared for what he revealed to them from his angry childhood, deep inside his tormented trance.

After the first twenty-four hours, Jeffrey was wearing down, but he still had a high level of resistance. His mother came to the institute with a box of organic vegetarian snacks. She did not want her son eating anything that had not first passed her inspection. The staff took her box of goodies, but she was not allowed to see Jeff.

That same morning, Jeff had broken out of his handcuffs and wriggled free from his listening station. He burst out of his prison and slipped past his therapists, out onto Sunset Boulevard, just as Martino learned of his escape. The ex–bail bondsman ran after him. He chased Jeff down, wrestled him to the ground less than half a block away and dragged him back. It was still early and the cops weren't cruising the Strip. Martino got his thrashing young charge back inside the clinic with only a couple of jaded pedestrians noticing anything unusual.

Several hours later, Jeff escaped from his cuffs again, but this time the therapists knew enough to barricade the door until Martino could be summoned to get him back into his chair.

Neither the American Institute of Hypnosis nor Martino was so cruel that Jeffrey was not given time to sleep—so long as he did so in the reclining chair where he was supposed to be undergoing his nonstop therapy. But the marathon regimen still called for intense and unrelenting pressure. By the time Frank Dana and another therapist had their six-hour turn with Jeffrey, he was still able to generate enough saliva to spit in Dana's face.

"Why'd you do that?" asked Dana, wiping the glob from his cheek while he pointed out to Miller that he, Dana, was not a mean-spirited oaf like Martino.

"God told me to do it," Jeff snarled.

"If God told you to get a gun and shoot me dead, would you do it?" Dana asked.

"Yes," said Jeff without hesitation.

Jeff's eyes were so pewter-dull and unblinking that they appeared to be lidless. Dana shuddered.

But despite his stamina and his God-inspired resolve, Jeff did wear down. He became rational enough to cooperate in a word association test.

After working with him for hours, the therapists were able to put him into a regression trance that carried him back through troubled recent incidents, including his breakup with Tracy Conrad and the disturbing relationship with Father Ed Cordero. They heard him reveal details of his love-hate relations with both Marguerite and Roy and his fears concerning his own ability to love and be loved, especially by a woman.

But the rudest shock of all came when Jeffrey's eyes darted and jumped behind closed eyelids and the words spilled out of him in the voice of a four-year-old child, creeping into his parents' bedroom shortly after Marguerite returned home from the hospital with his new little brother. In the darkest recesses of Jeffrey's secret memory, he retraced his movements one morning in 1962 as he moved to a kitchen drawer to retrieve a pair of scissors and walked in to see the new baby in its crib. He held the scissors aloft for a moment over the infant and pondered what exactly would happen if he were to plunge them into the center of the baby's chest, deep into its heart.

Dana momentarily exchanged raised eyebrows with the therapist who had teamed with him during his six-hour stint with Miller. Then they turned back to Jeffrey in his hypnotic state as he backed out of the nursery and left the sleeping infant unharmed, carefully replacing the scissors in the kitchen drawer.

The underlying idea of regressive therapy in Jeffrey's case seemed dangerous to the two therapists. The theory, as Dr. Bryan first wrote about it, was to get far enough back in a patient's memory to predate the traumatic events that warped the patient's personality in the first place. Once the trauma was relived, the patient could be reprogrammed to minimize the impact of the trauma on his adult behavior.

In Jeffrey's case, they had returned all the way to four years of age, when he and his family were living a sitcom-perfect existence in the Pasadena foothills.

And there was still inexplicable horror in this little boy's behavior. Where had such loathing and barely checked fraternal violence come from if it was there even when Jeffrey was only four years old?

Despite the lingering questions, when the weekend was over, the treatment seemed to have worked. It was as if the physical and hypnotic ordeal had purged an incubus from Jeff Miller's body and mind.

"Before, he couldn't even communicate. Afterwards, he was totally lucid," Dana recalled.

Jeffrey was returned to his parents a reprogrammed young man with no sign of the violent behavior that had brought him there. When he checked out, he was advised that therapy was far from over. He was to listen to the tapes that Dr. Gamsky had prescribed for him and return for hypnosis sessions at the institute three times a week. Jeff smiled and agreed. He seemed to be the Jeff Miller of old, at least for a time.

*   *   *

Larry Gamsky had a short fuse. He seemed the antithesis of a therapist for the emotionally disturbed. Sometimes he broke into epithets, shouting sarcasm at patients in the middle of a therapy session. He reserved his deepest contempt for those who could not pay. He didn't like Medi-Cal patients because they didn't really want to get well, he told Robert Matirko.

"His method of therapy was more on a short-term basis and he wanted results. That's the type of therapist he was," Matirko said.

Gamsky also didn't like the fact that Medi-Cal patients generated less revenue than those willing to pay cash on the barrelhead and that they also put the institute under the magnifying glass of state regulatory agencies.

The standard rate at the institute was $65 an hour, but Medi-Cal patients paid far less. The cash flow averaged out to about $17,000 a month: $15,000 from patients who paid in cash and $2,000 from those who were reimbursed through Medi-Cal.

Meanwhile, institute overhead came to about $19,000 a month. The institute only earned about $3 to $4 an hour on Medi-Cal patients, but their contribution was enough to keep the institute operating until Gamsky could figure out how to boost revenue. If their claims hadn't helped pay the rent, he would have gladly turned them away. He preferred patients like Martino's, like Jeff Miller, whose parents could pay the freight of therapy without having to fuss with government forms. When Martino found a parent willing to write a bank draft for $10,000 or $20,000, he shared the wealth with Gamsky's operation, but Gamsky would have preferred getting the entire fee for the American Institute of Hypnosis.

Money was a constant worry to Larry Gamsky: every time he got some, it slipped through his fingers. Gamsky encouraged his son to become an accountant so that he could help handle the institute books, and he hired Carolyn Brown, a former institute patient, to handle Medi-Cal claims.

"Basically, Larry said, 'I don't want to deal with this. This is driving me crazy. See what you can do.' And I did it," Brown said. She lasted four months and quit. Don St. Michael replaced Brown in January 1979.

While Carolyn Brown was efficient at the billing game, St. Michael was a whiz. He figured out which diagnosis and billing codes to put in the claim forms to get the most money out of Blue Cross and Blue Shield and Medi-Cal. During one phone conversation after he had taken over her job, Brown said, St. Michael told her, "Hi, how are you? Fine. I found a new procedure code and I'm getting money like mad. Talk to you later, babes."

The complaints had been coming into various state and local agencies about the institute even before Dr. Bryan had died.

On July 30, 1979, state medical board investigator Ed Perkins had heard enough from frustrated institute clients and their families about suspect treatment and exorbitant fees charged by hypnotists who passed themselves off as doctors. He wrote a five-page report recommending that Gamsky and Mingarella be prosecuted for practicing medicine without a license. Then he launched an undercover sting to get inside the institute and see what was going on. Perkins' operation hadn't been under way three months before Mingarella and Martino found themselves in hot water concerning a completely unrelated predicament.

On the afternoon of October 3, 1979, detectives in the Los Angeles Police Department's narcotics division got wind of an impending coke sale at a home in the Hollywood Hills. The home was occupied by a fat, fortyish psychologist who flew the narcotic in from Miami, the detectives were told by a confidential informant.

Acting on that tip, LAPD Lieutenant Clark Wardle made a blind call from a phone booth in North Hollywood to the home at 6312 Mirror Lake Drive.

"The cops are getting a search warrant," he whispered breathlessly when a man answered the phone. "If you have any dope, you had better get it out of there. Don't tell them you got a call."

Wardle hung up, went to his squad car and radioed narcotics detectives Donald Girt and Donald Joachimstaller, who had parked their own unmarked car across the street from the Mirror Lake address. Within seconds of Wardle's phone call, screams poured out of the house, according to Girt and Joachimstaller.

The front door flew open and a flabby man ran-waddled to a red Camaro parked in the driveway, tossing a Standard Shoes shopping bag in the backseat. It was Frank Mingarella.

As Girt approached him, his gun drawn, Mingarella froze. He saw Girt eyeing plastic Baggies containing about a pound of white powder that lay at the bottom of the shopping bag. Mingarella babbled that someone inside the house told him to get rid of it.

"They got a phone call and then told me, while handing me this bag, to get it out of here quick, take it to the clinic," Mingarella told the officers. "I do not know what is in the bag."

Girt and Joachimstaller went to the front door and knocked. Another huge lump of flesh answered: Richard Martino.

"Go ahead," Girt quoted him as saying. "There is no more narcotics here. You can go ahead and search."

But there were two more vials: one in the master bedroom upstairs and one in the study. The officers did find scales, a coke spoon, a freebasing kit, a revolver, airline tickets from Miami to L.A., an ID that showed Martino had once been a security officer and a freebasing pamphlet titled "Johnny's Snowflake Snow Duster."

There were also two younger men living at the Mirror Lake address. After the officers took their names and where they could be contacted if they were needed, they were dismissed. They held Mingarella and Martino on $10,000 bail each, however.

Martino swore that a former hypnotherapy patient who had later gone broke was the one who had turned him in, but he was never able to prove it.

The two men who led Jeffrey Miller in restraints into reprogramming therapy were themselves led away in chains. To add insult to injury, Mingarella lost his toupee during the arrest.

— 8

His cocaine bust and subsequent court battle hadn't helped Frank Mingarella's position at the struggling American Institute of Hypnosis. The word of mouth on the institute's marathon therapy successes, like Jeff Miller, had begun to draw in more patients, but the business side of the operation was still in the red.

The gruff and officious Larry Gamsky had switched roles with therapist Frank Dana, abandoning all of his administrative duties. Gamsky decided to devote full-time to hypnotizing and reprogramming. Mingarella handled marketing. He started a regular program on a Glendale radio station, KIEV-AM, that sold blocks of time to anyone who wanted to air their own talk show. Mingarella's show featured testimonials from patient and therapist alike, chatting about the curative properties of hypnotism as practiced at the institute. Among his guests, Mingarella included the warm guttural utterances of Richard Martino and the soporific voice of Larry Gamsky. Meanwhile, Gamsky ordered Dana to step up the Medi-Cal billings.

By the spring of 1980, Jeffrey's marathon and follow-up treatments seemed to be holding. Even though he had turned more and more to his born-again friends at Hope Chapel, his reprogramming helped him fit back into the family. Though he had occasional lapses, he seemed to have turned out so well that Roy and Marguerite agreed to try the same marathon treatment, without the restraints, on Michael.

In his parents' eyes, Michael simply hadn't grown up. They agreed between themselves that, at nearly eighteen years of age, when he ought to have become more adult each day, their younger son appeared to regress instead. He insisted on sleeping on the couch or on Jeff's bed instead of his own, which was equipped with plastic mattress covers. When he had his inevitable nocturnal accidents, he showed minimal remorse about ruining the furniture.

Michael was due to graduate from Palos Verdes High in June 1980—if he earned enough credits. He had a solid B in his Shakespeare class and an A in Chorale with Gary McRoberts, but he was only getting a C in economics and had talked about dropping his other classes. His high school counselor, Don Brough, told Marguerite he had a real attitude problem.

Still, he was holding down a job at Lindberg Nutrition Center at the Del Amo Shopping Mall after school and he did seem to want to succeed. He just got so easily frustrated.

"Mike has a very sweet, sensitive side to him, but the hostility overshadows it much of the time," Marguerite told Dr. Martino.

The Millers made a deal with their younger son: go to the American Institute of Hypnosis and let the same people who treated Jeff act as arbiters in their ongoing dispute with Michael. Whatever they decided to do, the Millers would go along with. Michael agreed, but he showed up for his pretreatment interview with a chip on his shoulder.

There was little doubt that Michael and his parents had a generation gap between them. To the therapists of the American Institute of Hypnosis, the gap seemed more like a bigger problem than usual. Roy and Marguerite had already impressed Martino as a pair of well-meaning, well-bred and well-heeled—but very old-fashioned—nitpickers. And Michael was a typical teenager: alternately arrogant and insecure, easily distracted, self-centered and plagued with raging hormones.

Unlike Jeff, who still had episodes of acting out, Michael struck Martino and Gamsky as articulate, indignant and sophisticated— not even remotely the whining, underachieving, immature bed-wetter that his parents portrayed him as being. Michael saw himself as a prisoner of Palos Verdes or, at the very least, his parents' indentured servant. He had problems—anybody could see that— but the institute therapists sympathized with his plight.

Michael told Martino that he didn't mind contributing time to help the family by doing chores and lawn work, like he said his father wished, but not all weekend every week to the exclusion of beach trips or hiking with friends. Michael told Martino, "I'd feel a lot more inclined to make a contribution that will make them happy if I felt I could have some freedom to go out and do some things that make *me* happy. I'm sure that's fair. They want me to do everything with family. Fuck 'family.' I've gotten to the point where I don't want to do anything with family. If they want me to start making up *now* for what I haven't done for seventeen years, they're full of shit."

Michael complained that any typical week in his life was taken up by school, job or family—usually with Marguerite dictating how he was to fill every waking hour. He hated going to church, but had never been able to get his parents to let him out of that weekly obligation. When his father told him he expected yardwork from him each Saturday to boot, Michael went ballistic, decrying the "teenage jail" he lived in and saying that if they wanted him to just be a happy, productive person they had to give him some freedom. Under their restrictions, though, he could turn to less ideal ways of tuning them out—like alcohol.

Rheo Blair had given him a taste for Scotch whisky—the nutritionist used to tell Michael a shot after dinner helped the digestion. He gloated to friends that he lifted Jeff's passport as ID to buy beer. But outside of an occasional drinking party on Friday night, Michael maintained that he stayed away from booze in high school. Not so marijuana, however, and he didn't mind telling his parents about the quantities he smoked.

"It eases the pain *better* [than alcohol]. Then my mom asks,

'Why do you do these things to yourself?' Well, why doesn't she look in the mirror? No, Mom, actually I get high because you're fair and understanding and compassionate and you've caused me to have a lot of self-respect."

Michael's pitch to the institute staff was not simply self-indulgent rage. He spoke with insight into the situation, even if his parents did not believe that he played by the same set of adult rules that they had learned from their own parents. Michael said he knew they cared about him—they were just lousy parents.

Michael said he didn't mind contributing to the family. And he didn't totally dismiss the silver spoon he found in his mouth when he was born. But that was never the point. He liked his lifestyle and home and was grateful for their generosity with things, but "even if I had been raised at San Simeon, I still might be miserable. Money and wealth aren't the same as *love*."

Roy said that his son might not be four years old, but he sure did act the part at times. His son might have a sweet, sensitive side, as Marguerite maintained, but Michael was also selfish. He invariably chose immediate gratification over long-term goals. Roy's own success was based on self-discipline and hard work. His sons—especially Michael—wanted everything *right now*.

The boy had trouble getting up in the morning, had a driving record full of violations and fought with Marguerite incessantly, peppering his arguments with foul language. He hadn't gotten as physical in his fights with Marguerite as his older brother had, but there was an occasional shove.

"He needs to understand cause and effect," Roy told the therapists. "He seems to feel he 'deserves' things without working for them."

Roy was out of his sons' lives most of the time. As he had done since both boys were small, Roy often worked late at the office while leaving most of the discomfort of rearing and disciplining the children to his wife. The result was that the boys reluctantly respected their father and saved their most caustic sarcasm for their mother. As her younger son passed from adolescence toward manhood, Marguerite felt Michael's hostility welling up a little more each day, like the first blasts of a torrid Santa Ana wind.

She told Martino that Michael had ceased to respect her authority and that "for years it has been necessary to give Roy a list of particulars at night for him to handle." Michael would then have to reckon with his father over these issues and tasks. Marguerite complained of "having to burden Roy with so much trivia."

She called Michael irresponsible, easily distracted, unrealistic, unable to keep family secrets. He would purposefully reveal things that his mother and father had asked him to keep quiet about. Private things, and secrets like Jeff. They felt they couldn't trust him.

He had taken to telling her to shut up or to simply "fuck off," she told Martino. Once, during a flash of temper, Michael kicked a chair and broke it. And he obsessed about never having had a little brother—something for which he blamed and badgered his parents constantly. It never seemed to dawn on him that his mother had passed beyond her childbearing years, according to Roy.

"He demanded [a brother]," said Roy. " 'Do it! Have one for me.' Like we owed it to him."

When Marguerite asked him to bring in the groceries, clean up a spill, vacuum dog hair from the kitchen—to do the simplest things—Michael told her "Later" or ignored her altogether.

"He seems to think we owe him so much," she complained to Martino.

It was the attitude, she said. Instead of coming to her where she might be working or reading in the kitchen or living room or some other part of the house, Michael would summon Marguerite into his room like a prince whenever he wanted something. He stalled her and made excuses when Marguerite wanted him to get a haircut. He helped himself to money from Marguerite's purse without asking. He took Marguerite's tape recorder to school without permission and wound up getting it stolen out of his locker. He didn't even bother to apologize to her when he told her he'd lost it.

And, as Roy had charged, he had a taste for fine things. When the family went to restaurants, said Marguerite, Michael always ordered the most expensive thing on the menu. When they went to the grocery store, Michael piled filet mignon and porterhouse steaks in the shopping basket. He searched out the highest-priced vitamin supplements and refused to take anything else. He liked the best clothes and expected his parents to pay for them. On top of it all, despite his willingness to spend their money, he boasted to his mom that he shoplifted now and then.

Marguerite felt that he behaved as if he were out of touch with reality; blaming others for his mistakes or misfortunes and refusing to understand what was really going on. She said he acted like something was literally wrong with his brain.

According to Michael, his mother was missing some rational thinking capacity too, especially when she got behind the wheel of a car. As she was driving him to the institute for his interview with Martino, he said, she almost missed the turnoff and swerved over three lanes of traffic on the Hollywood Freeway.

"In the process, she cut off one guy who almost shit!" he said.

Nonsense, said Marguerite. Michael was a backseat driver who refused to keep quiet while she chauffeured him places. His criticism was just one more way that he could show his ingratitude, she said.

Michael was adamant. He called his mother a maniac motorist from hell. Not only did she drive too fast, he said that she nagged other motorists about their car maintenance. "Drivers are always looking at her as if she's nuts. It embarrasses the hell out of me."

Michael had no respect, said Marguerite.

In fact, she did everything she could to help him, and Michael never even seemed to notice, she told Martino and Gamsky. When he came home late from work at the health food store, she saved dinner for him. When he didn't eat it, she was hurt. She wrote out his schedule and posted it on the refrigerator for him. When he didn't follow it, she was hurt.

When Marguerite spoke about her son, Martino noted, she often sounded more like a neglected wife than a concerned mother.

Martino advised her to keep careful notes about her son's behavior patterns. She did. They showed what a typical aggravating day was like with her younger son, from her point of view. In their own way, her notes were a better diagnostic tool that all the angry shouting matches combined.

Two days before Michael's formal therapy at the institute was to begin, Marguerite wrote a telling account of an occurrence with Michael in her journal, which she later turned over to Martino.

That Friday night Michael came home from work at 10:30 in an ebullient mood, pleased with a productive day at work. Even though he had gotten off an hour earlier, he didn't eat the dinner that his mother had saved for him, saying instead that he had eaten at work. He did make sure to tell her, though, that his manager had asked him if he would definitely come in for work the next day. Since Michael had taken so many days off, he really wanted him in. When Marguerite asked him when he had to catch the bus, he said he'd determine that in the morning, but he did ask his father to wake him up at eight. He retired to his room and proceeded, not to get some sleep, but to lie awake listening to music until early in the morning.

Telling Roy not to bother getting up on his day off, Marguerite rose to the 8 A.M. alarm and went to wake up Michael. She then had to return fifteen minutes later and try again. And again at 8:30. She recorded in her diary later that she finally got him up at 8:35.

She fixed his breakfast and agreed to drive him to the bus stop to catch a 9:28 bus to work. Then Michael fed the dog and returned to his room, donning his earphones to listen to music. Marguerite let him listen for the next hour and he missed his bus to work.

At 9:40 Michael called his boss to tell him he had rearranged his schedule, but that he could still come in to work. His boss told him he had already gotten somebody else and didn't need him. Mike turned from the phone and told his mother, "Isn't that great? I don't have to go! He has somebody else."

Marguerite was mortified. Later she confessed in her diary that at that very moment she had wanted to burst into tears. She couldn't believe that he could be so insensitive to her that he would wake her up early and make her pointlessly chase around after him and his responsibilities that way.

Michael didn't, however, return to his room. Instead, he started weeding out in the yard. Marguerite asked him if he would interrupt long enough to sweep the porches first so they'd look nice for the weekend.

"Later!" he snarled.

She asked again. Again he refused. When she asked still a third time, he very rudely said he just would *not* do it—he refused on principle, he told her. He would only do something if he—not she—thought it was worth doing. In the end, Michael did sweep the porches, but only because he had decided that their appearance that day was a good thing. These ritualistic skirmishes were no longer just a part of their lives. As the therapists had already come to appreciate in their grueling therapy sessions with Jeffrey Miller, the daily struggle between Marguerite and her sons *was* the Millers' life.

In therapy interviews, Michael reiterated that he felt his mother was just too nosy and pushy with him. He continued to complain that she never left him any privacy and also always had to be the one to finish an argument. Michael said that she wasn't just nagging, but hostile and sarcastic and put him down.

Marguerite, for her part, insisted that Michael "needs to dispel the idea that we owe him so much. . . . Even when [a task] is inconvenient, why should other people, for whom it's also an inconvenience, do it instead of him?" She was sick of his excuses for not doing what he was supposed to and felt that even the few commitments he did make were false promises he would break with another easy out.

One thing was clear: from their polarized positions, Michael and his parents saw things utterly differently. It would take a lot of work to achieve harmony.

Martino and Gamsky prepared for Michael's reprogramming therapy to begin first thing Monday morning, April 14, 1980.

* * *

On Monday, April 14, 1980, two Los Angeles police officers accompanied Board of Medical Quality Assurance inspector Ed Perkins on a 3 P.M. raid of the American Institute of Hypnosis. The officers handcuffed Robert Matirko, Frank Dana and Larry Gamsky while Perkins spent the next two hours confiscating several boxes of material. Matirko was arrested while he was counseling a patient. Gamsky, who had recently suffered a broken leg, had to use a cane to get to the patrol car. Frank Mingarella was arrested later at his home. They were all charged with practicing medicine without a license.

"They went through everything, every single file in the place," said receptionist Jean Clarke. "They just took anything of any consequence whatsoever. They even took my file of correspondence, you know. They went through all the file cases in the place."

Perkins was perfectly justified in doing so, of course. He had a search warrant, executed after a six-month undercover operation to see just how the American Institute of Hypnosis conducted business. The "patients" that Perkins sent in for treatment came back with enough eyewitness accounts of questionable treatment and medical mismanagement to merit a court order to search the place.

During the raid, a tall, gangly high school senior from Palos Verdes with a thatch of tousled brown hair and a bad complexion identified himself to the officers as one of the institute's patients. His name was Michael Miller and he had recently joined his brother as a regular patient at the institute.

Michael was indignant. His mother had signed a contract with Dr. Mingarella just one week earlier, promising to pay $6,000 for a seventy-two-hour marathon hypnotherapy treatment for Michael, just like the ordeal his brother had been through the previous summer. Michael raised his personal objection to the raid and began telling the police they had no right to do what they were doing.

"Shut up, kid, or we'll arrest you," said one of the officers.

Michael sat back down and didn't say another word until Perkins and the officers had taken what they needed and hustled everybody who had not been arrested out of the building. The men who had been treating them for anywhere from $65 to $90 an hour were not doctors, as they liked to call themselves, Perkins said. They were flakes.

By summer, the California Attorney General's Medi-Cal Provider Fraud unit had joined Perkins' investigation. Christine Smithson, a state investigator, began looking at the American Institute of Hypnosis books in the final quarter of 1980. She started by asking Blue Shield to turn over 131 claim forms and benefit explanation forms. She finished by filing 131 charges of Medi-Cal fraud against the owners of the institute.

Frank Dana and Robert Matirko, who had been arrested with Gamsky and Mingarella during the April raid on the institute, were subsequently exonerated. All charges and their names were expunged from the record, but both men agreed to testify against their former colleagues during their trial on Medi-Cal fraud.

Mingarella got out of the hypnosis business. What money he did have went for legal bills, fighting the cocaine charges and the nonstop trouble surrounding the American Institute of Hypnosis. When he filed for bankruptcy protection in 1983, he listed his profession as insulation contractor. In all, his debts amounted to more than $240,000.

Dr. Kuska maintained that he knew nothing of the institute's billing practices nor the fact that his medical license hung on the lobby wall, justifying its status as a medical clinic. When questioned by investigators, he steadfastly held that he had been involved strictly as a business partner and that he never intended to leave his thriving practice in Denver. He maintained he knew nothing of the kind of patient treatment his business partners were administering back in Hollywood.

Of the three original partners who bought the institute from Dr. Bryan's estate in 1977, Larry Gamsky alone remained a full-time hypnotherapist. After the state shut down the institute for good, Gamsky simply made a deal with Martino to sell him the institute's tape system. Then he moved six blocks east on Sunset Boulevard to join Martino in the lucrative business of selling tapes and deprogramming.

Andy DiCarlo and his mother, Helena Salt,[*] knew Richard Martino as Dr. Martino, after he was recommended to them by Dr. James Julian.

After he graduated from Rutgers University in the late 1970s, Andy DiCarlo's life seemed to parallel those of the Miller brothers in many ways. He couldn't seem to hold a job. He was alternately depressed and elated. He ate like a bird.

Andy left home and went to Los Angeles to get a fresh start. The first thing he did was call himself Drew DiCarlo. Later on, he went a step further and became "Drioux DiCarlo" because the spelling sounded exotic, French and somehow show-biz flashy. His mother protested when she found out, but he explained to her that everybody changed their names and reinvented themselves when they came to Hollywood. That's what it was all about.

He made new friends and kept at his avocation of writing song lyrics. He even copyrighted several and began work on what he hoped would become a Broadway musical. His mother helped him pay to put the songs to music and get demos made to send to recording companies.

But Drew still had no job months after he left home. After paying his rent and sending money for food one time too many, Helena flew to California to see how he was doing. What she discovered was a pale, thin, nervous remnant of her son who had taken to drowning his depression in quart bottles of wine. He couldn't sleep. He wouldn't eat.

Drew's drunk-driving arrest was the last straw. Helena wired him the $250 for his bail, but then began asking friends what to do to pull her son out of his tailspin.

In July 1980 a lawyer acquaintance advised Helena Salt to send her son to Dr. Julian. She made an appointment, paid $250 for tests

[*]Not their real names.

and got Dr. Julian's diagnosis: Drew suffered from dysinsulinism, acetonuria and hypoaminoacidemia. In other words, he was starving to death.

Alarmed, Helen suggested that Drew be hospitalized, but Dr. Julian assured her he could deal with her son as an outpatient. The treatment wasn't a Rheo Blair diet change. Dr. Julian prescribed a series of megavitamin and amino acid injections three times a week at $50 a shot. He also wanted $123 for vitamins. An up-front payment of $500 with another $500 within the month would handle everything, he told her. She paid with her VISA card and flew back to Ohio.

In early September Helen got a note from Julian's assistant:

> Thank you for your check of $2,000 received today. I am enclosing your receipt. Andrew is doing beautifully. Dr. Julian had a Lithium Test done earlier this week and we are awaiting results. He looks great—looked especially "well-turned out" yesterday in his tweeds. Looking forward to seeing you again.

The assistant ended the note with a happy face and her signature.

But there was more. A few days after Helena got the note, Dr. Julian called. He wanted Drew under Dr. Richard Martino's care. Martino had been very successful with something called psychosynthesis, she remembered Julian telling her. It was a process of deprogramming and reprogramming that involved sodium pentothal. There was nothing to worry about because Julian told her he would be the attending physician, Helena said. Julian wanted a $2,500 retainer fee. Then he advised her to return to California to see Martino.

When she showed up at Martino's office, just a few blocks from the institute, Martino was flanked by Dr. Julian and a man he identified as his assistant, Dr. Larry Gamsky. For the next hour, Martino regaled Helena Salt with miracle stories about youths who were suicidal, homicidal, alcoholic, anorectic and cult slaves.

People came from miles away and from other states to seek his help, he said.

Helena was impressed with Martino's stories. But she wanted to know just one thing: could they *really* help Drew lick his alcohol and marijuana addiction?

In one month's time he would be normal and able to sustain himself financially, she remembered Martino promising her.

"I was thrilled and said it will be a miracle," she recalled. "They said 'absolutely no problem.' "

She flew back to Ohio to discuss it with her husband. Martino wanted $100,000 for his services. Helena and Drew's stepfather didn't have that kind of money, but Martino assured Helena that Blue Cross and Blue Shield would reimburse about eighty percent of her fees if she put "Hypnotherapy by RX" on her checks.

Finally, after much haggling, he told her he would give her a special discount: $15,000 for Drew's cure. She agreed and gave him Drew's medical insurance identification number.

Neither Gamsky nor Martino thought it would be a good idea for Drew to know how much his treatment cost.

Mr. Salt balked at paying anything more for his ne'er-do-well stepson who had already cost him and his wife untold thousands while he fooled around trying to "find himself." If her husband had a problem fronting the money until the insurance company reimbursed the Salts, Martino counseled Mrs. Salt to simply not tell him. Drew's future was more important than money, he said. No sooner did she send a down payment of $1,500 than Martino wanted more.

The $15,000 fee would wipe out her passbook savings, but Helena started to write out a check anyway. Martino stopped her. Write two checks, he said: one for $10,000 and one for $5,000. He also advised her not to tell Dr. Julian how much she was paying. That was because the fee was unusually low, he explained.

Then he invited her to California to watch Drew's treatment begin. What she witnessed was called a "marathon": seventy-two hours of nonstop therapy. But Mrs. Salt was disappointed. The rigorous therapy she had been promised was breached from the beginning.

"Drew was fully awake during the whole seventy-two-hour period," she complained. "He even met me in the Jolly Roger [restaurant] for dinner."

In fact, after the therapy was over, Drew's drinking continued. Dr. Martino had told him that drinking wine to calm down and help him sleep was all right as long as the wine was diluted with water, he explained to his mother.

On September 22, 1980, Dr. Martino called her at her husband's office. He told them that she had to pay $2,750 for tapes that Drew had been using in addition to the money she had already paid.

"Well, all hell broke loose in the office," she said. "Needless to say, I had been under a great deal of strain, since Drew is not Mr. Salt's son."

Helena protested. She reminded Martino that she was retired and only received $174 per month Social Security. All her money was in both her name and her husband's name. Martino told her to insist that her husband divide their property evenly. He even suggested she get a divorce and offered to help her find a lawyer.

Drew had also been borrowing money from Dr. Martino. Every week or two, Martino called Helena to ask for repayment.

"In the beginning, I reimbursed him, but said 'no more' unless I consented," she said. By then, she felt Drew should be working at least part-time, as Martino had promised.

In October Martino called Helena with news that Drew had been arrested again. A lawyer whom Martino had found for her son conferred with Drew and now wanted $4,500 for his services—$2,500 up front as a retainer. Bail was set at $1,250.

Drew spent six days in jail before his mother posted bail. He was released and bail was refunded with the proviso that Drew enroll in six months of substance abuse classes and attend Alcoholics Anonymous meetings once a week. The total fee for the counseling was $675.

A few weeks later, Drew appeared to be back on track. When

he called home, he sounded steady and optimistic. Helena figured the hypnotherapy must finally be paying off.

"It seems the therapy he is now getting had helped him considerably," Mrs. Salt wrote in her diary at the time.

Drew disagreed. He wanted to quit his therapy. He called one night to say that, since he began seeing Dr. Martino and Dr. Julian, neither his insomnia nor his hypertension had improved. Helena told him to continue his therapy regardless. Not only was she certain that it must be doing some good, she had already paid Martino and Julian $25,000 for his treatment.

She heard silence on the other end of the telephone line. Then he hung up.

A few moments later, Drew called back.

"I'm sorry, Mother, but I was so shocked I couldn't talk," he said. Helena remembered his voice cracking.

On her last visit to California, she went to see Dr. Martino. She couldn't pay any more money and the one insurance claim that she had filed on Drew's behalf had been rejected. Blue Cross would not reimburse the Salts. During their visit, Dr. Martino told her he had earned $250,000 in 1979 and only paid $11,000 to the IRS. He urged her to talk to his accountant.

"He also suggested again that I get a divorce and said he would retain a lawyer for me," she said. That was enough. She left and never went back.

Drew continued to have problems. He didn't wind up back in jail, but he was nearly thirty years old and still unemployed. Still Helena always thought of him as having real perseverance and a great mind. Drew would have made a great paralegal, she said. He also had a big heart.

"He used to pick up musicians on the street," Helena recalled fondly. "He'd call and say, 'Ma, I need twenty-five dollars.' He had quite a deep voice with a flair to it."

Helena doesn't remember if she ever met Roy or Marguerite Miller, but is sure that they probably passed each other in the waiting room at the Institute of Behavioral Science. By the time she and Drew made the acquaintance of Julian, Gamsky and Martino, Michael Miller was among the constant parade of patients who came and went at the institute, clutching his reprogramming tape cassettes and mumbling to himself.

She wishes that she had been introduced to the Millers. They might have shared their pain. It might have helped them all. She believes she understands their ordeal: the stigma of loving and caring for a troubled young adult, the expense of buying great expectations and the embarrassing denial that goes along with acknowledging the reality of a mental breakdown—or worse.

One day several months after his treatment had ended, Drew went home to his tiny apartment in North Hollywood, pulled all the drapes shut and took a razor blade out of his shaving kit in the bathroom. When police found the body several days later, the spectacular spray had coagulated to a pattern of dull brown spots on the sink, the walls and the side of the tub. It was hard to tell that it was dried blood. About two years later, the Salts filed suit against Gamsky, Julian and Martino alleging that they had misrepresented the therapy and the results they projected their son would receive. The three men denied the claims and ultimately the suit was dismissed due to the Salts' financial inability to pursue their claims.

9

In June 1980 Michael graduated near the bottom of his class at Palos Verdes High.

He was tired of being constantly compared to Jeff. Of course, what most of his classmates and teachers did *not* know was that Jeff had gone off the deep end in his born-again Christianity, while Michael—despite his poor scholarship—felt himself actually coming into his own, now that he was finally past high school. He wasn't so defensive anymore when a classmate cut up about having to sit next to the guy who ate Limburger and bean sprout sandwiches. His mom's diet had helped in one way: he learned who his friends were. At June graduation, he gratefully wrote in classmate Ken Anderson's yearbook: "Even when I disgusted you with my off-the-wall natural lunches, you still accepted me."

In fact, a number of his classmates had begun to accept him. He was no athlete like Jeff and never made the baseball team he repeatedly tried out for, but he did get into many of the same singing groups, including Madrigals and Chorale. He also joined the Shakespeare Club and developed an interest in acting, even though a role in one of Palos Verdes High's musical extravaganzas was forever beyond his grasp.

Women no longer regarded him as a malignant pest, even though he could not seem to get his relationships beyond the friendly stage. He was constantly being described as "sweet."

"He was a really nice, gentle guy, but he was not my type," said fellow senior Patricia Strauss, who used to go to choral practice with him. "He was like a big brother to me."

He drove Strauss home one night, blew a tire on the way and kept on driving, despite her protests that driving on a flat tire was dangerous. On the back of a graduation photo he gave her months later, Michael wrote: "To Pat: I hope life's treating you right and you're staying out of trouble. My car's been running pretty well lately but it probably wouldn't stall if you'd stay calm and wouldn't panic."

She carried the picture in her wallet, where she kept all of her "closest friends," she said.

At eighteen, Michael was still a virgin. To his knowledge, neither of his parents had engaged in premarital sex. Virginity was not at all unusual, particularly for a child of privilege like himself. Even in the emancipated 1980s, Michael knew very little about teen sexual activity and national averages. All he knew was that Jeff had gotten laid in high school and he had not. He was determined to correct that in college.

During Michael's senior year at Palos Verdes, the movie version of the Who's *Quadrophenia* was released. It quickly became a teen cult film on the order of *Eraserhead* or *The Rocky Horror Picture Show*. That summer, before he drove up to Palo Alto to start his freshman year at Menlo College, Michael saw the film again and again. He joined other high school fans who went to midnight screenings at a Redondo Beach theater, not far from Hope Chapel, Jeff's new home away from home.

That summer as well, Michael found himself identifying less with his tormented born-again brother and more with *Quadrophenia*'s teen hero, Jimmie: a working-class kid who participated in the 1964 Brighton Beach gang wars between Britain's Mods and Rockers. Sometimes, when the house lights dimmed and he watched the rock opera unfold, Michael smoked a joint in the seats at the back of the theater, vicariously rebelling along with rock star Sting, who sang the Who's bitter lyrics about being young, alienated and Mod.

Quadrophenia's Jimmie hates useless, stupid people who kibitz while the world grows worse daily. Wars and starvation. Old people ignored by their own children because they haven't got time for them. All these injustices make Jimmie so furious he wants to "smash things up." Meanwhile, his shrink says he isn't crazy. But Jimmie scoffs at his psychiatrist, saying, "He should see me when I'm pissed."

By film's end, the hero finally realizes that the Mods, for whom he fought so selflessly, live a lifestyle as artificial and empty as those of the psychiatrists and parents he originally rebelled against. Michael told Dr. Martino, Gamsky and the others who used to work at the American Institute of Hypnosis that he had the same problems Jimmie had. He also noted that Jimmie rode his scooter off a cliff at the end of the picture.

Michael's summer break between graduation and college was as rebellious, and as meaningless, as Jimmie's. He continued to experiment with cigarettes and pot. He downed his share of vodka and beer with other summer companions as they roamed from the hills of Palos Verdes to the streets of Hollywood, looking for adventure.

"We used to break into condominium complex Jacuzzis and sit around all night until somebody found us and kicked us out," remembered Doug Kaback, one of Michael's classmates. "We used to play a game we called 'beer hunter,' based on the movie *Deer Hunter*. We'd go to a golf course late at night and shake up beers and chase each other around. You'd pick up one beer at a time, shake it up and try to spray the other people.

"We'd get gunpowder too and blow it up in the wee hours of the morning. And we'd take people's sailboats and make little trips down the coast in them. We broke into nurseries to get potted plants and flowers and leave them on the doorstep of the girls we liked."

Michael was defiant. Because Marguerite asked him to, he

wouldn't sweep the porch. Likewise, he regularly and conveniently forgot to walk or feed the dog. He played his stereo loud over his mother's protests. He had a summer job, but he was often late. Sometimes he didn't get up in time to go to work at all.

He also had his own car, and, by summer's end, had chalked up a half dozen traffic tickets and more than $600 in fines. Roy and Marguerite were furious but helpless. They could do nothing with him. They breathed easier after they saw him off to Palo Alto.

After visiting the campus with his parents during the summer, Michael enrolled in Menlo College in September 1980. The school was just a half mile north of Stanford University on the San Francisco Peninsula, but it did not share the same academic standards. Tuition at Menlo was nearly as expensive as Dartmouth or Stanford, but it required little more than C high school grades and an average SAT score for admission. The school offered a four-year degree in business administration, but only a two-year junior college diploma if a student wanted to pursue liberal arts.

"I got the feeling that the junior college was a glorified day-care center," said Chris Morphy, a business major and one of Michael's contemporaries at Menlo. "It was the place where, if September rolled around and nothing was going on for you, you could call up and find a spot. Every region of the country has a school like Menlo: nothing works out for you, so you have Daddy write a big, fat check and that's where you wind up."

Michael arrived with high hopes. The first week of school, he wrote Larry Gamsky, praising him as "the most fantastic person I have ever met" and giving him the credit for helping him overcome his emotional immaturity.

"I'm finally settled in my room with everything in its place, and bought all my books yesterday," he said. "Everything's going fine and classes start tomorrow."

But eventually, Michael himself began to describe Menlo to his parents as a "dead" school with a limited selection of subjects. Nevertheless, Michael chose the two-year course in liberal arts. He studied French and acting. He took literature classes and read novels like *Catcher in the Rye* and *Cannery Row* and plays like

Hamlet and *Oedipus Rex*. He studied hard enough to make the dean's list his first semester, but he made few friends.

When he called home, Michael was contemptuous. It was the kind of campus where undergrads had food fights in the dining hall, he told his mother. The student body seemed more interested in beer parties than education. Meanwhile, he was drinking beer with the handful of friends that he did hang around with. He also dabbled in recreational drugs and ate burgers or chocolate or pizza whenever he pleased, five hundred miles out of his mother's critical sight.

While away at school in Northern California, he also remained in touch with the therapists at the American Institute of Hypnosis. Since the institute's closure the previous spring, the therapists operated out of Dr. Martino's Institute of Behavioral Science. Michael called on them often for advice and wrote occasionally. In his judgment, he told them, they had turned out to be friends who had done him remarkable good.

Thanks to Rheo Blair's encouragement, he wasn't as ashamed of his body, despite the weight loss he'd suffered since returning to his mother's vegetarian diet. And, thanks to the American Institute of Hypnosis, he no longer felt as shackled by his inhibitions. At Menlo, he felt less like the gawky loser he was in Palos Verdes.

If he hadn't been encouraged by his hypnotherapists, he might not even have gotten through his senior year at Palos Verdes High. He credited Mingarella and Gamsky for programming him to succeed.

After high school, both Mingarella and Gamsky recommended that he physically get away from his parents' smothering influence. Gamsky was even more outspoken about his leaving home than the others. At times, he even raised his voice at Marguerite when she came by the institute to check on her sons' progress. The way she tried to channel both boys' lives was flat-out wrong, he told her, and he was especially antagonistic about the way she treated her younger son. She had no right to keep him away from red meat, candy bars and the opposite sex.

"Either take him to bed or leave him alone!" Gamsky once yelled at Marguerite in a frustrated moment, giving voice to an angry undercurrent Michael had felt throughout his high school years about his mother's controlling ways.

Gamsky's counseling technique had grown bolder since the shutdown of the American Institute of Hypnosis. During their sessions, he asked Michael to speak frankly about his mother: How often did Roy and Marguerite have sexual relations, if at all? Did her need to control everything, including what he ate, mean that she was sexually starved? Why did Marguerite schedule her sons' lives so rigidly, down to where they were and what they were doing during every waking hour?

"As long as I can remember, Michael had this schedule he had to adhere to," recalled one of the Millers' neighbors. "If he wanted to play ball, but it wasn't between, say, 4 P.M. and 5 P.M., he couldn't."

Marguerite wrote his schedule down and posted it.

"His mother set the schedule for him and it would be, 'Practice violin from 3 P.M. to 5 P.M.; homework 5 till 6,' " the neighbor said. "He had to do exactly what it said."

In an act of defiance, Michael sometimes wrote "Have fun" into a block of time that his mother had not already scheduled for something else.

Gamsky's counseling sessions, coupled with the hypnosis cassettes Michael listened to on subjects ranging from sexuality to religion to motivation and separating from one's parents, had begun to make sense to Michael.

And, now, just as Gamsky had advised he would be, Michael was finally on his own at Menlo.

Several years later, recalling his visits to both the American Institute of Hypnosis and Dr. Martino's Institute of Behavioral Science, Michael gave credit where credit was due: Mingarella may have gotten him through high school, but Gamsky got into his head.

"Gamsky told me lots of filth about my parents," he said. "It made the ideas in my head speakable."

As part of his therapy, Michael was asked to fill out a questionnaire detailing his feelings about sex, religion, relationships, etc. For his therapists, it was tough to tell whether or not he was being serious in his answers at times. In the questionnaire, for instance, he revealed that he and a male friend had once stripped together when they were both twelve years old—a normal enough event in the developing sex life of a pubescent boy. But he also claimed to have had relations with a boxer dog.

And under the portion of the questionnaire dealing with religion, Michael said he was raised Methodist and believed God must exist, but when asked what organized religion his parents belonged to, he wrote "the Republican Party."

In Washington, D.C., a revolution was under way.

After four years of trying to jump-start the country, President Jimmy Carter was turned out of office in November 1980, and California Republicans, led by Ronald and Nancy Reagan, were given the keys to the White House. Roy and Marguerite Miller were among the celebrants, rejoicing that commonsense conservatism had finally prevailed.

On January 9, 1981, Ronald and Nancy Reagan formally signed over power of attorney to Roy Miller in its entirety. He now acted on their behalf on all personal legal matters. His workload at the office leaped. His first order of business was to sell the Reagans' five-bedroom ranch-style home in the exclusive Pacific Palisades area of West Los Angeles. It went on the market for $1.9 million the same week that the Reagans flew back to Washington for the Inauguration. Their first tax return as First Couple was due in three months and it was up to Roy to prepare it.

The day after Inauguration, the Gibson, Dunn and Crutcher partner who gave Roy Miller his job as the President's personal attorney walked into the Department of Justice to assume his new job. William French Smith was an outsider to official Washington and he would remain an outsider throughout his four-year tenure as Attorney General. He didn't trust eastern liberals and he didn't like the weather. He was in Washington to do his duty and nothing more.

Ronald Reagan, William French Smith and Roy Miller all sang the same anthem about pioneer spirit, free enterprise and the Protestant work ethic. There would be no room for freeloaders and felons in a nation run by the Reagan White House.

Smith asked for seven new federal prisons and thirteen regional antidrug task forces almost as soon as he took charge of the Justice Department. His message was clear: no coddling for criminals, especially those who dealt or dabbled in drugs. Felons went to prison to be punished, not psychoanalyzed on the public's time.

On the civil law front, deregulation became the rallying cry of the Reagan Administration, and William French Smith was one of its chief standard-bearers. The Attorney General's policies favored corporate America over organized labor; free enterprise and rugged individualism, as long as the individual was willing to work hard.

Roy Miller couldn't agree more. One of his first recommendations to the new administration was to turn the President's focus on successful nonunion companies, where hard work was rewarded and malingering was not tolerated.

Miller urged the President to publicly recognize Lincoln Electric Company as an example of the conservative work ethic. The successful Cleveland corporation had been a leading manufacturer of electric motors for decades, sharing profits with productive workers in the form of high paychecks and big bonuses. Workers got no sick leave, paid holidays or other benefits, but those who worked hard were rewarded with big paychecks.

Lincoln Electric reflected Roy Miller's own cool determinism and pride of achievement. The company's policies were not unlike those of the La Verne Fruit Exchange, where his father had worked so hard for so many years. La Verne's labor policy had been simple: those who grew and packed the most and best-quality citrus were rewarded. Those who did not, lost out.

Reaganomics implied survival of the fittest. Unfortunately, when Roy tried applying that same Darwinian principle to his own children, tolerance and compassion always seemed to get in the way.

* * *

Besides the election of Ronald Reagan, the Miller family experienced another significant event in the fall of 1980. After years of robust health, Harold Bruner died at eighty-seven on the last day of November. Of all the Millers, Jeffrey took his grandfather's death the hardest.

In his final years, Harold seemed to have become more keenly aware of the problems of young people. Jeff wasn't the only one who noticed. Members of the Claremont United Church of Christ remarked on it, pointing to the social conscience Bruner encouraged in his church, particularly during the campus uprisings of the sixties and the Vietnam protests of the seventies. While he criticized "disrespect for property," Harold had come to appreciate the sense of powerlessness young people felt. Time had mellowed Marguerite's stern father. He listened to his grandchildren with a patience and sympathy he had rarely displayed to his own daughters.

When Harold Bruner died, Jeff felt as though he had lost one of the last nonjudgmental adults in his life. He went to pieces.

The marathon and follow-up treatment at the American Institute of Hypnosis turned out to have been only a temporary solution. He retreated further and further into himself. Jeff was beyond control, alternating between long periods of stony silence and rages that the Millers feared might lead to a violent attack, either on Marguerite or on someone else.

Their son was schizophrenic. There seemed little doubt about that. Dr. Thomas Talbot Seeley was the last resort for the Millers.

In Seeley's opinion, the American Institute of Hypnosis treatments had done inestimable harm—especially the mind-bending tape sessions emphasizing the stifling influence of an overbearing mother and a young man's need for sexual release.

"Anybody who messes with hypnosis and tries to apply a dynamic influence with schizophrenics often makes it worse," he said. "With schizophrenia, the mind is already overanalyzing. 'Should I do this? Should I do that?' By firing up their conflicts and fantasies, that kind of therapy gives validity to their delusions and grandiosity."

But Marguerite was part of the problem too.

"She was a very obsessive mother," recalled Dr. Seeley. "When you have a mother who is obsessive and sort of smothering in an overly protective way, it can create a smoldering pressure. A son can't get free to develop the social skills to go out and form the kind of relationship you have to have to get sexually satisfied."

The Millers placed Jeff under Dr. Seeley's care at Ingleside Hospital, an upscale psychiatric center near Pasadena that specialized in short-term recovery programs for emotional problems ranging from grief and fear to all kinds of chemical and mental addiction. Though Ingleside's image was that of secure warmth—its logo featured a homey hearth fire burning in a brick fireplace—it also had a locked ward for violent or absentminded patients who might wander off unattended in the hospital's regular wards.

Jeff's stay at Ingleside was longer than that of most patients, according to Dr. Seeley. First he got better. Then he got worse.

Seeley was a veteran of treating young men and women from good middle-class homes for schizophrenia or clinical depression. Unlike the therapists of the American Institute of Hypnosis, Seeley was a real medical doctor: a 1969 graduate of the University of Rochester Medical School who had been granted American Board of Psychiatry and Neurology certification the following year. He became a successful working psychiatrist during the 1970s, rose quickly among his peers and had been formally commended by the nationally known UCLA Neuropsychiatric Institute.

He knew about schizophrenia. It could not be harnessed by vitamins, vegetables and hypnosis.

Most schizophrenics were dangerous only to themselves. Once in a great while, however, they became very dangerous to others, obeying the murderous whispers that only they could hear.

Before he became Jeff Miller's psychiatrist, Dr. Seeley had treated dozens of severe schizophrenics, some of whom tried suicide repeatedly to still the voices inside their heads. At least one of his patients found relief from the voices another way.

"I had a case of a fellow who was driving down the highway one day and it suddenly came to him that he had to go home," said

Seeley. "He'd been in a fog all day, he said afterwards. He went in the house, stabbed his wife while she was still in bed and then he went next door and killed both of his parents. He didn't remember a thing."

Schizophrenics hear voices in the beginning—often while they are still in their teens. If they mention the voices to anyone else at all, they normally get disbelief followed by scoffing. Relatives tell them they are crazy. There are no voices. It's all in their imagination.

The patients's embarrassment over his condition is usually enough to stifle any detection of the first symptoms of schizophrenia, according to experts like Seeley. The more schizophrenics try to ignore the voices, however, the louder they get. The voices order them to do or say outrageous things. Unchecked, the voices become a cacophony, inducing fear, confusion and hallucinations—or worse.

Young men under twenty-five, who only occasionally show a genetic predisposition to schizophrenia, are its prime victims. Even the most conservative estimates put the percentage of schizophrenics in the general population at nearly one percent. Some of Seeley's colleagues said the figure could be as high as three or four percent. But sons of the poor are eight times more likely to suffer schizophrenia than the rich. Most well-to-do families keep this mortifying malady under wraps.

Harold Bruner's death had reignited Jeffrey's schizophrenic episodes. None but those closest to Roy and Marguerite, however, ever knew Jeff had a problem.

Just before Jeff had to be returned one more time to the hospital, all four Millers gathered together for an informal family portrait. They all smiled for the camera. The Millers reproduced the photo as a greeting card that they mailed out to friends and relatives for Christmas 1980.

Marguerite stood between Michael and Roy, her arms wrapped around both of their waists. Jeff stood beside his father, looking for all the world as if he were still the bright, cheerful but serious young man who had planned to become a theologian just a year earlier. Both boys were dressed casually and Marguerite wore a simple straight dress. Roy was in a suit, white shirt and thin, dark tie. Roy held his wife's hand in the photo.

And Michael smiled an innocent smile for the camera, while his left hand curled slightly in such a way that his middle finger extended further than the rest of his fingers.

"I took about twenty-six years of French to avoid taking math and I got pretty good at it," said Peggy Sweeney, who met Michael in Madame Hester's French class at Menlo. "He ended up coming up to my room for informal tutoring."

She lived on the women's floor at the Kratt Hall residential dorm on campus and, at first, she didn't mind tutoring. She was one of her French professor's shining lights, so she wound up tutoring everyone, it seemed, including her own roommate, Laura Belfry. But practicing French phrases with the intense, looming kid from Palos Verdes got to be a bit too much. At first, she felt sorry for him because he seemed so awkward and alone, but Michael's presence grew oppressive after a while. Instead of warming to coeds who were often as skittish and tentative as himself, he seemed purposely aloof. Even a little ominous.

Peggy remembered one evening during Michael's first year at Menlo when she and Laura were sitting on their beds in their room, rehearsing the guttural *r*s and flowing phonetics of the French language.

"Our door was open a crack and I got up to get something across the room and there he was standing outside my door," she said. "He'd just been standing there at the door, listening to us! Not saying a thing. Just listening. After that, we nicknamed him 'Creepy.' "

When Creepy found reasons to see her, she found reasons to avoid him. Once, when he asked to borrow her typewriter, Peggy concocted a plan to loan him the machine in such a way that she would not have to see him face-to-face. When she saw him coming her way across the campus, she found a more circuitous path to her next class.

"He had these piercing blue eyes," she recalled. "And he'd say things like, 'Gosh, you have such beautiful hair,' and run his fingers over your hair. He was soft-spoken, but always kind of weird—this tall scary guy. He was *not* your typical idea of a typical college guy. You wouldn't picture him out throwing a football around."

Back home in Los Angeles, Jeff's condition worsened. Dr. Seeley recommended long-term care and a more radical type of treatment—the kind that Ingleside Hospital could not offer. Jeff was transferred temporarily to Arcadia Memorial Hospital, where he was officially diagnosed as suffering from acute paranoid schizophrenia.

The first week of March 1981, Jeff was transferred again, this time to the Anne Sippi Clinic—a long, brown T-shaped building in the hills of East Los Angeles that more closely resembled a low-rent motel than a treatment hospital.

Since the clinic first opened in 1978, Dr. Seeley had been one of its biggest fans. When nothing else seemed to work, and if the family could afford the steep price of the therapy, Seeley recommended his own toughest cases to Anne Sippi.

The man behind the Anne Sippi Clinic for the Treatment of Schizophrenics did not believe in conventional treatment. Jack Rosberg was a gravelly voiced clinical psychologist from New York with a cigarette habit. He held a master's degree in psychology from New York University, but was not an M.D.

Rosberg spurned electroshock therapy, lobotomies, Thorazine, Elavil, locked mental wards and most of the other traditional methods of treating schizophrenia. They were inhumane and served the needs of the doctors and nurses, not the patient, he argued. Most mental health professionals just didn't want to invest the "damned hard work" required to help a schizophrenic exorcise his or her devils, he said.

Part witch doctor, part Pentecostal revivalist and part parent, Rosberg oversaw a staff that used direct confrontation to get inside the patient's insanity. Sometimes he took on their same crazy behavior himself.

If a patient shrieked and babbled in Swahili, so did Rosberg—even though neither of them spoke the language. If a patient shrank back into a corner, trying to ignore or get away from his therapist, Rosberg followed, keeping his nose no more than a few inches from the patient's nose. If a patient insisted that he was being pursued by aliens or that he was Jesus Christ, Rosberg went along with it. To a point.

"God told me I was His son," insisted one patient, stretching his arms out against a wall as if he had been crucified.

"Oh, yeah? God told me there was some bastard going around claiming he was His son and gave me a contract on him," answered Rosberg. "Because He told me *I* was His son."

Direct confrontation demanded persistence and patience. Most of those who wound up at the clinic had spent years building up bizarre defenses that didn't dissolve with a few sessions. Anne Sippi was usually the last stop before a one-way trip to the nearest asylum.

"I get them after everyone else has had them," Rosberg told his critics and disciples alike. "I'm the garbage collector."

He taught his therapists to treat schizophrenia in much the same way teacher Annie Sullivan taught Helen Keller how to speak and write. Rosberg assumed that there must be a logic to a schizophrenic's erratic behavior; that their insanity was a form of self-preservation—simply a way of coping with the terror of real or imagined annihilation. New York psychoanalyst John Rosen, who took Rosberg on as his apprentice for three years in the early 1950s, blamed the disorder on "malevolent mothering." A successful therapist had to be a tough-loving parent, he said.

Rosberg took reparenting a step further than Dr. Rosen. A therapist gained trust by being just as wacky as his patient, but always strong and always in control, said Rosberg.

"I confront the person with the fact he's nuts," Rosberg told one interviewer a few months before opening his clinic. "It's important that he knows he's nuts—that he has a distorted view of the world, and acting on this view, he makes misjudgments and says weird things. The idea, of course, is abhorrent to him; and the harder I push, the more he resists."

Therapy at the nonprofit clinic—named for one of Rosberg's patients—was unusual, occasionally harsh, always intense and quite expensive. The cost of full-time care and treatment in the thirty-two-bed facility was about $2,000 a month when Jeff entered the program. The good news was that the average patient walked out of the clinic within fourteen months, able to cope with his or her disability enough to function in the outside world.

"Nobody is beyond hope except the therapist," Rosberg liked to joke with his apostles.

After Harold Bruner's death, the voices inside Jeff's skull stepped up their orders that he beat up anybody who got near him. He had already commemorated himself at Ingleside as violent to himself and others, despite the antipsychotic drugs Dr. Seeley had prescribed.

Jeff clashed with Rosberg and his staff from the very beginning. On March 11, just a few days after he entered the clinic, he leaped on a staff psychologist and began pounding him to a pulp. It took three or four attendants to pull him off. The psychologist could come up with no apparent reason for Jeff's assault.

Just over two weeks later, on March 28, 1981, the *Palos Verdes Peninsula News* reported that Renee Taylor, author of *The Total Health of the Total Person*, was coming to Palos Verdes to show her film *Health Secrets of Shangri-La*. She also planned a workshop she called "A Healthy Diet—A Happy Body." Marguerite Miller planned to attend.

The *News* also reported that an entire class from Chadwick, the Peninsula's premier private school, had flown to Washington for a special visit to the White House. The article noted that two of Reagan's own children, Maureen and Michael, had attended Chadwick back in the 1950s.

What the *Palos Verdes Peninsula News* could not report on March 28, 1981, was the story of the year, which was about to unfold three thousand miles away. It was the story of an agitated twenty-five-year-old college dropout who couldn't hold a job, was obsessed with a movie star and had been kicked out of the house by his

disgusted parents. This young man's story was typical of a generation of pampered young adults who alternated between infantile
dependence and frustrated aggression. During one of his fits of
anger, he physically attacked his mother. When his parents
couldn't put up with any more of his lackadaisical, whining ways,
they sent him packing.

It was not a story about Jeffrey or Michael Miller, though it
could have started out the same way. The young man in question
was raised in an affluent Colorado home, the son of a born-again
Christian father and an equally religious mother who had grown
up as the daughter of devout Disciples of Christ.

What made this young man's story different from the Millers'
was the .38 pistol in his pocket and the obsession in his head.
After he left home, he traveled to Washington, D.C.

On March 30, 1981, John W. Hinckley, Jr., stepped into the
history books as he lay in wait outside the Washington Hilton,
preparing to ambush the President of the United States. Hinckley
was certain that act of violence would win the attention of actress
Jodie Foster and silence the voices inside his head.

Television carried the story first. The biweekly *Palos Verdes Peninsula News* wouldn't carry the news until several days later.

But Roy and Marguerite Miller paid scant attention to the video
replay of the shooting of Ronald Reagan, over and over and over
on the television news programs that week, or the reporters trying
to interview Jo Ann and John Hinckley, Sr., about their schizophrenic son. On March 30, 1981, as surgeons wheeled Ronald
Reagan into an operating room in order to extract the flat bit of
lead a half inch from his heart, Roy and Marguerite Miller were
too preoccupied with grief of their own to pay much attention to
the attempted assassination.

On March 28 Jeff Miller swallowed an entire bottle of aspirin,
and the following morning he was dead.

Dennis Bidsdorf and Ernie Valenzuela were the LAPD robbery/
homicide detectives dispatched to the Anne Sippi Clinic from the

Hollenbeck Division to investigate what Valenzuela later called "an undetermined death." In dispassionate police prose, they detailed a case that had all the signs of a crazy kid who killed himself.

> Last night, March 28, he told one of the attendants that he had taken 100 aspirin tablets. He then handed her the empty bottle. He was administered Ipecac or some vomit-inducing agent. He appeared to be all right after vomiting.
>
> This morning, March 29, his roommate saw him hitting his head against the bathroom walls. The patients in the next room also heard the noise. The roommate states that the decedent then fell to the linoleum in the sleeping area of the room they shared.
>
> The roommate, who is also a mental patient, did not think there was anything wrong as he had seen the decedent go into a catatonic state on several occasions. This would even happen while the decedent was walking through the halls of the clinic.
>
> When the police arrived, they observed the decedent lying on his back, alongside the roommate's bed. He was dressed in shorts and a shirt. There was a pool of blood under his head. A cursory examination revealed an open wound in the scalp, in the parietal-occipital area. No apparent weapon was found in the room. There was no other blood, except for the puddle under decedent's head.
>
> At this time, the police do not have a suspect in custody. They are carrying the case as undetermined, pending results of autopsy and toxicological tests. There is a distinct possibility that the decedent fell to the floor while lapsing into one of his catatonic states.

Jeff Miller's system was drug-free—no narcotics or alcohol or barbiturates. Officially, he died at 8:42 A.M., March 29, 1981. He had a long shallow gash across his forehead, but the medical examiner concluded that he must have cut himself when he collapsed. Following an autopsy, the medical examiner decided acute salicylate intoxication, or aspirin overdose, was what killed him.

There was speculation among Jeff's old friends at the United Methodist Church and his new friends at Hope Chapel that there must have been more to his death than an aspirin overdose and a coroner's verdict of suicide. Aspirin poisoning was essentially acid eating away the lining of the stomach, triggering an excruciatingly painful death by internal hemorrhage. It seemed strange that even a catatonic Jeff Miller would be able to die such a death in silence while the twenty-four-hour staff walked the corridors outside his room.

The rumors about his suicide never went anywhere. The obituary published in the *Palos Verdes Peninsula News* was terse and mysterious, providing no clues as to how or why such a promising young man could come to his end so early or so tragically.

> 23-year-old Jeffrey Bruner Miller of Palos Verdes Estates died Sunday morning in Los Angeles.
>
> He was born Sept. 29, 1957, in Los Angeles. He grew up in Pasadena and in 1969 moved to Palos Verdes.
>
> Mr. Miller was graduated from Palos Verdes High School in 1975 and from Dartmouth College in 1979. He was a member of the First United Methodist Church of Pasadena and Hope Chapel in Hermosa Beach. He was an Eagle Scout.
>
> Surviving are his parents, Roy D. and Marguerite Miller, and a brother, Michael, all of Palos Verdes Estates; and his grandparents Mr. and Mrs. Roy G. Miller of Claremont.
>
> Services will be held Sunday at 3 P.M. at the United Methodist Church in Pasadena.
>
> Private burial will be in Oak Park Cemetery in Claremont. . . .
>
> Memorial contributions may be made to the First United Methodist Church, 500 E. Colorado Blvd., Pasa-

dena 91101, or the Hope Chapel, 2420 Pacific Coast Highway, Hermosa Beach 90254.

"We lost him," said Hope Chapel's Rev. Ralph Moore. "We did the best we could. But we lost him."

— 10

"We went up [to Menlo] to tell him that Jeff had died instead of calling him by the telephone or writing him," Roy Miller recalled later. "And it seemed as if he almost blocked it out, as if a curtain had come down over him, that he was trying to shield from whatever emotions might naturally flow from such a tragic event."

Michael couldn't bring himself to go to his brother's funeral. He drove to Dr. Julian's home and found sympathy there. Dr. Julian's sisters and mother were kind, even solicitous. They made him breakfast in the morning and tried their best to console him during the day.

"I've always been good with young people, since I first started working in my dad's store," said Helen Giuliani. Her mother was especially taken by the "quiet, unassuming, bright young man," she said.

Michael remembered spending nearly a week at Dr. Julian's house. Julian and his sisters remember it as being far less time than that. But time was only one of the dimensions in Michael's life distorted by Jeff's death.

The Millers had taken a tape recorder to Jeff's funeral and taped the entire memorial service. They gave Michael a copy, and when the mood hit him weeks or even months afterward, he popped the cassette into his car tape deck when he was out driving by himself, or while he was alone in his room, much the way he listened to *Quadrophenia* or the self-help tape cassettes that Dr. Gamsky had sold him. The sad sounds of mourners and the minister's words as his brother's casket was laid into the earth at Claremont's Oak Park Cemetery brought back an imagined tableau of Jeff's dozens of friends and family members, bowing their heads at graveside while his parents stood at the forefront. The tape induced waves of cathartic emotion in him, continually reigniting his grief.

Michael spent the next weeks asking questions of himself and those few friends he trusted, trying to make sense of his brother's death. Mostly, though, he stayed to himself, brooding.

It was the middle of the spring semester at Menlo, but his classmates rarely saw him after Jeff's funeral. When he finally did return to campus, he seemed dramatically different.

"After Jeff died, all he wore was black," said Peggy Sweeney. "Black sweatshirt, black sweatpants, black sneakers. Even when it was a hundred degrees outside, he wore black. He was always all covered up."

He didn't make the dean's list at Menlo the second semester. He almost dropped out altogether. The one area where his scholastic interest intensified was French class. He practiced phrases on anyone who would listen—especially women. France and French culture became an obsession. French had been Jeff's ticket to sophistication, it could be Michael's as well.

It was almost as if Michael's green-eyed jealousy of his older brother had suddenly escalated one more step following Jeff's death. Michael literally wanted to *become* his older brother. Jeff had spent a semester in France during his sophomore year at Dartmouth. Michael reasoned that he should go too. He talked his parents into letting him go to France for the summer.

He found a blue-collar job in Le Havre on the Normandy coast, cleaning telescopic slides for a company called Chambrelan: a *métalurgerie* that made parts for trucks and defense vehicles. One of Chambrelan's managers, M. Couppey, let Michael board with his

family in their beachfront home, where Michael immediately ingra-
tiated himself with Madame Couppey, buying her flowers and candies. He immersed himself in French culture, language and
philosophy. He also immersed himself in French romance.

On July 6, 1981, Michael wrote to his old therapists back in Los
Angeles. The stationery was decorated with sun and palm trees—
more California than France. He wrote that he had just moved out
of his room at the Couppeys' home and was now sharing a small
apartment with a secretary he had met at the company where he
worked.

Her name was Christine. She was a few years older than himself,
but she was French and female and willing to end the curse of his
virginity. They had been living together for nearly a week, "and
life is like a dream," he told Dr. Martino.

On the day he wrote Martino, Michael planned to drive an hour
north of Le Havre to a beach at the French coastal town of Etretat.
It was hot—nearly eighty degrees. And life was wonderful. He and
Christine had made love often, he exulted, and he was staying in
good shape for her by lifting weights, swimming and running. She
lived inland in her apartment, so he couldn't run along the beach
every morning the way he had at the Couppeys', but he still jogged
regularly.

Christine took him shopping and bought him clothes: socks,
pants, shirt, a sweater. She made him help her pay for food and
keep the apartment clean, but she was not tough enough, Michael
said. His one big problem with her was his own desire to be "moth-
ered and directed," he confided to Martino, adding paradoxically,
"but I know I'm old enough to take care of myself."

He kept finding himself relating to Christine the way that he
related to his mother. He was also haunted by dreams and "bizarre
thoughts" that made it difficult for him to concentrate when he
was at work.

He dreamed that he had strangled Marguerite one night. In
another dream, he raped her. He also had been experiencing flash-
backs to his childhood, when he was the happiest that he could
ever remember being. He wanted Martino's advice about every-

thing. For, though his parents gave him life, Martino got the credit for "raising me to be the capable person I am today."

What he did not write in his letter was that he had begun to miss work at Chambrelan. A short time after he mailed his letter, he was fired and moved out of Christine's apartment, Christine's life and Le Havre. He spent a few days in Paris and met Michelle, another young woman.

But there was no job and no prospects of income. He cut his summer sojourn short when it became clear he wasn't going to be able to make it there on his own. He flew back to Los Angeles less than a month after sending Martino his glowing, disturbing letter from the Normandy coast.

The nightmares he described in his letter continued to haunt him long after he left Europe. The recurring rape dream was particularly frightening. In one of the dreams, he smothered Marguerite with a pillow instead of strangling her. He was convinced these nocturnal visions had all been influenced by demons.

After he got back to the United States, Michael made a beeline for Hollywood to see his therapists.

The American Institute of Hypnosis was no longer in business. Its debts had climbed to $222,901.21 before the institute declared bankruptcy and stiffed most of its creditors.

But Martino's Institute of Behavioral Science was thriving. Dr. Martino had established his practice further west on Sunset Boulevard, near Beverly Hills. Before leaving for Chicago to join his son Joe, Larry Gamsky (who had formally and legally changed his name to Ryan Hunt) had sold Martino the entire American Institute of Hypnosis electronic hypnotism system including monitors, master control console and the library of Dr. Bryan's self-help tapes.

Though Gamsky was gone, the cast of characters who had originally treated Michael and Jeff remained substantially the same: Matirko, Mingarella, Martino. They offered to continue his treatment, but pointed out that he was responsible for helping himself too. The therapists had already begun to teach Michael self-hypnosis before he went to Europe. With the aid of handpicked tapes from Dr. Bryan's library, tailored to Michael's specific needs, he would be able to reprogram himself, even when he wasn't able to come in for a session.

One of the tapes they prescribed for Michael was new. Gamsky had produced it himself before he left California, to augment Dr. Bryan's collection. It was designed to help young men and women who suffered from a domineering mother.

Gamsky called his creation *Smother Love*. He started out on the tape by ordering the patient to completely relax mind, body and psyche. Then he launched into an odd Socratic monologue:

"What would be the natural defense mechanism if you were going to be dominated by a woman, or anyone as far as that's concerned?"

Not physical domination, he said. Not even cruel domination. But domination nonetheless. "Nagging" might have been a better term, but "domination" made Gamsky sound more scientific.

"You would feel overloved, smother-loved, if you will," Gamsky's voice continued on the self-hypnosis cassette.

Too much "smother love" could cause a child to reject his own mother, Gamsky conjectured. When the child grew up, he kept right on rejecting anyone who duplicated that same smothering behavior, whether it turned out to be his boss or girlfriend or wife.

"To get deeply involved with a woman, as a friend, or on another level, or any person who has a tendency to overlove, or smother-love, would represent to you the submergence of your ego to that person," Gamsky spoke, enunciating every syllable in his dull, plodding, baritone voice.

The way to overcome the conflict of interacting with other adults who might have a hovering, maternal side to them, Gamsky carefully explained, was to follow his posthypnotic suggestion and shut the smother lover out of the patient's life.

"Let's break that connection right this very minute," he said. "Concentrate your mind on just breaking that connection.

"Picture your mother there, put plugs into her or whatever you want to imagine, but do it symbolically. . . . Pull out all the plugs, cut the umbilical cord, do whatever you want, but break those connections.

"Picture her talking and then her mouth becomes frozen tight and once you break all the connections, picture her fading, fading away out of your life. Not an important factor in your life at all. Then picture yourself feeling free because that's what you are."

No more domination from male or female smother lovers, Gamsky counseled. Armed with his posthypnotic suggestion, the patient was assured he could no longer be dominated.

"You, from this moment on out, will treat all men, all women, especially the dominant mother type—the smother lovers—on the basis that you will evaluate them one at a time," he said.

Michael took Gamsky's hypnotic advice to heart—perhaps deeper and more profoundly than any of the institute therapists ever suspected he might. He played *Smother Love* over and over, listening hard to the message and dwelling on that picture of a domineering mother, silenced and fading from his life.

He had been keeping a diary since Jeff's death and wrote paeans to himself that often reflected the advice he got from his counselors. Sometimes Michael seemed to interpret the intended message on the institute tape cassettes in an odd and offbeat manner.

"Be direct!" read one of Michael's diary entries. "Women do not want you to fail! . . . Marguerite wants you to fail! . . . That bitch caused you more misery than anyone else in this world—but she's gone! Marguerite is no longer a part of your life!!"

In another entry, Michael summed up what he had learned about dealing with women. He believed that women will allow people to manipulate them, and willingly acquiesce, if they like those people.

If Michael's theories about women, or his more specific diatribes concerning Marguerite, ever surfaced in his counseling sessions with Martino or any of the other therapists, they made no note of it.

Near summer's end, just before Michael was to return to Menlo College for the fall semester of 1981, therapist Robert Matirko—the state-licensed counselor on Martino's staff—ran a routine word association test with Michael. The results were alarming enough that he got on the telephone immediately and advised Roy Miller that something was seriously wrong with his son. He needed more than the self-help hypnotherapy that Dr. Martino had to offer, Matirko told Miller. He needed psychiatric treatment. Soon.

Two-thirds of the way through the fall semester, Michael called collect to Palos Verdes from a Palo Alto pay phone. Marguerite accepted the charges.

"I've been doing a lot of thinking about what I want to do," he told his mother.

He had quit his job, he said. He'd been working part-time at a store in the Stanford Shopping Mall near Menlo College, but the management had found someone who could work every day.

He didn't like school anymore. He intended to complete the semester, but he also felt like giving his mind a rest. If he dropped his classes after the twelfth week, it would mean Fs and he didn't want that on his record.

Still, he was restless.

"I went to San Francisco and had an interview at a modeling agency," he said.

Actually, he hadn't been to just one agency. He visited three different modeling agencies, he said. They all told him he had good bone structure, good posture and terrific facial features. One of them was the Barbizon School for modeling, but Don St. Michael, the secretary at Dr. Martino's office, had advised Michael against going there. It wasn't very good for male models, he said. In fact, it was a joke. Maybe it was okay if you were a woman, St. Michael had told him, but he didn't think Michael was looking for a course in etiquette.

No, Michael told his mother. He was very serious about this. He wanted to be a model and earn a lot of money fast. He could continue with college *after* modeling school.

Wasn't modeling kind of a vain profession? Marguerite asked.

"The time to model and sell yourself is when you're young and you have a lot of market value," he answered. "You're only young once."

The Millers had always made a point of wanting their son to look good in front of their friends and "for your own ego," he told

Marguerite. So why wouldn't his parents be happy with him selling himself as a product? He was sure he'd be successful if he gave it a try, but he'd grown frustrated at Menlo College, not knowing if he could make it or not.

Acting appealed to him as much as modeling. People had asked him more than once if he was an actor or a model, he told Marguerite. He had been talking to the mother of one of the few friends he had made at Menlo and she, too, recommended that Michael go to acting school. He reminded Marguerite that she and Roy had already promised him they would be willing to put him through school in New York or Los Angeles. Why not acting school?

Marguerite was pleased to hear him effuse about something, even if it was as impractical as acting or modeling. She had heard him depressed often enough, when she heard from him at all. She went along with his flight of fancy, scribbling down notes as fast as her son talked and offering her own advice to encourage, yet temper, his exuberance. Perhaps she could talk him into studying acting closer to home.

UCLA offered fine arts majors. USC was probably equally good, she said. And up near Menlo, San Francisco State University had a good drama department.

No, said Michael. He wanted to go to a private school.

"If I want to go to acting or modeling school, it's $2,400 a year for one in San Francisco," he told his mother. The school he had in mind was the only school in the country that placed all of its graduates in jobs, he said.

Michael liked the idea of New York even more, however. It had the cachet of Broadway and the legendary Lee Strasberg Actors Studio.

"That's where the theater is. I know I can do the work here, but I want to explore other avenues," Michael said. "I care a lot about my looks. It's not egotistical. I'm selling myself. Is it wrong to want to sell yourself? I like to appear that way [like a model]. And I love acting."

He admitted that it was more practical to act in film than on stage, of course, but either way would cost some money. In order to get on TV, he explained, you had to have pictures shot so that you could send them out to casting directors.

"I know you want the best for me and I do too," he said.

He wasn't just calling to hit his folks up for money, however. He also wanted to call and tell both of the Millers that he loved them very much, he said.

He wanted to please his mother, but he wanted to please himself too. He could not fathom himself working at a desk job. He had scant admiration for the white-collar career routes his cousins had taken.

"They don't want me to be this good-looking," he said without a hint of arrogance.

He grew pensive and philosophical about his future. When Plato discussed the concept of beauty, Michael said, the Greek philosopher speculated that offspring raised to shun things that are ugly become nobler and stronger.

"Intriguing," Michael mused.

He asked Marguerite to run interference for him; to convince Roy to trust his judgment and let him go into acting and modeling. Then, he said, he could be truly grateful to his mother.

He ended the conversation by boasting to her that he had just eaten a half pound of chocolate. Then he hung up.

For the first time since their 1980 graduation, Michael's old friends saw him at a New Year's Eve party in 1981. Several members of the old Palos Verdes High Chorale group threw the bash as a kind of reunion, and it was the first time that most of the old crowd had seen Michael at all since his brother died. They weren't prepared for the apparition that showed up. Mike McLaughlin remembered Michael looking haggard and shiny-eyed, silently gliding through the throng of college kids in a very out-of-place dark three-piece suit and a beard, mustache and long hair.

"He looked like Abraham Lincoln," said Beth Pearson. "His eyes were sunken in. He looked so scary. I remember thinking he was on drugs. I remember being in the kitchen. He was looking at me, staring, and he was talking in a monotone voice and he really scared me."

The Michael Miller she saw at the New Year's Eve party was not the goofy, eccentric but generally outgoing Michael Miller that she had known in Gary McRoberts' classes.

"He seemed much more introverted than he was in high school," said McLaughlin.

When he did try to socialize, Michael inspired dread among his former peers instead of the easy laughs he once got for being a nerd.

"We were all trying to get away from him," said Pearson. "He was mumbling things that didn't make sense. He was way out of it. We couldn't believe how he had digressed."

After the holidays, Michael again tried talking his mother into letting him go to New York to find his way in the theater. Marguerite still thought acting was vain, but he wore her down with his constant harangue about looks and beauty and the importance of selling one's talent while one was still young. Roy was not so easily convinced. He told his son he was more apt to support him if each thing he started he actually completed.

But Marguerite wanted to keep Michael happy.

"We are taught in the U.S. that you must be the perfect mom, the perfect wife, the chauffeur," said Marguerite's friend Sally Alonzo. "Wife, mother, Suzy Homemaker. We're the only country in the *world* that makes a woman be all those things. And some women act like they can do it all."

Marguerite did her best. Alonzo says she gave far too much of herself to her family and did not keep back anything for herself.

"She never raised her voice. She *lived* for those boys," said Alonzo.

Michael got his way. He didn't return to Menlo for the spring semester. In March 1982 he flew to New York to become an actor. For the next several weeks, his transcontinental telephone calls came into Roy Miller's office like clockwork.

Harold Aumock Bruner and Marie Buxton *(right, center)* both attended Iowa's Drake University in the years prior to World War I before marrying, starting their family and migrating to Southern California. Both Michael and Jeffrey Miller were unusually close to their maternal grandparents. *(Drake University* Quax *yearbooks)*

Roy George Miller *(left, center)* and Ednabel Loofbourrow *(above, center)* graduated from Pomona College during the 1920s, starting their own family in Claremont, California, with the birth of Roy David Miller in 1929. *(Pomona College* Metate *yearbooks)*

Roy Miller plays cello and Marguerite Bruner plays violin in a Claremont
High School music class, circa 1945. (*Claremont High School yearbook*)

Pomona College graduation photo,
Marguerite Joan Bruner, 1952.
(*Pomona College* Metate *yearbook*)

Pomona College graduation photo,
Roy David Miller, 1951.
(*Pomona College* Metate *yearbook*)

Mr. and Mrs. Roy David Miller on their wedding day, August 9, 1952. (*Reproduced from the* Claremont Courier)

Michael David Miller, high school graduation photo, 1980.
(*Palos Verdes High School yearbook*)

Jeffrey Bruner Miller, high school graduation photo, 1975.
(*Palos Verdes High School yearbook*)

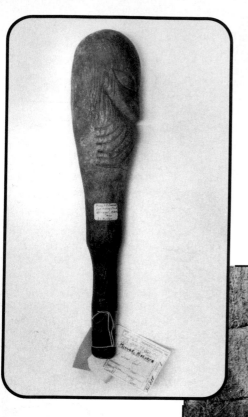

Klingkit Indian fishing club, brought back from Wrangel, Alaska, in 1920 by D. H. Buxton, Marguerite's grandfather. Used by Michael to club his mother to death. (*Dennis McDougal*)

Jeffrey Miller as Will Parker in the 1975 Palos Verdes High School production of *Oklahoma!* (*Palos Verdes High School yearbook*)

Let every heart prepare Him room, and heaven and nature sing.

WE WISH YOU A BLESSED CHRISTMAS!

THE MILLERS
Michael, Marguerite, Roy, Jeffrey

Miller family Christmas greeting, 1980. (*Frank Dana/private collection*)

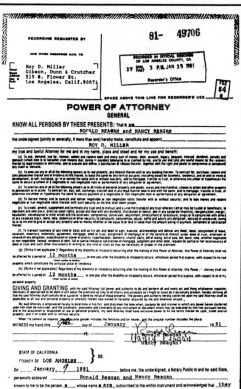

Power of attorney, dated eleven days before Ronald Reagan's inauguration, granting Roy Miller "full power and authority to do and perform all and every act and thing whatsoever requisite, necessary or appropriate" in the name of Ronald and Nancy Reagan.
(Los Angeles County Recorder's Office)

Ronald and Nancy Reagan photo autographed for Roy Miller. *(Courtesy of the Ronald Reagan Library)*

Roy Miller residence, 2019 Via Visalia, Palos Verdes Estates. Upper left room is the master bedroom where Marguerite's body was found. *(Dennis McDougal)*

Roy and Marguerite Miller during a vacation retreat. *(Herald Examiner Collection/Los Angeles Public Library)*

Mrs. Marguerite Miller, shortly before her murder. *(Herald Examiner Collection/Los Angeles Public Library)*

Michael Miller's defense attorneys, Tom Nolan and Stephen Miller. (*Jack Lardomita/ Daily Breeze*)

Michael Miller arraigned on charges of raping and murdering his mother, Marguerite. (*Herald Examiner Collection/Los Angeles Public Library*)

Michael Miller and defense attorney Tom Nolan. (*Jack Lardomita/ Daily Breeze*)

A dour Roy Miller during the sanity hearings for his younger son, Michael Miller. (*Herald Examiner Collection/Los Angeles Public Library*)

Roy Miller faces the bench in Torrance Superior Court, his son Michael at far left with defense counsel Tom Nolan and Stephen Miller. (*Herald Examiner Collection/Los Angeles Public Library*)

Michael Miller, flanked by attorney Tom Nolan and a court bailiff, is found not guilty by reason of insanity in the rape/murder of his mother and is consigned indefinitely to Patton State mental hospital.
(*Jack Lardomita/Daily Breeze*)

"I would send him money to pay the hotel bill and it would either be used for something else or wouldn't get applied," said Roy Miller. "And I was almost having to send him money every two or three days to cover certain bills rather than give him an allowance. He was just unable to handle money because he kept coming back and saying, 'I need more money. I used it for this or I used it for that.'

"And it was apparent to me that he was just not able to handle money or to look for an apartment or to look for a job."

On Michael's twentieth birthday, May 31, 1982, Roy and Marguerite met their son's return flight at Los Angeles International Airport. He had spent less than three months in Manhattan, in a cheap hotel. He went out for food and exercise, but he never got a job or found an acting school that would take him. In New York he had begun to think about killing his therapists. He also began to hear his brother's voice criticizing him and calling him an "idiot."

He looked like hell when he got off the plane.

"After the initial greeting—which was somewhat distant but also included a certain cordiality—we were going to a place to pick up his baggage," remembered Roy Miller. "He preceded us by several steps. And then, when we got to his baggage, he turned around rather suddenly and looked, and looked me straight in the face and exclaimed, 'I don't even know you!' And it took me aback."

Roy and Marguerite stared at their disheveled son for a few heartbeats. When Roy finally recaptured his attorney's savoir faire, he fired back at his son: "Well, would you like to get acquainted?"

"And he said, 'Well, I guess so,' " Roy remembered.

Michael seemed very distant. He wasn't exactly aloof, but he appeared distracted, or absorbed in something else. It took several seconds for him to realize that someone was talking to him. If his parents asked him a question, it could remain unanswered for a minute or longer.

"And it didn't usually help to ask him two or three times because he would sometimes get upset if we would do that," remembered

Roy Miller. "But then even after minutes, sometimes, he would answer the question. And sometimes he wouldn't. Or sometimes we would give up and go on to something else."

Though they weren't sure if he was listening, Roy and Marguerite tried to reason with their son. He needed help and he needed it quickly.

"I persisted and told him that I thought he ought to get some counseling; that when people are ill or might be ill they needed experts to counsel them," said Roy.

But Michael had had his fill at the American Institute of Hypnosis and it hadn't helped him. He told his parents he wanted no part of any more counseling.

"Why don't you take all the money that you might spend on a psychologist or psychiatrist and just let me have it and I could take a boat trip around the world or do something like that and further my education?" Michael asked.

The Millers stuck to their line, and before the end of June, Michael began regularly seeing Dr. Sumner Shapiro, a psychiatrist and accredited psychoanalyst who practiced in the San Fernando Valley.

"We asked him how come or how he happened to get in touch with Dr. Shapiro," said Roy. "And he said, well, he had called a local psychiatric association and asked if they would refer him to a psychiatrist who spoke French because . . . he had been to France and had studied in France. And he thought that it would be to his liking for some reason for him to have a psychiatrist that spoke French."

Roy and Marguerite didn't think that was a very good way to select a psychiatrist, but after they had had a chance to interview Dr. Shapiro, they decided he'd do.

"And since he was somebody Michael had selected and was somebody he would be willing to go to, it was better that he go to Dr. Shapiro than not go to anybody," said Roy.

When he first started seeing Dr. Shapiro, Michael insisted they speak to each other in French. Shapiro went along with it. For his part, Shapiro insisted their sessions be confidential. He made a practice of taking no notes during his sessions. Michael saw him three times a week.

Within weeks, Michael showed signs of recovery.

"He signed up for a summer school course in each of the [two summer] sessions at UCLA," said Roy. "And I know at least the second one he finished with a satisfactory or passing grade."

One integrated arts course he took through UCLA Extension was about Greek mythology, art and culture. He might be speaking French to his analyst, but he was switching academic allegiance to Greece. He had read *Oedipus Rex* his first semester at Menlo, but he reread the Sophocles tragedy at UCLA and spoke of it often with Dr. Shapiro. He spoke of his family tragedies too, including Jeff's and his own. But Shapiro kept the details to himself, even though Marguerite called often to check on Michael's progress.

At home, Michael showed great impatience with the Millers' housekeeping, especially their failure to sort through Jeff's room.

"When we were away he would just sort out the cupboards and rearrange the cupboards, putting dishes in this place and that place and really berating us for not having our dishes and our possessions in a way that he thought was the orderly way," Roy recalled.

Dr. Shapiro didn't tell his parents specifically what went on in therapy, but he did tell the Millers that their son was improving.

"And it seemed to us that he did improve," said Roy.

He took a more active role in the family, keeping his room neater and attending social functions with his parents. And those mental blanks, when he simply did not respond to questions, were fewer and fewer. By autumn, they seemed to have gone away completely.

GHOSTS

Sex crimes are always male, never female, because such crimes are conceptualizing assaults on the unreachable omnipotence of woman and nature. Every woman's body contains a cell of archaic night, where all knowing must stop.

CAMILLE PAGLIA
Sexual Personae: Art and Decadence from Nefertiti to Emily Dickinson

⟶ 11

When Officer Karen Belcher arrived at 2019 Via Visalia on March 24, 1983, Mrs. Marguerite Miller had been dead about fifteen hours. Belcher and Robert Conner, a young reserve officer riding with her, got the radio message at 10:57 P.M. near the end of their routine evening watch. The dispatcher for the Palos Verdes Estates Police Department described the call as "an unusual circumstance."

An "unusual circumstance" normally had a rather narrow, and negative, definition on the Peninsula. In this sumptuous seaside city of fifteen thousand, the status quo was sanctioned, but the peculiar was not. Here, an unusual circumstance usually added up to a possible crime or potential scandal.

Now and then a high-strung executive might beat up his wife or an intoxicated stockbroker might run his car off the hillside. There was the male prostitution ring that Belcher's department busted up after the suspects had been turning tricks for wealthy businessmen in the hills overlooking the ocean for several months. There were the cliff divers—despondent souls who, for whatever reasons, chose the Palos Verdes ocean cliffs to plunge headfirst to their bloody deaths on the rocks a hundred feet below. There were the body dumps: a shooting or drug overdose victim from one of the flatland communities like Torrance or Compton or Carson, tossed from a moving car into the freeway daisies planted along the shoulder of Palos Verdes Drive.

Unusual circumstances sent a temporary chill through City Hall. Municipal officials privately expressed astonishment that such *unusual* circumstances could occur in Palos Verdes at all. Publicly, they said nothing. Palos Verdes was the opposite of Malibu or Beverly Hills, where the very rich often seemed to bask in attention of any kind. Palos Verdes was discreet. Even the movie stars who moved here did so to stay out of the limelight. Whenever vice or violence reared its head, Palos Verdes civic officials collectively held their breath, letting it out only after it became clear that the news media had given scant attention to (or better yet, ignored altogether) the latest unusual circumstance. There hadn't been a murder in Palos Verdes for over two years.

Not until this cool March evening in 1983.

Belcher pulled her squad car up in front of a long, low ranch-style home with white sandstone boulders strewn across a front yard covered in dark green ice plant. Many of the residences along the street were surrounded by high stone walls or chain-link fences, but not the Millers' home. An eclectic assortment of plants and bushes sprouted around the yard: here, an orange hibiscus newly in bloom; there, a cactus; off to the south side of the house, a bed of pink and red roses.

A hand-painted tile just outside the entryway read: "Along the way take time to smell the flowers."

Joe Hall, an officer in charge of one of Palos Verdes' canine units, had already arrived. He had been through the house quickly to ascertain that no one was inside, but when Belcher arrived, Palos Verdes Watch Commander Ron Echols told her she was to take the official report. Hall pointed her toward Roy Miller, the owner of the house. The only other thing Hall told her was that there was a body inside.

Standing near the front door of his home, Roy Miller looked ashen but composed. His long, thin features seemed drained and deliberate at the same time. Belcher had never met him, but she'd interviewed her share of unsettled crime victims and suspects. Miller could have been either type. He didn't wince at all as he answered her short list of questions.

When he unlocked his front door and stepped inside, he told her, he found a bloody towel and broken spectacles in the doorway. He called for his wife, but she didn't answer. He ran next door to his neighbor's house and called the police.

Belcher flipped her notebook shut and ordered him to stand by. She and Conner then carefully retraced Miller's steps into the Miller household, listening intently for any sound of man or animal lurking inside.

"I entered the residence by means of the front entry and observed broken eyeglasses with several pieces of broken glass lying on the entryway rug," Belcher later wrote in her incident report.

She also saw the broken, red plastic flashlight lying on the floor and a heap of bloodstained night clothes. Roy Miller had mistaken them for towels. She heard the stereo playing in the living room. Strange music. An eerie oriental sort of mood instrumental, she recalled much later. It gave her a sudden feeling of unease. There, in the soft lamplight, she saw something odd.

"I saw a wooden club-like instrument lying on the floor near the clothing, also in the living room," Belcher wrote.

It was a dark brown cudgel, heavy at one end like an Irish shillelagh, about a foot and a half long. Officer Belcher gave it the once-over, blinking at what appeared to be dried blood on the blunt and heavier end of the club. But she didn't touch it.

She moved a little more cautiously down the hallway toward the master bedroom, located just across the entryway from the living room in the northwest corner of the house. When she peeked carefully around the doorjamb, she caught her breath.

"I observed a nude female lying on her back in bed," she wrote. "I saw blood stains on a pillow which was partially covering the victim's face. Traces of blood were noted about the face and mouth. I could see no movement and the body color was very pale. I observed lividity about the body. I saw no respiratory movement.

Due to the above listed facts, I was of the opinion that the victim was deceased."

What she didn't write was the look on the dead woman's face when she lifted the pillow slip that covered her head. There was a panic in the mouth and eyes, even in death, that would haunt Belcher for years afterward. And there were marks on her neck that Belcher likened to claw marks. In the years ahead Belcher would see nothing quite like the sad, frightened corpse she did that night in the Millers' master bedroom.

Belcher backed out of the room, now as shaken as Roy Miller. She and Conner walked quickly out the front door, exactly the same way that they had entered. Roy Miller was waiting.

It was Belcher's first murder case and she had no real frame of reference for how a survivor behaves when he or she hears that a loved one has been found dead. Miller's reaction struck her as peculiar when she broke the news. Instead of fury or tears, she saw shocked approbation in Roy Miller's haggard eyes. He seemed numb.

She tugged Miller by the sleeve and guided him back to the neighbor's house to report in by telephone. Despite her shock, Belcher still had the presence of mind to know that what she had to say would best not be said over her car radio, where it could be picked up by scanners.

There was a dead white female in the Millers' master bedroom, she reported after getting through to dispatch. A naked dead woman. All the victim was wearing was an engagement ring, a wedding band and a pair of earrings. She was thin and middle-aged and may have been beaten pretty badly. She was not breathing, and her skin was chalk-white.

Sergeant Ed Jaakola, senior detective on the tiny, two-dozen-member police department, relayed the message through dispatch that he would be right up the Hill to see the crime scene for himself.

Still at the neighbor's house, Belcher asked Miller a few more questions before reinforcements began to arrive and cordon off the neighborhood.

She surveyed his hulking, bent, six-foot-three-inch frame, still clad in medium-starched white shirt, thin, dark tie and an impeccable but quite undistinguished business suit. He looked like a kindly, retiring man, not a wife beater. Still, routine and common sense dictated that she ask the question anyway:

Had there been any recent marital problems?

Miller shook his head. Marguerite hadn't been under the care of a physician either, he told her.

Miller's answers didn't automatically rule out the possibility of spousal abuse, suicide or an accidental drug overdose, but they did set the parameters for questioning. Belcher asked him to remember anything unusual, any clue from the past twenty-four hours.

Drawing every ounce of his professional cool, Roy recounted the events of the day, beginning with his breakfast meeting in Los Angeles. He had his business appointments through the day and his hospital board meeting in Arcadia in the evening. By the time he recalled again the horror awaiting him just inside his own home shortly after 10 P.M., his disciplined lawyer's façade began to crack. He hyperventilated, his long slender fingers raking across the crown of his skull, uselessly smoothing strands of hair that would never return to their proper place.

Sergeant Jaakola arrived during the questioning, as Miller sat on the edge of his neighbor's living room sofa mumbling his answers in a slightly trembling voice, his elbows resting on his knees and his head hung down. While Belcher continued to go over the information, Jaakola went to the Miller house.

He didn't need to look at the crime scene for more than five minutes to know he needed outside help on this one. The Palos Verdes Estates Police Department was well equipped to handle pranks and burglaries, but murder was not one of the tiny department's specialties.

As bureau commander, Jaakola made a decision to call on the L.A. County Sheriff's Department for help. The request went through a homicide lieutenant at the seedy old Hall of Justice building in downtown L.A., not four blocks from Roy Miller's office. By calling in sheriff's deputies, Jaakola surrendered jurisdiction over the case, but he also washed his hands of responsibility. And, from what he had been able to ascertain, this was going to be far more than some routine domestic violence that had gotten out of hand. The man who sat in the living room next door with his face buried in his hands, Jaakola had just learned, was Ronald Wilson Reagan's personal lawyer.

At three minutes past midnight, Los Angeles Sheriff's Sergeant Al Sett and his partner, Detective Jerry Beck, were rousted out of bed. The homicide duty commander told them to get dressed and get to Palos Verdes. By the time the two men dressed, rendezvoused at the Hall of Justice and drove together to the adobe-colored stucco house with the red tile roof on Via Visalia some forty miles to the west, it was nearly 2 A.M.

Sergeant Jaakola had already dispatched a couple of his troops to knock on doors around the neighborhood, asking if anyone had seen anything. When Sett and Beck drove past the Montemalaga Elementary School a quarter mile from the Miller house, Jaakola had already set up roadblocks with reserve officers manning the barricades. The detectives had to flash their badges to get by.

Jaakola met them at the front door. He'd conducted murder investigations before, but only when it was fairly obvious who had committed the crime. This one began as a genuine mystery and Jaakola felt way out of his league. On the one hand, he told the two sheriff's detectives, the entryway to the house was strewn with evidence of a violent struggle, indicating that a burglar or some other intruder might have happened upon Mrs. Miller and beat her into submission. On the other hand, the front door was securely locked—double dead-bolted, as a matter of fact—and intruders who commit murder are rarely concerned with seeing to it that the dead bolt is in place when they leave.

A quick check of the windows and doors around the rest of the house indicated no forced entry.

She also had been dead for several hours, meaning that she had probably been killed in broad daylight, Jaakola pointed out. Even in a neighborhood where houses were twenty to thirty yards away from each other and often surrounded with brick fencing, it was unlikely that some stranger could beat a woman to death in her own home and leave completely unnoticed.

A sheriff's photographer was on his way, but Sett and Beck didn't wait. They asked Jaakola to join in if he wanted and began a meticulous investigation, starting where Roy Miller had first called out his wife's name several hours earlier. One detective took notes while the other announced in painstaking detail exactly what he observed.

As they described it in Sett's notebook, the rug in the entryway was 6½ by 4½ feet and strewn with bits of the broken lens and reflector of a red plastic flashlight. Two red slippers had been carefully placed, side by side, on the north edge of the rug while one-half of a pair of eyeglasses, broken at the bridge, rested on the west edge of the rug. The other half of the glasses lay on the floor, just a few inches beyond the rug.

The pile of clothing in the living room that Roy Miller mistook for towels was actually bathrobes and pajamas. Marguerite's pink bathrobe covered blue-and-gray-striped pajama bottoms and a pair of size 34 Jockey shorts. They were all bloodstained.

A man's orange bathrobe lay next to the pink one. To the right, Marguerite's pink nightgown was heaped over a pajama top that matched the bloodstained bottoms. The brick-red hue typical of dried blood was splattered across the nightgown and pajama bottoms too. Beneath the pile of clothing, more bloody spots marred the living room rug.

Between the pink and orange bathrobes, Beck saw something else. He described it as Sett wrote: a one-and-a-half-inch-long curved, bloodied, plastic-like substance that was almost certainly a human fingernail.

But it was the long, heavy black cudgel near the living room fireplace that Karen Belcher had first spotted, six feet west of the entryway, that drew the full and immediate attention of all three detectives. Sergeant Sett designated it Item No. 1 on his inventory of evidence before he went any further in the investigation. There was the same dark shade of brownish red on the heavy end of the club as there had been on the night clothes piled on the other side of the living room. Without touching it, the three men squatted down to study the foot-and-a-half-long club. There was a white tag hanging from the slender end, as if it had been a cataloged museum item. Sett flicked the tag over with the eraser end of his pencil, careful not to touch it. It read:

"Klingkit Indian Fish Killing Club, Wrangel, Alaska, 1920, D. H. Buxton."

The entourage left it in its place, along with all of the other bloody evidence, and moved on to Roy and Marguerite's bedroom.

There were more specks of blood, coagulated in an uneven dot-to-dot trail along the stone floor leading into the bedroom. A bloody pillow was jammed between the nightstand and the bed. Marguerite Miller lay flat and still on the sheets, her head covered with a pillowcase. She was faceup and naked, her belly and breasts deathly white, but apparently unscratched. A greenish bruise stretched along the lower right side of her torso, as though she had suffered a brutal body blow, but the bedspread and blankets hid from view any injury she might have suffered from her knees down. The detectives could not see her face or her feet, but her left hand was visible. The fingernail on the middle finger was missing, a darkened red blotch marking the exposed quick and cuticle where a nail ought to have been. It was clear that Mrs. Miller had not submitted quietly to what looked more and more to the detectives like a violent rape as well as a murder. When the forensics were done, Sett speculated the fingernail found on the living room carpet would be a perfect match for the one missing from Mrs. Miller's finger.

The official police photographer showed up at 2:30 A.M. and began firing off his strobe through all nine rooms of the house. At the same time, Sett and Beck began scouting every inch of the 2,700 square feet of the house for signs of fingerprints. Wayne Plumtree, the criminalist assigned to the case, didn't arrive until almost 4 A.M., giving Jaakola time to talk with the two sheriff's homicide investigators about traffic control and the impending media blitz.

In a few hours it would be daybreak and joggers would be in the streets, along with housewives walking their poodles and Pomeranians. By 6 A.M., people would start driving down the Hill to the city to go to work. By 7 A.M., teachers and children would begin to arrive at nearby Montemalaga Elementary School.

And, by 8 or 9 A.M., Jaakola said with undisguised contempt, the newspapers and wire services would be all over the Peninsula like flies on a fresh turd.

There would have to be a press release and probably a press conference, Sett told Jaakola. Chances were that most of the media wouldn't even know where the Palos Verdes Estates Police Department was, which was a big plus. If they played it right, the police could dispense with their responsibility to inform the public without having to do much more than deliver the minimum information: a murder had been committed and they were conducting a thorough investigation. Period.

But Beck and Sett were veterans of this sort of thing. Fending off the media was always nettlesome because reporters were trained to be persistent. In a case involving the President of the United States, even peripherally, they were not going to go away. Ideally, it was best to have rapport with the men and women of the press anyway. Though it was Jaakola's show, they said, the two sheriff's detectives would be glad to deal with the press and help take some of the heat off Jaakola's department.

But there was still much to do before sunup. Fortified by hot, black coffee, reinforcements from both the sheriff's homicide division and Jaakola's department and the natural adrenaline that accompanies the opening phase of any murder investigation, all three men redoubled their investigation efforts.

On a countertop in the kitchen, Sett found a stack of loose-leaf notebook sheets containing several months' worth of handwritten notes. A quick scan indicated that it might be a diary kept by Marguerite Miller. He told Plumtree to give it a number and an evidence tag.

In a bathroom on the northeast side of the house, Sett and Beck found more bloody evidence. A wet hand towel, stained a blood-brown, rested on the sink. A tissue that also looked as though it had been used to daub away blood lay on the tile floor next to the toilet. A pair of knit, multicolored sock-shoes or mukluks were also on the floor with a white sweat sock tucked inside each of them. There were bloodstains on all of them.

The bedroom adjacent to the bathroom also had bloody artifacts: a large handkerchief and another pair of size 34 Jockey shorts. The adolescent bric-a-brac, books, record albums and clothes strewn around the room were clues as to who lived here. The bedroom had to belong to the Millers' son.

Beck and Sett asked Plumtree to catalog everything they had found, including the blood-spattered sheets and pillowcases found in the Millers' bedroom. They also wanted the hairs inventoried that they had found in the bed where Marguerite's body still lay at 4 A.M. George White, the investigator from the County Coroner's Office, had yet to make his appearance.

White, who arrived shortly after 4:30, apologized for being late, but quickly made up for lost time. He slipped the pillowcase off Mrs. Miller's head while a group of about a half dozen law enforcement officials gathered around the foot of the bed craning for their first close look at the blow that killed Marguerite Miller.

The fatal bruise to Mrs. Miller's forehead resembled a maroon star. The blow had cracked her skull, stunning her but not killing her. An autopsy later in the day would confirm that she died of asphyxiation. Her dilated gray-blue eyes stared at the police officers. Her shoulder-length brunette hair was matted with the blood from two other crushing blows to the top and back of her head. Her left hand, with its missing fingernail, lay parallel to her body, but her right hand was crooked up, as though it were positioned there to protect her face. Her legs were spread apart, right knee slightly bent.

White would check for drugs, semen and other discharge, but not until he got the body down the Hill. Rigor mortis had already begun. He took the temperature of her liver to try to get a fix on how long she had been dead and then ordered the body loaded into a waiting ambulance for transport across the L.A. Basin to

County USC Medical Center, where headquarters for the county medical examiner, or coroner was located.

It was 5 A.M. The temperature outside was sixty-three degrees.

According to George White's thermometer, Marguerite Miller's liver was sixty-nine degrees. She had been dead for nearly twenty-four hours.

Sett and Beck didn't get around to their own interrogation of Roy Miller until 6:30 A.M., back at the Palos Verdes Estates Police Department. Sett saw Miller as "the perfect Reaganista Republican, all the way down to his cuffed trousers." The two detectives didn't discuss their own suspicions with him, but they did ask Miller to phone his sister-in-law's house in Santa Monica before they got started. They wanted him to ask his son to come to the police station for an interview.

Jaakola had already told them he thought Jeffrey Miller might have had something to do with the murder. The bloody tissue and mukluks in the bathroom seemed to point in that direction. The elder Miller boy had been applauded by teachers and classmates alike as a great kid and a terrific student when he graduated from high school in 1975, but Jaakola seemed to recall that Jeff had had his run-ins with the authorities too. He was a wiseass, according to Jaakola. In his own opinion, Jeff Miller was "kind of a jerk," he told the two sheriff's detectives.

When Jaakola ran Jeff Miller's name through the computer back at the station, however, it came up blank. He told the detectives that the only name in the data bank was that of Michael David Miller, Jeff's twenty-year-old younger brother. He'd had a traffic conviction for reckless driving the previous autumn and he was apparently the only one living at home.

In fact, he was the only one living at all. Shortly after Sett, Beck and Roy Miller had all settled down for Miller's formal debriefing in the captain's office at the police station, Miller confirmed that his elder son had committed suicide two years earlier. Michael had had trouble adjusting to the loss ever since, he said.

Miller remained remarkably composed and lucid in detailing his recollections of the previous day for the two officers. Despite the trauma compounded by twenty-four hours without sleep, he recited the same story he'd given Belcher and Jaakola hours before: a normal workday, beginning at 6 A.M. and ending at 10 P.M. with the horror of finding the aftermath of violence and murder inside his own home.

The broken flashlight and the fish club belonged to the Millers, but they were normally kept in the family room, he said. The broken glasses were Marguerite's. She needed them for reading and distance.

Questions about Michael were a little more difficult for his father to answer. The boy was having the same difficulty adjusting to adult responsibilities that many kids his age were having, but the death of Jeffrey only made Michael's coming of age worse, according to Miller. Michael had tried making it on his own—even spent some time living in New York. By May, the Big Apple had gotten the best of him and he returned to live, temporarily, in his old room. In June his parents saw that he needed professional help to rise out of his depression and sent him to see a psychiatrist. He had been seeing Dr. Shapiro almost every week since that time, said Miller.

The morning sun was beginning to burn through the cloud cover when the detectives finished the interview. Outside the department, the first two or three reporters had already shown up and were cooling their heels, waiting for information. Sergeant Jaakola was perplexed and a little angry at how quickly the word had gotten out. His guess was that ambulance drivers who took the body to the coroner must have tipped off some wire service reporter. Jaakola hadn't even had time to prepare a press statement.

But he was interrupted when a pair of automobiles pulled up outside the station. A tall, emaciated young man got out of the driver's side of one of the cars and walked inside, where a small but growing crowd of police officers, journalists and just plain curious citizens were gathered in the tiny lobby of the tiny police department. When a trembling Roy Miller spotted the young man, he stepped up rapidly and hugged him, holding on tight for a moment.

Michael Miller squeezed his father back just as tightly. Al Sett let them share a smile and a greeting for a moment before steering the elder Miller outside. Jerry Beck asked Michael to follow him back to the captain's office.

Beck barely got the door closed before Michael sat down, turned to him and calmly spoke.

"I did it," he said. "I killed my mom and then I raped her."

Beck stared, trying not to show his astonishment. The clock on the wall read 7:30 A.M. Neither Beck nor Michael nor the hands on the clock seemed to move at all until Al Sett reentered the room several moments later.

— 12

Jerry Beck grabbed Sergeant Sett by the wrist the moment he walked into the room and skewered him with a look. His eyes told Sett everything: the kid had confessed. After a few whispers from Beck, Sett nodded and reached in his coat pocket for the small crib sheet he carried with him everywhere, just in case. It bore a shorthand version of a criminal suspect's constitutional rights, to be read before any formal questioning.

Michael had the right to say nothing more until he had an attorney present. Further, if he waived that right, anything he said could be used against him in court. Those were the rules, and that's what Sett recited from his card. Still, the pale, thin youth who sat before them agreed to talk, attorney or not. He had nothing to hide. Rarely blinking and never showing much facial movement beyond a blank frown, he seemed almost matter-of-fact about the events that led up to the murder and rape of his mother. It all actually began the night before, he said, when he lay awake in his bed, staring at the ceiling and toying with an obsession that had tormented him time and time again.

What if he killed his father, then raped his mother and killed her too?

Michael kept several knives in his bedroom, he said. He had a
sword too. Sometimes he carefully ran the tip of a finger over their
edges to test how keen they were.

He could kill them both with a knife. Block. Thrust. Twist the
blade.

He fantasized about how it would be, ending both of their lives,
one at a time. Their panic. And fear. And his own power over
both of them.

After toying with the knife for some time, he set it aside and
nodded off to sleep in the only escape from his obsessive fantasy.

But he didn't sleep long. He awakened at 5:45 A.M., hearing
quiet rustling through the bedroom door, coming from across the
hall. He recognized it as his father, getting ready to leave for work.
It was an opportunity that Michael couldn't let pass. He leaped
from his bed and pulled on his mukluks over a pair of socks he'd
slept in. While his father shaved and dressed, Michael stole into
the kitchen and made breakfast for him, making sure to liberally
butter the oatmeal and toast before setting it on the table. It might
not be as quick or effective as a knife in his heart, Michael reasoned,
but the butter might clog Roy Miller's veins and arteries to such
an extent that his father would suffer cardiac arrest. He'd just keel
over at his desk.

Michael smiled as he watched his father nibble at the food. By
the time Roy Miller left, he hadn't eaten much and showed no
signs of keeling over. In fact, he smiled and thanked his son for
getting up so early just to make breakfast for him. Then he was in
the car and backing out the garage door, driving down the Hill in
the thin morning light.

Michael went back to his room to brood for a while. He lay on
his bed and stared at the ceiling, rehearsing the scenario again.
The knives were still there, but they were no longer the key. He
moved aimlessly around his room, pacing and dwelling on the idea
of murder. He drifted out to the family room, eyes darting about
for some weapon other than a knife. Something . . .

At a little past 8 A.M., Michael entered the master bedroom. He
saw his mother, still stretched out beneath the sheets in the big,

king-size bed. She disgusted him. He'd told her as much. A contemptible Palos Verdes housewife with no ambition to be anything but a leech, spending her husband's money. The previous evening, she had asked Michael to count the pieces in her mah-jongg set so that he could take it to her sister's house. His mother was a shallow butterfly. She had wasted her life.

Michael wore an orange robe over his striped pajamas. He still had on his shorts, white socks and mukluks when he sat on the edge of her bed.

Her eyes fluttered open and she stretched, smiling at her son. He hugged her and said good morning. She rubbed the sleep out of her eyes.

Suddenly, Michael asked if he could crawl into bed with her.

She cocked her head and gave him a weary, inquisitive look. Get into your own bed, Marguerite told him.

He couldn't, he told her. During the night, he'd had one of the accidents he'd been having lately. His bed was wet.

His mother turned away from him and waited for him to leave. Michael got off the bed and paced the floor in his robe and pajamas, looking like a skinny, orange panther. He wasn't feeling all that well, he said. It was his teeth again, he said. His wisdom teeth. They were cutting up through the gums at the back of his mouth, making his rear mandibles feel as though they were going to explode inside his face. It hurt. Bad. He wanted Marguerite—that was what he called her instead of "Mother"—to examine them. Now.

She sighed, shook her head and sat up, slowly pivoting so that she sat on the edge of the bed. She donned her pink bathrobe and looked past her son.

It was not the first time Michael wet the bed or wanted his molars examined. When he got this way—regressing to bed-wetting and compulsive behavior—it had been Marguerite Miller's experience that the best thing to do was simply ignore him. She got out of bed and walked by him to the family room to make a phone call. Michael could hear her chatting with one of her friends about a health food lecture they planned to attend that night, but he wasn't interested in eavesdropping. There were urges welling up inside of him and it was all he could do to concentrate on keeping a cool head.

After she hung up, Marguerite went into her bathroom, trying her best to ignore her son's inappropriate behavior. If she enabled it by offering to help him or by even just listening to him, he'd keep it up, demanding more. She'd seen his childish regressions transform into equally childish rages countless times before. She calmly waited until they passed before attempting further communication. Trying to talk to him in the midst of one of his tantrums was like talking to a kindergartner: bright but emotionally wrapped up only in himself. She shut the bathroom door behind her.

Michael wasted no time. While she was in the bathroom, he slipped into the living room, disrobed and raced back to his parents' bedroom. He hid in the closet.

Earlier, beneath his robe he had hidden the Alaskan fishing club. When he stripped down to nothing, it was the only thing that he took with him into the closet.

Then he waited.

Marguerite left the bathroom, reentered the bedroom and began to fix her hair in the mirror. It was then that she saw Michael, stark naked, standing amid the hangers and dresses with his fishing club in his hand. Her eyebrows arched, but more out of consternation than fear. She turned away from the mirror and abruptly walked out of the room. She would have none of his foolishness. Michael followed her into the living room, grabbing her by the shoulder, falling to his knees and pulling her to the floor with him.

Again his mother showed no hysteria, no fear. She had seen him this way before. He was being unreasonable and acting out inappropriately. It had not been the first time and could only be treated if Michael developed the right attitude. Instead of play-acting his obsessive fantasies, he should talk them out with Dr. Shapiro, she told him. It was wrongheaded behavior. It was not right or good for anyone. It was inappropriate and should be dealt with in the proper setting with a professional.

Even lying on the floor with him straddling her, she tried reasoning with him.

Michael burst.

He began clubbing her. He didn't know where the first blow fell. It was probably on the forehead, just above her right eye, but it may have been the back of the head. It was a frenzy after that, his breathing as excited as his loins. Perhaps she screamed. He didn't remember. He struck her again and again and again. Perhaps a dozen times in all. He wasn't sure.

Michael's next moments would understandably be a blur. Sergeant Sett had done enough confessions to know that suspects got the big picture as well as the details wrong in the midst of their emotional delirium. He was prepared for the wringing of hands, the shedding of tears and the raking of fingernails through the scalp. He was prepared to put a fatherly arm around the boy's shoulders as he spoke the worst. What he was not prepared for was a calm, almost clinical explication, as Michael described how he raped his own mother.

"When she was on the floor, he pulled up her night clothes and, even though he did not have a full erection, he began having sex with her," Sett wrote in as dispassionate a tone as Michael spoke.

Michael pulled off Mrs. Miller's robe and nightgown and continued to rape her, only to stop after a few moments. He told the two detectives that the living room rug was hard on his knees. The fibers were rubbing them raw while he wrestled with his mother's naked body. He saw no way to avoid rug burns unless he moved her somewhere else, where it was softer. He grabbed her beneath the arms and hauled her into his parents' bedroom. He laid her on the bed and resumed his position.

There, he consummated the act.

Was she conscious? asked Beck.

She was still warm, but she didn't respond to his touch or voice, said Michael. No resistance. He grabbed one of the pillows on the bed and pressed it over her face while he raped her, he added.

When he was finished, he took a shower. Then he got dressed and went into the kitchen for something to eat. For the next four hours, he puttered around the house, reading and listening to music. He returned to the bedroom three times to see if she had moved. She hadn't. Each time he came back, he sat on the bed and went through a ritual to ascertain that she was dead. He held the pillow over her face, pressing her chest at the same time to force any remaining air out of her body.

At noon, he left the house to run some errands, making sure to double-bolt the front door when he left. He hadn't kept his appointment with Dr. Shapiro that morning, so he dropped by the Encino office sometime after 2 P.M. to apologize and set up a new appointment. Michael promised to show up the next day without fail, and without mentioning a word to the psychiatrist about what he had done.

His next stop was his aunt's house about twenty miles to the west in Santa Monica. His mother had asked him to drop off the set of mah-jongg tiles and that was exactly what he did. He got there around 3:30 and suddenly felt very, very tired. After handing the mah-jongg set to his aunt, Marilyn Adkins, he asked if he could take a nap in his cousin Bill's room. She told him to go ahead. He slept like a baby.

When Bill Adkins came home at 10 P.M., Michael was asleep in his room.

Adkins, a twenty-three-year-old college student who lived at home, picked up the story for the two sheriff's detectives after Michael left the captain's office, accompanied by Ed Jaakola and another Palos Verdes Estates police officer.

Marilyn Adkins asked her son not to awaken his cousin. Michael seemed exhausted, she said. So Bill slept in a different room. He woke up at about the same time as Michael: after the phone rang at about 6:15 A.M., rousing everyone in the household.

It was Roy Miller on the line, asking to speak with Michael. He had tragic news. Marguerite was dead. Bill and his parents stood petrified at the door to Bill's room as Michael took the phone and listened. He said little. Just listened. The Adkinses stood by, ready to help if they could, though Marilyn had to be comforted herself upon hearing the news of her youngest sister's death. After promising to get to Palos Verdes right away, Michael hung up the phone and stared at his cousin.

"My mom is dead," he said. "I killed her."

Bill and his parents nodded, reaching out to Michael and holding him tight. They all believed they understood what the boy was trying to say. Michael was three years younger than Bill, but he had been through so much more. Michael had lost his older brother. He was having terrible problems adjusting to growing up. Everyone in the family knew that he was seeing a psychiatrist.

And now this. It was no wonder that Michael felt psychologically responsible for his mother's death.

But Roy Miller was alone at the house now and undoubtedly devastated. Mr. and Mrs. Adkins, Bill and Michael quickly dressed and climbed into their cars. There was no time to dwell on the details of Marguerite's death. Bill could only assume that it was an accident of some kind. It was ugly to contemplate, but it might have been suicide. Perhaps that was the reason Michael kept repeating, over and over, that he had killed his mother.

Bill offered to drive, but Michael insisted that he could handle it. Bill nodded sympathetically and let the younger man drive. It was a way for Michael to occupy his hands and his thoughts and get his mind off this latest tragedy in the Miller family saga. They sped down the freeway toward Palos Verdes Estates while Bill's parents followed them in their own car.

Michael didn't drive to the house, however. He went straight to the Palos Verdes Estates Police Department. Bill was confused. As Michael parked, Bill asked why they had driven there first instead of going to the Millers' house. Michael acted as if he didn't hear him. He turned off the engine and, without waiting for his cousin, marched straight into the lobby of the police department.

Roy Miller was there. Bill watched as father and son embraced. When Bill Adkins' parents arrived, they accompanied the senior Miller back to his house while Bill stayed behind to wait for his cousin.

It was after 9 A.M. when Sergeant Sett and Detective Beck were finished with Michael Miller. He asked to make two phone calls before they went any further. He tried reaching his father, but the line was busy, so the first call went to his psychiatrist.

Beck dialed the number Michael gave him and waited until Dr. Shapiro answered. Then he told him he was Jerome Beck with the Los Angeles County Sheriff's Department and handed the receiver over to Michael.

"I killed my mom," Michael said into the receiver.

In a brief reprise of what he had just spent nearly an hour telling the detectives, Michael described what had happened. When he began spouting something in French, Beck ordered him to speak English or hang up the phone. At that point, Shapiro asked to speak to Beck. Michael handed the receiver back to the detective.

The psychiatrist was volubly upset—the first real expression of unbridled emotional distress from anyone that either Sett or Beck had heard since they had first received the call to investigate the night before. Dr. Shapiro pleaded with the detectives to hospitalize Michael immediately. Beck thanked him for his concern before hanging up.

Michael's next call went to his father, now back at the house with his aunt and uncle. With an unnerving calm that sent an ice-water chill trickling down Sergeant Sett's spine, Michael explained that he had been responsible for his mother's death.

"I did it," he said.

At 9:17 A.M, his conversation with his father was finished. And, just as Bill Adkins surmised, the talk behind closed doors where the two sheriff's detectives finished their interrogation of Michael Miller did turn to suicide.

But it wasn't about Marguerite Miller. The suicide that Al Sett and Jerry Beck were concerned about was that of Michael Miller. Before Ed Jaakola marched him out of the interrogation office, past Bill Adkins and into booking for fingerprints and photos, they asked Michael whether he had ever attempted suicide.

He hadn't. But he'd given it serious thought several times.

That was enough for Sett to put in a call to the Los Angeles

County Men's Central Jail in downtown L.A. after Michael left the room. After the paperwork was completed and Michael Miller was on his way to the world's largest indoor jail, Sett wanted him kept out of the general population. It would be best if he were put somewhere by himself, perhaps in the medical wing. Sett requested special handling for Michael and ordered a twenty-four-hour suicide watch.

The media onslaught that Ed Jaakola had feared was in full swing before Michael finished his confession. The reporters had been dribbling into the closet-size lobby of the Palos Verdes police station since dawn.

Daniela Wild, a crime reporter for the *South Bay Daily Breeze*, was among the first to show up.

A little after 6 A.M., still sleepy, Wild made her routine round of calls to local police departments from the *Breeze* city room. When she had worked her way down her police call list to Palos Verdes, the watch commander told her over the phone that the department was investigating a murder. She cut her calling routine short and drove as fast as she could to the Peninsula.

Nobody ever got murdered in Palos Verdes unless it was something big.

She arrived at the police station front desk before 7 A.M., while Michael Miller and his cousin were still en route from Santa Monica. When she stormed through the front door of the station, there was only one other civilian in the lobby. He was tall, gaunt and motionless, in a disheveled business suit, with a blank face and a shock of dark, graying hair that needed combing. He sat and stared straight ahead. Daniela brushed on by, paying him scant attention as she hung over the front counter and asked the dispatcher if she could see Jaakola. The dispatcher waved her through a security door to the back of the station.

Only after the sergeant had given Wild a brief rundown on the night's events did she learn that the man sitting out in the lobby was the victim's husband. Wild excused herself and was back in the department lobby in a flash, asking Roy Miller in a sympathetic voice if he wanted to talk about his wife. He didn't. Wild shrugged and raced back inside for more notes on the homicide investigation.

Jaakola laid it out for her: female . . . Caucasian . . . fifty-two . . . found dead . . . apparent homicide victim . . . no suspects in custody . . . still under investigation. While Jaakola rambled, she scribbled his descriptions of the murder scene in her notebook. An Explorer Scout who had volunteered to help out at the station tapped Wild on the shoulder, startling her out of her concentration. The scout motioned toward the lobby. Mr. Miller had changed his mind. He wanted to talk.

But he didn't want to talk about himself, Wild soon learned. Also, she was no longer the only reporter there. By this time, several others had arrived, their notebooks out, their tape recorders whirring.

"I married the girl next door," Miller told the reporters in a monotone. "We went to high school, grammar school and Pomona College. She was a beautiful, beautiful woman."

Wild scribbled phrases like "a breath of fresh air" and "devastated" as Roy Miller talked about his wife.

But Wild also made a mental note about Miller's peculiar detachment. At first, she wrote it off to the kind of nerve-numbing shock she had witnessed in the next of kin of victims of fatal auto accidents. Still, Miller's manner seemed almost resigned, as if he were talking about events from long, long ago and not the murder of his own wife less than twenty-four hours earlier. There was no modulation in his voice at all.

"You don't need to talk about me," Miller told the reporters. "Let's talk about my wife. It's her death. It's her life we're celebrating. The world is richer for her being here. Everybody's life is richer who touched her."

Later, in the *Breeze* city room, Wild would describe Miller's impromptu eulogy as unnervingly calm. When a rewrite man on the *Breeze* copy desk snatched up her notes and incorporated them into a wrap-up for the next day's paper, he couldn't resist describing Miller as "choking back emotion."

Upon reflection, Wild wished that she had insisted that the rewrite man use a different phrase. Miller wasn't choking back emotion. From where she stood, it looked as though he had choked it *off*. Completely.

"The word 'flat' keeps coming to mind," she said years later. "He was flat. A flat affect is what I believe the shrinks would call it."

When Michael Miller showed up at the station, Wild watched the two of them hug. If there was emotion, it remained well hidden from Wild's eyes during the short embrace. After a few moments, sheriff's deputies shuttled Michael past Wild and the other reporters and into the captain's office for interrogation.

Wild had enough information to get started, though. The story was all unfolding so quickly that she had her news article half-written in her head before the police put out the first alert to Associated Press, City News Service and United Press International. An hour later, after Michael was brought out, booked and shipped off to county jail, the news had already begun to leak out all over Los Angeles. By 9 A.M., the network news vans were there. Wild watched as an anchorwoman for KABC-TV's Channel 7 Eyewitness News Team did a stand-up interview with Roy Miller, getting the same sotto voce epitaph he had given the print journalists an hour earlier but this time doing it on videotape. Once the interview was over and Miller had left, Wild remembered the TV newswoman leaping in the air like a cheerleader, shouting "Yessssss!"

Then Roy Miller was gone, driving back to the asylum of his hillside home, away from the media madness down below.

Inside the station, Jaakola briefly drafted Wild into service to help answer phones. The lines lit up like Christmas trees once the story hit the wires. There were not enough police or volunteer Explorer Scouts on duty to handle the deluge from all over the country. One caller even purported to be from the White House Press Office. Everyone took the caller to be a crank, but Wild speculated that the call was probably real. The death of Marguerite Miller was no ordinary murder.

Jaakola, who was used to operating in a quiet little police station in a quiet little community, began looking more than a little apoplectic. Wild took him aside. Instead of explaining the case to everyone who called, she suggested, why not draft a press release and host a one-stop press conference, just as Beck and Sett had recommended several hours earlier at the murder scene? Wild even volunteered to write the press release herself.

Just after 10 A.M., Jaakola sat down to reread her draft.

> On Thursday 3-24-83, at approx. 11 P.M. the Palos Verdes Estates Police Dept. received an unknown trouble call from Mr. Roy Miller at 2019 Via Visalia, Palos Verdes Estates.
>
> Mr. Miller stated that when he arrived home he entered the front door and saw blood and a pair of broken eyeglasses on the floor. He called his wife's name and when there was no response he went to a neighbor's house and called the police.
>
> Responding police units found Mrs. Marguerite Miller, 52 yrs. old, dead in the master bedroom, an apparent murder victim.
>
> The cause of death appears to be blunt force trauma but the specific cause of death will be determined by the coroner's office.
>
> At 9 A.M., 3-25-83, Michael David Miller, 20 yrs. old, was arrested and booked at the Palos Verdes Estates Police Dept. for the murder of his mother.
>
> The Los Angeles County Sheriff's Homicide Bureau is assisting in the investigation.
>
> E. A. Jaakola, Sgt. 716

Jaakola smiled. He looked up to thank her, but Wild was already gone. While the rest of the Los Angeles media were still arriving in news vans and car pools for the noon press conference, Wild was leading the way up the Hill to the Miller house to get a look at the murder scene.

13

Joann Hicks and Judy McFarland worried about Marguerite when she didn't show up at Dr. Bruce Halstead's health talk.

The gals, as they called themselves, used to joke that "late" was Marguerite's middle name. She was rarely on time. In fact, she was almost *always* late.

If the gals planned to carpool to a nutrition lecture down the Hill in Redondo Beach or Torrance, or a speech by Focus on the Family founder Dr. James Dobson, Marguerite would usually call Joann ahead of time and offer to drive.

"I'll meet you at the corner of Palos Verdes North and Crenshaw," she would say.

Joann would answer "Fine" and then go to the corner and wait. And wait. Finally, when Joann was fuming, Marguerite pulled up, sometimes a half hour late. The thin, bright-eyed Mrs. Miller with her girlish laugh and crooked smile would shrug and explain: "Well, uh . . . I had a phone call."

Marguerite seemed to spend half her life on the telephone. When she was engaged in conversation, she didn't let anything interfere, especially punctuality. It wasn't that she was scatterbrained or indifferent or unfeeling. Quite the contrary. According to Joann,

Marguerite was always late because she could never say no. If a relative or someone down at the church or even Gilberto the gardener needed help, she dropped everything to focus her attention on their problem and failed to keep her appointments. Thus, Joann interpreted her friend's perpetual tardiness as a natural outgrowth of Marguerite's compassion and hyper personality.

Joann and Judy considered themselves Marguerite's closest comrades. Joann had come to accept Marguerite's busy, busy nature shortly after Judy first introduced them to each other years earlier, when Joann joined the South Bay chapter of the American Nutrition Society. Marguerite and Joann became fast friends, and much of the gabbing that Marguerite did on the phone each day was to Joann.

Joann knew that Marguerite might be late, but she never stood people up. Until recently, Marguerite had rarely missed a lecture. Since her troubles with Michael began escalating, her absences had been on the rise, though. Being a good mother put a crimp in her lifestyle. But both she and the other gals agreed that family came first, over everything else.

Dr. Halstead was one of Marguerite's favorite speakers. He had gained quite a reputation as a New Age doctor with the publication of his "complete guide" to the history and use of dimethyl sulfoxide. DMSO, as it was known among health enthusiasts, was an industrial wood-pulp solvent that had gained cult notoriety as a pain reliever and anti-inflammatory balm. He also championed a theory known as "chelation": altering blood molecular structure in such a way that prevented the need for heart bypass surgery.

The auditorium at the United Methodist Church in Redondo Beach was packed on Thursday evening, March 24. Through their connections, the gals had been increasingly successful in getting dozens of national holistic medical experts to speak for free at American Nutrition Society lectures and the crowds grew accordingly. Soon, they also brought in men and women with cancer in remission, regenerated hearts or recovery from multiple sclerosis, all as an apparent result of dietary change. The society's free monthly lecture series had become de rigueur among enlightened Peninsulans, often drawing as many as three hundred people. Marguerite, who edited the chapter's newsletter, deserved a lot of the credit. The gals began to see themselves as a team with a mission.

Judy had even written a book about the importance of nutrition. She and her mother, dietary pioneer Gladys Lindberg, coauthored *Take Charge of Your Health*, a 1982 Harper & Row handbook on nourishment, exercise and the teachings of Jesus Christ. The right combination of all three of these life elements could prevent or retard everything from heart disease and cancer to impotence and schizophrenia, according to the book. And with Gladys' retirement, Judy had taken over managing the famous Lindberg Nutrition Center.

Both Mrs. Lindberg and her daughter were disciples of West Coast nutrition guru Adelle Davis, whose series of books on eating right had attracted an international following during the 1970s. The Lindbergs, in turn, influenced friends and friends of friends to join in the crusade. They had turned Joann, Marguerite and dozens of other Palos Verdes housewives and mothers into converts.

Joann used to quote Leviticus: "The life of the flesh is in the blood."

Well, what did that mean? Joann asked rhetorically. Wasn't oxygen in the blood? Oxygen and nutrients from *food*? Sugar drew fat into the arteries, sparking spurts of energy, but ultimately leaving the body depleted and one step closer to disaster.

Like the other gals, Marguerite approached hypoglycemia more as a national threat than as simple blood sugar imbalance. Feeding a child ice cream and candy bars was tantamount to feeding them arsenic and cyanide. The result was the same, only slower and more agonizing. A sugar rush didn't just hurt the gastrointestinal system and half of one's internal organs. It went right to the brain too, triggering wild mood swings, manic depression and often catastrophic behavior.

As Judy had written in her book, "A typical hypoglycemic victim is, in fact, an emotional yo-yo, strung out on a chemical reaction he cannot control, with reactions so severe they frequently resemble insanity."

In fact, improper nutrition didn't just *resemble* insanity, according to Joann. It *caused* insanity.

"There don't have to be schizophrenics," counseled Joann. "If you have enough oxygen going, the body has a natural balance."

Joann saw a pattern between holidays and madness. During the sugar-saturated days before and after Halloween, Christmas and Easter, some of the worst atrocities and perversions were inflicted by human beings on one another. Beatings. Knifings. Rapes. Murders. Accounts filled the newspapers every year.

It was a truth that did not escape Marguerite in her pursuit of ways to help fight Michael's mood swings. Of all the members of the South Bay chapter of the American Nutrition Society, Marguerite probably took the information most seriously. In Marguerite's eyes, the lectures were not just interesting. They were vital to her sons' mental health.

That's why both Joann and Judy were quite concerned when she never appeared for Dr. Halstead's lecture and never called to offer an excuse. It wasn't like Marguerite not to call.

As she was driving home late Thursday night after the lecture, Judy suddenly developed a "terrible, ghastly feeling—a foreboding," as she would later describe it to Joann. She couldn't explain it. It came upon her like some nauseous sense of doom. Something awful had happened. She couldn't shake the feeling, even after she had gone to bed.

When Joann called her early Friday morning, Judy was already half-braced for some bad news. She didn't know how bad.

"Marguerite's gone," Joann said. She wasn't hysterical, but there was a tense, serious vibrato to her voice.

"Gone? Gone where?" Judy asked.

"She's dead," said Joann.

There was shock, then disbelief and anger in Judy's reaction. That was impossible! They had just seen each other!

It was murder, said Joann. That much was clear.

How could it have happened? Judy demanded.

The word telegraphed over the Peninsula grapevine was that her son might have done it.

Another impossibility. Marguerite had her problems with the boy, they'd quarreled at times, but they had him in treatment.

Michael had worked for Judy at the nutrition center during the summer. He was a little slow but gentle as a lamb. In fact, he had come by the store the previous afternoon and showed no signs at all that anything had been amiss. It was preposterous to think he might have done it.

Judy and Joann commiserated, running the facts back and forth across the telephone line before they decided that they had to do something. Still on the telephone to each other, they began by saying a prayer together. Then Judy suggested they take their prayers to the Miller house and try to offer some comfort to Mr. Miller.

Joann and Judy met Roy Miller at the door, just after he returned home from the police station. There wasn't much he was able to add. His house was as lifeless and empty as his face. Marguerite was gone, he told them, taken away to the county morgue. Michael was on his way to the county jail after being booked on suspicion of murder. Roy would try to find the best criminal defense lawyer he could to handle his son's case.

Roy was efficient—some would say coldly efficient. Judy and Joann knew better. He was a fine husband and good father who had gone on automatic pilot to get through this unbelievable nightmare. His perfect family had been insidiously and inexplicably shattered. Judy and Joann were filled with conflicting waves of faith and consternation. The facts of Marguerite's death remained all so unnervingly contained, yet gruesomely incomplete.

But they had no time for reflection. While they were talking with Roy, the front doorbell began buzzing and buzzing. The media had arrived. Marguerite's friends saw their duty and went to it. Roy remained inside while the gals headed off the TV crews that had descended on Via Visalia. Judy was blinded by the camera lights as she emerged from the house.

"We're all here to pray for Roy and help him," Judy told them. "What else can we do? What he needs right now is a lot of prayer."

The two women stationed themselves at the front door like

sentinels, ready to field the reporters' questions, but even more determined to block media access to Roy Miller's private agony.

"They were very private people," Joann explained. "A very wonderful, compassionate, priceless family. The best. The pinnacle."

They did answer reporters' questions about each of the Millers. Marguerite, they explained to the press, was simply the best of the gals who lived and socialized with each other on the Peninsula. She gossiped a bit, especially about the high-and-mighty types that Roy Miller knew through his associations in highflying Republican circles. But Marguerite was down-to-earth.

When the reporters questioned her about Michael, Joann had just as ready an answer. Michael was good-natured, sweet and devoted to his parents.

"He was a really precious person," she said. "He loved his mother and father."

It was a great family, said Joann. A beautiful family—a note that Judy McFarland echoed when it was her turn to step up to the microphones again.

"They are an All-American family," she told the newspaper reporters and TV cameras. Judy was so caught up in the moment that she did not see the irony in using the present tense to describe a family that no longer existed. "An intimate family, raised in the church," Judy continued. "They went everyplace together."

She didn't dwell on Michael's problems. He had never been as handsome or as talented or accomplished as Jeffrey. If his older brother had been poised and bright, Michael was coltish and average. When Jeffrey died, Michael took it especially hard. He was actually quite fortunate to have a mother like Marguerite there for him during that tragedy, Judy told the press.

What she didn't tell them was that Marguerite was very particular. Exacting, actually. Her finicky nature extended to her children, whom she held to a high—some might say, impossible—standard.

Judy remembered when the boy first came to work at the health food store. She had given Michael the simple task of operating the carrot juice machine. He caught on quickly enough. Judy saw him grinning broadly to himself at his own little routine of slice, juice and bottle after half an hour at the machine.

But when Marguerite came in to see how he was doing, that all changed. Michael tried to show her how he made the carrot juice and she immediately took over. She had a way of cutting the carrots that would *improve* on Michael's method, she explained. It was more efficient and less time-consuming her way. She took over, taking the knife out of his hands and slicing, crushing and juicing the carrots in half the time that it took her son to do it.

She didn't even look up from her carrots to see the smile fade from Michael's face. But Judy saw. His eyes drooped like a dachshund's, his expression as crushed as the carrots Marguerite jammed quickly and efficiently through the juice machine. Marguerite wasn't acting out of ill intent. She just seemed oblivious.

But the carrot-juicing tale wasn't a story she was prepared to give to the newspaper that day. Marguerite was gone and recalling such an incident might give the wrong impression.

Up a twisty road, no more than a minute by car from the afternoon traffic of Ventura Boulevard, Dr. Shapiro had practiced psychoanalysis from dawn to dusk each day for more than twenty years.

He normally took a break at noon, but the early morning phone call from the Los Angeles County Sheriff's Department on the last Friday in March 1983 left him without much of an appetite. Michael Miller would not be keeping his rescheduled appointment this particular Friday.

He had just confessed to murdering his own mother.

Shapiro remained in shock for several minutes after he put the phone back in its receiver.

His patients varied from browbeaten housewives with personality disorders to young professionals with floating anxiety to conflicted youngsters like Michael David Miller, with their hungry nameless demons ranging inside their souls. They were all very different. All they had in common was the drive up to Shapiro's sprawling, rustic estate at least once a week for an hour's worth of exorcism.

Sometimes, if it was close to lunchtime, the doctor would share a hot dog with one of them in the kitchen of his main house. Sometimes he grew as fond of his patients as he did his own children. After all, a sizable number of them wound up in his hands because they had been abandoned emotionally and, on occasion, physically by their own parents.

Shapiro saw himself as a free spirit with a profound sympathy for his fellowman. Jacqueline, his beloved wife of more than thirty years, had herself become subject to psychotic episodes in recent years. In tones of abject fear, she described how radio commentators and TV talking heads specifically directed torments and taunts at her that nobody else in the family heard or saw.

And Jackie was not the only Shapiro with psychological problems. The eldest daughter, Carolyn, had been through an intense bout with alcohol and cocaine abuse. Sumner Shapiro did not merely empathize with his patients. He must have sympathized with them too, feeling their pain as he experienced his own, within his own family.

Shapiro was a Massachusetts native and a Harvard graduate who had gone on to take his medical degree from Boston University. Later, when he migrated to California, he became certified as a Freudian analyst at the Los Angeles Psychoanalytic Institute.

But Boston remained in his blood. Politically, Shapiro was an academic liberal, but when it came to things like family, home and property, he was as conservative as Ronald Reagan. He was punctual, demanded the same of his patients and charged by the hour.

He and Michael hit it off instantly. He had been seeing the young man for nine months, during which Michael seemed to be making considerable progress toward breaking the ties with his family and establishing his own identity.

As he had explained to Marguerite Miller during a phone call just a month earlier, her son's mood had seemed to be shifting away from the angry, immature attitude that he had displayed when Michael first came to him the previous summer. Shapiro tried to encourage this more serious side, dwelling on the boy's academics and employment future.

Shapiro teased Michael about his roguishness. The boy often seemed to contradict strictly for the sake of contradicting. Shapiro gently cajoled him to take greater command over himself.

He admired the Millers' patience and told them as much. Both Roy and Marguerite were doing everything a therapist could ask, he told Mrs. Miller. The therapy took patience, understanding and time.

Michael still spoke often about Marguerite's late parents, Harold and Marie Bruner, and Jeff's untimely death. All three had passed away within a three-year period, leaving a gaping void in Michael's life. He was still in crisis two years later, moving from grieving to anger to acceptance. But he did appear to be coming to the realization that he had an identity of his own, Shapiro had told Mrs. Miller.

"He's a very individual guy," he told Marguerite.

Michael appreciated the finer things in life—an attitude that reflected the love of culture instilled in him by Roy and Marguerite, as well as the Bruners.

He still had a long way to go, though. He was a young man harboring a lot of frustration and anger, especially about Jeffrey. It would take time and tolerance to work through.

Shapiro tried to lighten the resonance of even the most ghastly of his patients' anguished memories. Treating the macabre with laughter was one way of deflating its potency. Connecting the dots of their dreams with earliest childhood memories was another. He wasn't opposed to sifting through a patient's biography for symbols, but his approach was not strictly traditional analysis either.

His patients eventually came to appreciate how effective and important his therapy techniques were, but Michael Miller knew little about his techniques when he first came to Dr. Shapiro for help the previous summer.

Back then, Marguerite had confided in her closest friends that she and Roy had been seeking help for the boy for months. Ever since he'd returned from New York, he had gone from therapy to therapy. The Millers had tried everything, from traditional counseling to hypnosis.

At one point, Marguerite found a British remedy called the Bach Flower Stock Essences that aligned with her thinking on natural cures. The "essences" consisted of thirty-nine different kinds of condensed tree leaf or flower petal pressings, bottled in England and shipped around the world to the holistic faithful for relief from a host of emotional afflictions. Crab apple essence was supposed to relieve symptoms of self-disgust or shame. Water violet essence combated excessive pride or aloofness. Honeysuckle fought nostalgia and homesickness. And so on.

In Michael's case, Mrs. Miller selected six of the Bach Essences to feed him: holly, for jealousy, envy, hatred and suspicion; impatiens, for irritability and impatience; mustard, for deep gloom; seleranthus, for uncertainty and indecision; star-of-Bethlehem, for the aftereffects of trauma and all kinds of shock; and willow, for resentment and bitterness.

She made Michael take the dosages that she prescribed for him on a regular basis, mixing two drops of a natural Bach Essence with one ounce of spring water and administering the concoction to him at the rate of one teaspoon four times a day, like medicine.

In emergencies, the Bach Centre in Wallingford, England, recommended that a patient take undiluted Bach Essence drops as a "rescue remedy." "For immediate or emergency uses in shock, emotional stress, dentistry, 'stage fright,' severe bites or stings, take four drops in a small glass," read the instruction pamphlet that came with the small vials of flower essence. The essences were also good, the pamphlet claimed, for sprains, open wounds, burns and massage and benefited animals and plants as well as human beings.

Marguerite's insistence that Michael keep up his dosages didn't seem to make much difference. By the time he arrived at Dr. Shapiro's office, the essences had not helped him at all. He remained alternately angry and morose, and even Marguerite's strict supervision of his diet didn't seem to improve his moods. She had even tried sending him to Santa Monica to see a counselor who specialized in biofeedback. The theory was that a patient could control his own moods by training himself to alter his involuntary bodily functions, such as blood pressure and heartbeat. That hadn't worked either.

Michael rebelled. After Marguerite reluctantly agreed and Roy promised to foot the bill, Michael went to Dr. Shapiro.

At their first sessions they found common ground in their mutual appreciation of music and the performing arts. Like Michael, Shapiro's daughter Carolyn aspired to become an actress. Michael had been to Paris and Shapiro made much of the fact that they both spoke French with some fluency.

And there were the boy's sexual frustrations. He talked a good game, but it seemed apparent that his female companionship was limited. He was pleasant enough. Dr. Shapiro advised trying to casually meet and date a variety of girls.

Before Michael's scheduled appointment; a teenage girl who was always accompanied by her mother also came up the hill for her session with Dr. Shapiro. She and Michael ran into each other from time to time and she soon developed a crush on him. Given Michael's late-blooming adolescence and painful shyness around the opposite sex, it was not a bad happenstance. But Michael was either oblivious to it or too shy to do anything about it.

In retrospect, Shapiro acknowledged to himself that he had seriously underestimated just how disturbed Michael was.

Then Detective Beck's phone call came. Michael would no longer be driving up into the Encino hills once a week to seek Shapiro's services as referee between Michael and his inner demons. Shapiro now had to visit his patient in jail.

While Michael Miller finished the booking process and found his way to his bunk in the medical wing of the five-story Los Angeles County Men's Jail, his mother underwent an autopsy to determine the exact cause of her death.

At 2:22 P.M. on Friday, Marguerite Miller's slight, battered body was wheeled on a gurney to the operating room. Just after 6 P.M., the City News Service wire blurb told the tale in a nutshell.

A three-hour autopsy today by Los Angeles County
Coroner Dr. Ronald Kornblum showed that Marguerite
Miller, wife of President Ronald Reagan's personal attor-
ney, died of blunt force trauma to the head.

The autopsy, which concluded about 5:30 P.M., determined that Miller, 52, suffered no other significant injur-
ies. And there was no immediate evidence of sexual
assault, coroner's deputy Bill Gold said.

However, tissue specimens taken from the woman's
body will be forwarded to the sheriff's crime laboratory
for further examination.

Specimens included microscope slides with smears from rectal,
nipple and oral swabbings, combings from the pubic hair and daubs
of discharge from the genital area, all tagged, sealed and submitted
to the lab criminologists in a routine package called a Sexual
Assault Evidence Kit. If there was semen anywhere, the lab would
find it and report back to homicide within three days.

Kornblum also sent blood and tissue samples for drug analysis to
search for traces of amphetamines, PCP, narcotics, alcohol or any
of the other unnatural drugs that Marguerite so abhorred.

And while Kornblum went through the autopsy protocol, with
a careful examination and the formal weighing of each internal
organ, Al Sett and Jerry Beck stood by as witnesses. They had
spent afternoons like this one inside the coroner's Forensic Science
Center before, watching assistant medical examiners perform this
dreadful surgery. It was rare that the county coroner himself did
the duty, however, calling out the results as he proceeded through
this publicly little-known exam: "The body is unclothed and unem-
balmed and is that of a well-developed, well-nourished 52 year old
White female which measures 68 inches in length and weighs 94
pounds. The body is cold. Rigor mortis is present and all joints are
beginning to dissipate. . . ."

Forensically, there was nothing particularly unusual about her.
She had a healthy heart and kidneys and liver. Kornblum kept his
observations on a purely scientific plane, however, even as he

described Marguerite's bluish-gray eyes and her light brown hair, all matted at the back of her head with dried blood.

Kornblum observed cuts to her forehead, right scalp and the top of her head. Though her nose had not been broken, it bore abrasions and contusions, like those on her right cheek and chin, as though she had been dragged facedown across a floor. The tip of the middle finger of her left hand had been torn away. The base of her skull had been hit with such force that both orbital plates had been fractured, the cracks extending all the way to the front of the skull.

Kornblum also noticed that her lungs were partially collapsed but grayish pink and moist. They appeared healthy. But Kornblum's scalpel revealed a darker truth inside the lungs. The lower lobes of the lungs were heavy, dark and red—the color of large quantities of blood. He confirmed for the two sheriff's detectives what they had already suspected. Officially, Marguerite Miller died from perhaps a half dozen vicious blows to the head. Technically, however, she asphyxiated on blood that trickled from her hemorrhaging skull into her lungs while she lay unconscious and helpless on her back in her own bed.

— 14

There already seemed to be subtle but steady pressure from above at the sheriff's department to take it easy on the Miller case. Nobody ordered Sett and Beck to let up on their investigation, but the entire homicide division knew exactly who Roy Miller was.

The elder Miller had officially gone into seclusion by Saturday, and all his comments were now being channeled through another Gibson, Dunn and Crutcher lawyer: F. Daniel Frost.

Frost had blue-blood credentials very nearly as extensive as those of William French Smith. Like Miller, Frost was a tax special-ist whose forte involved estate planning and the art of pushing corporate and personal income to new highs while keeping taxes low. He, too, was a California native, a Reagan conservative and one of the near-anonymous but powerful white Republican men who wielded genuine and unquestioned authority over Southern California.

In addition to being a member of the board of governors of the Los Angeles County Music Center, Frost was president and over-seer of the Music Center Foundation's $45-million endowment and a former vice chairman of the Claremont University Center board of fellows, in Roy and Marguerite Miller's hometown. Since 1962,

Frost had also been managing partner of Gibson, Dunn and Crutcher. He was credited by many with transforming that legal institution into the city's richest and most powerful law firm.

Frost had one further distinction. His wife was the former Camilla Chandler, the older sister of *Los Angeles Times* chairman and former publisher, Otis Chandler. When reporters—particularly those from the *Times*—were routed to Frost for comment on the Miller case, they were made aware from the outset that Frost was not just another lawyer. He was a brother at the bar of Roy Miller and also the brother-in-law of the man who ran the all-powerful *Times*.

"Noel [Greenwood, the *Times* metropolitan editor] told me several times that Roy Miller was just a tax lawyer and that William French Smith was Reagan's *real* lawyer," former *Times* reporter David Johnston recalled years later. "He said that the whole case was being blown out of proportion because he [Miller] just happened to handle the tax returns for Ronald and Nancy."

Johnston and reporter Jerry Belcher, another *Times* staff writer who followed the Michael Miller story, said they were ordered by their superiors to tread lightly.

They joined a host of other newspaper and television reporters who were forced to accept Roy Miller's version of the unfolding story as filtered through Daniel Frost's noncommittal telephone conversations during the next several days. Frost's interpretation paralleled that of the *Times*' Greenwood: the Miller case would never have received the same media attention if Roy were not the President's personal attorney. Frost refused to tell the media whether or not Reagan had been in touch with Miller since the murder. According to Frost, fairness compelled those covering the story to dispassionately approach the killing of Marguerite Miller just as they would a similar homicide that did not tangentially involve the President of the United States.

The argument worked well in theory, but not in practice.

Al Sett knew by Saturday afternoon that he had a capital case against Roy Miller's son. The semen tests weren't back from the lab yet, but the confession was enough. In California, murder during the commission of a second felony was punishable by life in prison without parole or by death in the San Quentin gas chamber. And rape definitely qualified as a felony.

At 4:38 P.M. on Saturday, March 26, Sett issued the following order to county jail personnel:

"Transport Miller, Michael David, MW/20, Bkg No. 7045-270 to Torrance Municipal Court Monday, March 28 at 8:30 A.M. for arraignment on charges of 187 P.C., Murder, and 261.3 P.C., Rape."

While Sergeant Sett was preparing to arraign Roy Miller's only remaining son on first-degree murder, the elder Miller visited Dr. Shapiro's hillside office in Encino, where the two men discussed in somber tones both the tragedy of Marguerite and the plight of Michael. Roy unburdened himself while sitting in the same dilapidated easy chair where Michael had sat during his counseling sessions so many times before.

Because it was the weekend, Shapiro had asked his answering service to pick up all his calls. He wanted to talk with Roy Miller in total privacy.

When the phone rang through anyway during the middle of their discussion, Shapiro was more than a little irritated.

"Hello," Shapiro snapped into the receiver.

"Hello," answered a familiar voice. "This is Ronald Reagan. Is Roy Miller there?"

Shapiro handed over the receiver, his jaw hanging as loose as a one-hinged door on a potbellied stove. From Shapiro's position at the opposite side of his desk, the phone conversation between the President and his lawyer was short and sounded to Shapiro as though it was heavy on commiseration. There were no great words from the Great Communicator—only private condolences. That the conversation had happened at all impressed the psychiatrist so deeply that he related the yarn to his visitors for years afterward.

When he was off the phone, Roy Miller told Shapiro that he had retained a pair of top-notch criminal attorneys to defend his son. Tom Nolan and Stephen Miller—who was no relation, Roy assured Shapiro. Nolan and Miller wanted Shapiro to talk to the boy and then with them, Roy told the psychiatrist. Shapiro's assessment of the young man's sanity would be crucial to the defense that the two attorneys had in mind.

Shapiro agreed. He might not be able to meet with Michael before his Monday arraignment, but he did promise to make the trek to the county jail within a few days.

Monday morning, just before Michael's scheduled arraignment, the results came back from the lab. Criminalist Thomas McCleary confirmed for Beck and Sett that there had been semen on the swabbings taken from Mrs. Miller's genitals. When they met with Richard de la Sota, the mild-mannered young prosecutor that the district attorney had assigned to the case, the detectives were able to say with confidence that they could prove rape.

But even if Michael's confession had not been enough and the laboratory evidence had turned out inconclusive, the detectives had a third piece of evidence, which they had reviewed over the weekend, that should have removed any doubt. In fact, it should have been a neon warning to the Millers that catastrophe was headed their way, months before the murder.

The previous autumn, Marguerite had begun keeping a sporadic, loose-leaf diary of her daily activities, centering on the emotional problems and psychoanalytic treatment of her younger son. It was an odd hodgepodge of longhand notes and reminders, tossed together with grocery lists, phone numbers and often shocking, even graphic, accounts of Michael's bizarre behavior.

At times, it was hard to follow, like a stream-of-consciousness essay. It was revealing, insightful and chilling, even to a jaded homicide detective's eyes. But it raised just as many questions as it answered.

It was unclear in portions of the text exactly who Marguerite Miller was writing about and precisely what she meant when she engaged in her frequent and often volatile arguments with Michael during the weeks leading up to Thursday, March 24, 1983.

But in much of the diary, Marguerite was crystal-clear in her chronicle about her increasingly disturbed offspring. It began with her strangely detached, almost clinical assessment of the origins of Michael's summer-long despondency.

Michael was holding back a lot, she wrote in early June, just before Michael began seeing Dr. Shapiro. He was rigid and tended to stifle his emotions. His thinking was unrealistic, he distorted facts and he blew comments and criticism way out of proportion.

Marguerite saw her son withdrawing from interpersonal relationships. One moment he would be self-conscious and hypercritical of himself. The next, he was trying to control everything and everyone around him.

Dr. Shapiro, on the other hand, had a "very nice manner." He was polite, well spoken and gentle, according to Marguerite. Before Michael ever met with him, Shapiro set out the ground rules. He took Saturdays and Sundays off, "in the interest of self-preservation," he told Mrs. Miller. Michael would have to meet with him during the week. He also talked with his patients about "areas that are private" and liked to talk with parents about those areas separately first.

By the time Marguerite had made her first formal journal entry, the ground rules had been laid out and accepted by everyone, and the private areas Shapiro had mentioned to her posed no problems. As his sessions got under way, Marguerite kept careful track of Michael's odd behavior at home.

On Monday, August 30, 1982, Michael found his mother in the kitchen, asked her if she would mind cooking some beets for him and then returned to his bedroom. Marguerite found the beets in a meat drawer in the refrigerator, where Michael had put them. They were partially frozen, so she knocked softly at his bedroom door to let him know they weren't absolutely fresh.

He whipped open the door angrily. Why was she banging on his door? Though she was somewhat taken aback, Marguerite quickly told her son that there were hardly any greens left on the frozen beets. Would he like her to get spinach from the yard and cook it? Anything was fine, he grouched, and shut himself back in his room.

Marguerite went out to pick the spinach and Michael was back, following her onto the patio. He was totally naked, and screeched at her to not bother him again—he was cutting his wisdom teeth and trying to sleep.

Marguerite pointed out to Michael that there were workmen in the neighbor's yard who might see him naked, but he seemed to pay no attention. She held up some Swiss chard she'd found in the garden and said that she'd cook that with the beets, hoping that might please him.

"I don't care what you put with it," said Michael. "In fact, you can masturbate on it. I don't care."

Then he left, but he was back a moment later, still nude.

"In fact, you can cook yourself. You might be more tender," he said.

Marguerite puzzled over the incident the rest of the day. She had, in fact, been very sweet to her son. She did not understand what had made him so upset.

A little over a week passed and Marguerite was in a nutritional self-help mode. She made notes to herself to write a check to a radio program called the *Health Connection* for information on healthy, hearty lifestyles and to get three new Bach Essences to treat anxiety, weakness of will, and inner torture that she could then administer to Michael. She also made a note to herself to pick up *My Mother, My Self*, by Nancy Friday, a book about women interested in searching for their own identity among the detritus of their early relationship with their own mothers. It was a book that Michael had urged her to read.

Two days later, Michael was acting out again.

After she returned from a trip to the drug store, Marguerite found her son throwing away all of the jar lids in one of the kitchen drawers. He told her he was doing it to be a good son and to set her straight.

"You need a big daddy and you don't have *any* daddy," he told her nastily. He was not going to take on the additional role of parenting her, he informed his dumbfounded mother. If that was her plan, she could just get out. As he raved on and shook his finger in her face, Marguerite wondered if he really thought she and Roy would actually move out and leave the house to Michael.

Two weeks passed. Then Michael was on another rampage, this time lecturing Marguerite for two hours straight on a Tuesday late in September about how she hadn't yet read *My Mother, My Self*. She'd never understand him or understand Jeff if she didn't read the book, Michael insisted. They shared the same mother, but they were different. He told her: "Jeffrey killed himself. I'm a survivor. I'm strong."

He went on to shock Marguerite by criticizing his brother. He called Jeff a loser because he died without accomplishing anything first. He and Marguerite's family, the Bruners, were nothing.

She should start jogging, Michael advised. In one breath he told her she spent too much time trying to stay in shape and, in the next, he told her she was in terrible shape. She should become better organized. She needed to feel better about herself. The last thing she needed to do was go to church. Christianity was a fraud.

Nobody at their church was in shape, Michael continued. In fact, they were fucking losers, for the most part. Unlike many of their peers, the Millers had started out poor, Michael said, and their attitudes continued to be grounded in poverty instead of enjoying their affluence and their fine house in the Palos Verdes hills.

Then he turned all of his vitriol back on Marguerite. She wasn't worth talking to and didn't deserve the time he put in trying to set her straight. She was as big a failure as her own parents or her suicidal older son. In the old days, when they still lived in Pasadena, they were a family and life was good, spontaneous, fun. But those were the old days. Now Marguerite whiled away her time with few friends and no future. She needed to make more friends and feel good about herself.

His staunchly Republican parents might be critical of Communist Russia, he said, but at least they had achieved one laudable goal: they had wiped out the myth of Jesus Christ and put organized religion where it belonged—in the trash bin.

At month's end, he was still angry.

He grew irritated when Lance barked at the time of day that someone normally took him for a walk, but wouldn't walk the dog himself. Then he was at his mother again. Liberally sprinkling his speech with four-letter expletives, he shrieked at Marguerite again for not finishing the Nancy Friday book. That was the only way she could ever satisfy him, he yelled.

The greatest love that Marguerite had ever shown him was when she signed Dr. Julian's contract, paying out $6,000 for his marathon hypnotherapy and his $65-a-session follow-ups with Dr. Martino, Dr. Gamsky and the other therapists, he told her. He added that he knew she and Roy resented paying the money and didn't approve of the therapy, but it was the best thing that had ever happened to him.

Jeff had been a failure, he reminded his mother. Jeff's big flaw was that he believed that he had to marry the first woman he ever had sex with—a mistaken notion that the Millers had infected Michael with as well.

Marguerite contradicted her son. She had never told Jeff or Michael any such thing, she said.

Michael was unappeased. Jeff turned out to be a homosexual, he raged. He didn't even *know* his own brother, he said. He hung out with the losers at Hope Chapel.

"Your firstborn was a degenerate," he snarled. "He never did anything. The fucker never even married. Didn't accomplish anything."

Michael had to leave home, he told her. He had to get work and leave home in order to be his own person. And he could never come home again. If he did, he would be consumed, like his older brother.

Marguerite made a note to herself. She had to get down to the health food store and pick up Bach Essence No. 4 soon. It was the oil of the red flowers of the centaury plant, which—according to the Bach brochure—could be used as a remedy for people "who let themselves be exploited or imposed upon by others and who can allow themselves to be slaves."

This time, she wasn't as specific in her notation—as to whether she was buying the potion for Michael or for herself.

*   *   *

"Mike brought me a rose with flourish," she wrote a few days later. Marguerite recalled she had been delighted.

But within five minutes, while she was still admiring the flower he had given her, Michael turned vile. Instead of addressing his mother as "Mom," he called her "Marguerite" out of calculated disrespect. He referred to Roy the same way: by his first name, instead of "Dad."

"You wouldn't be anything if it weren't for Roy," he bellowed. "How would you ever have lived in Palos Verdes if you hadn't married your husband? Maybe if you got out there and busted your ass from nine to five, you'd stop hiding in your house and yard and do something."

Michael accused Marguerite of being filled with hate. She had never really experienced love, he said. Once upon a time, back when they lived in Pasadena, his mother had been a beautiful woman: spontaneous, smiling.

But that had all ended after they moved to Palos Verdes.

Then, out of nowhere, Michael waxed poetic for a few moments about scrotums. The sacs that hold the human testicles are the most beautiful things in the world, Michael told his mother.

The next day, he was at her again.

Her life was a sham, he told her. When she put on makeup and dressed to go out, it was all a pose. She was disgusting to look at. She looked more like a Polish peasant woman than a fresh and vital Palos Verdes housewife.

The home she labored on only reflected the lack of self-esteem she and Roy fostered in everything they touched, he continued. The house could have been elegant and estate-like with a pool and tennis court like the rest of the homes in their neighborhood— instead, it just didn't fit in.

In the kind of non sequitur that Marguerite seemed to have gotten used to, Michael switched his diatribe from his disdain for his parents and the home they provided for him and began raving about sex.

"Fucking a hippopotamus," he said. "Oh, that's what I'm going to do someday. Put your ears back and . . ."

A young person's clearest expression of spirituality in pagan, pre-Christian societies, he lectured his mother, was sexual orgasm with an elder of the tribe.

He stared into his mother's eyes and began to tell her again how beautiful he thought she had been when she was younger, years before when they had lived in Pasadena. Michael said that he had pored over her wedding pictures and observed that she had been remarkably lovely as a bride. But now, he spat out, he found her repulsive—unkempt and out of shape. The only way she could win back his love was by making herself beautiful and admirable again.

He blinked and looked up at the ceiling fan over the door. It resembled a scrotum, he told her. Or maybe a vagina.

Did Marguerite ever think about her cunt? he asked. Did she ever look at it? Really get in *touch* with it?

Primordial times were better, he rambled on. In ancient days, the princess of the tribe had to submit to sex with anyone in the tribe who wanted to take a poke at her. If Marguerite had lived back then, she might loosen up a little and not be such a slave to social mores. She wouldn't be a prisoner of Christianity and the United Methodist Church.

Marguerite had not simply been sitting by idly and listening like a doting mother to her son's ravings. She was writing it all down, keeping a careful record of his bizarre behavior. But that was not enough. She couldn't keep taking the abuse forever.

She needed to get some idea from Dr. Shapiro as to how long she had to listen to her son's insults and humor his unrepentant vulgarity. Did she really have to patiently listen to monologues about fucking animals or submitting to tribal sexual customs? Wouldn't it be better if she just left the room?

Michael had deteriorated to the point where his conversations with his mother turned to sex for no reason at all. She could make some remark in the kitchen about the weather and he would come back with:

"What do you want? My cock?"

Once, she just hugged him to show how she still cared for him. She told him, "Mike, you're so strong." Instead of responding abnormally by making one of his rude remarks, or responding normally by simply hugging her back, he seemed confused. He could not meet her eyes. He turned and ran out of the house into the garden.

Marguerite caught up with him and asked him what was wrong— why he suddenly bolted from the house like he couldn't bear to face her.

The question burst out of him like a bullet. Once, they had been as one—when he was in her womb. Did she ever want him back? He knew other mothers had sex with their sons. Did she want to— ever? (Only Michael didn't use phrases quite so polite.)

If she was shocked by his sudden outburst, Marguerite didn't show it. By now she had heard such language so often it didn't faze her—she had let him get away with it for so long and grown so numb to his worst outbursts that it rolled off of her. Instead, she patiently and logically tried to address each outrageous suggestion.

Fathers take advantage of their daughters more often than mothers do their sons, she told him. And, what was more, incest could be devastating. It could cause irreparable harm for a woman who later tried to have relationships with other men.

When Michael noted that Casanova was but one example of famous figures from history who committed incest, Marguerite held to her logical tack, trying to reel him in. However, Michael took the opportunity to question her in an appalling way. Cornered in her garden, Marguerite endured Michael asking her if she liked sex and how far she'd ever gone—two men at once? If she had lost her patience with his degradation, she made no record of it later. She did not stop him.

Finally, Michael zoomed in. Marguerite was told she'd made the wrong choice for a bedmate—she had selected her husband over her youngest son.

"I'm more desirable, but you can't have me," he taunted. "You made your choice."

The next day, Michael ordered his mother to sit down at the

kitchen table and write him out a check for a case of hydrogen peroxide. When she asked him why, he told her to stop concentrating on his prick and write the check.

"Where are you going to keep a case of hydrogen peroxide?" she asked.

"In my room," he snapped. "Does it matter where I keep my prick? Up or down? In someone's mouth?"

Dr. Shapiro said Michael had been making progress. In fact, he seemed better than at any time since he had begun seeing him. During their sessions, Shapiro told Mrs. Miller, he stressed to Michael repeatedly: Don't upset your mother, and respect your father.

But there was a fragility to the situation, he told her. He advised her to speak to her son with precision—to leave nothing open to interpretation. She needed to speak factually, not in the abstract. She needed to be compassionate, but should try hard not to nag.

During their sessions, Michael had been doing a lot of reminiscing about growing up in Pasadena, Shapiro told Marguerite. Michael lamented the fact that Roy and Marguerite had chosen not to have more children. He would have liked more brothers and sisters to play with as a child.

If anything, what Dr. Shapiro recommended for Michael was a social life. He didn't seem to have many dealings with anybody outside of church, Shapiro or his parents. He needed to date. He needed to get out and mingle.

His relationship with his father could use some work too. Roy had grown more remote from his family since he had become the President's lawyer. As he told Marguerite, Roy simply hadn't anticipated how demanding and how public his life would become when he took on the job. Since Michael had come home from New York, Roy had to fight for every private moment. Those moments had become fewer and further between with each passing day. The Reagan Revolution was well under way and like it or not, Roy Miller was a part of it.

But Michael didn't help improve his relations with his father either. Whenever he got a chance, he'd make some snide remark, like, "Which room in the house do you influence the President in?"

He didn't particularly like either of his parents, he told Shapiro. For one thing, the Millers refused to live life passionately. And Marguerite . . . in Michael's opinion, she was two different people inhabiting the same body. In the evening, she'd be bright and smiling. By morning, she'd look haggard and jaded. As his Grandmother Bruner had grown older, her mind deteriorated, he told the psychiatrist. Perhaps it was a genetic flaw. Perhaps Marguerite was also developing a deranged mind, he said.

Michael had been meeting each afternoon for a week with Dr. Shapiro when he asked Marguerite to join him in the living room one day. After they both sat down, he said:

"You tell the doc I'm being revolting when I'm just being Michael. I'm not going to take care of you when you get old."

Marguerite smothered those she loved, he said. She was all over Roy the minute he walked through the front door and she was all over Michael the rest of the time. She refused to give people their space. That was one reason that Michael quit playing the violin. She would not let him alone, he told her. He needed his space for his music, for himself. Everybody needed their space. But Marguerite would not allow it.

"Your husband doesn't love you," he said. "Do you think he does?"

Marguerite said that she did, in fact, believe that Roy loved her. Didn't Michael think so too?

"No," he said.

According to Michael, Roy loved his own mother more. Mothers and sons have an unbreakable bond, he explained. In a twisted bit of logic, Michael told her that he could never love Roy because Roy loved his own mother more than Roy could ever love Marguerite.

Marguerite hardly had time to put together a reply before Michael carried his brainstorm one vulgar step further. It was incumbent upon the parent to prepare the child to enter an adult, loving relationship, he told her. And the best way to do that was by example. Therefore, he explained, it made sense that Marguerite prepare Michael by having a sexual relationship with him.

Marguerite got up and left the room.

The first week of December, Marguerite went to Michael's room to tell him that he had better get going if he wanted to make it all the way to the Valley in midday traffic and keep his appointment with Dr. Shapiro.

When she stepped into his room, Michael had Paganini on the stereo and sheet music on his music stand. He held his violin in one hand and the bow in his other.

And he was naked.

"Get the hell out of here!" he screamed. "Don't you *ever* interrupt me while I'm studying!"

With that, he stepped forward and threw his mother out of his room by the scruff of her neck.

Five minutes later, a meek but indignant Marguerite returned to Michael's door. She loved him, but was he aware that he had hurt her when he tossed her out of his room?

He charged her again, yelling at her at the same time that her behavior was "inappropriate." While Marguerite cowered, he screamed that she could not love him. In fact, she couldn't love anybody because she'd never been loved herself and didn't know what it meant to love.

It was her father and his withholding of love that had made her this way, he said. Over his mother's protests Michael stated that neither Grandfather Bruner nor his daughter ever had a mother's love.

Marguerite was stunted—a pathetic little girl so scared of the world and everything in it, Michael tormented. But Marguerite countered that she did know quite a bit about the world, and furthermore it was more than enough to prove to her that there was a lot of evil out there that she wanted nothing to do with.

The harangue had come to a head and Michael asked finally, "What do you want from me? Do you want my cock?"

Later in the day, when she sat down to write out her thoughts,

Marguerite tried hard to look on the bright side. What he was doing when he said such awful things was what the therapists called "projecting," she believed. He was saying terrible things about her because he could not bring himself to say those same terrible things about himself, she guessed. He must be torn up inside. Thus, she would listen, but she would not let him rattle her. She would not take his vile spirit to heart.

Dr. Shapiro seemed to feel Michael was getting better, even if his behavior continued to be outrageous. Marguerite, too, was doing her best to focus on the positives.

After all, he did seem to be more agreeable at some moments than he had been in the months after Jeff's death. He joshed around now and then. When she chided him about yelling so loudly when they had their arguments, for example, Michael told her they could be just as loud and obnoxious as they wanted to be.

"I don't give a fuck about the neighbors. We were here first," he said with a sly smirk.

Three days before Christmas, Michael got stuck in traffic and was late for his therapy appointment. Marguerite took the opportunity to quiz Dr. Shapiro when he called to inquire about Michael's whereabouts.

Shapiro was doing everything that he as a therapist could, he told her. But there was good news. Things did finally seem to be looking up. The Millers' patience might be paying off because Shapiro had, in fact, seen a shift in Michael's mood recently. The boy's anger seemed to be slowly giving way to something Shapiro called "roguishness." He acted more like a rascally kid than an angry or mean-spirited adolescent. Shapiro was able to tease him about his calculated outrageousness without Michael blowing up at him. There was a sense of humor beneath the brooding depression.

Later that afternoon, after Michael had returned from Encino, he asked his mother to sit down with him in the living room again for a talk. He was very concerned about his wisdom teeth. They were coming in painfully, but he insisted that he did not want them pulled. He asked Marguerite to peer into his mouth to see the red swollen spots at the back of his jaws where the molars would soon be breaking through the gums.

Marguerite told him that they might have to come out. Impacted wisdom teeth could be a serious thing, she said.

"I've had them all my life! They're part of me!" Michael suddenly hollered.

He was up, pacing. He told her he would die before he let a dentist yank them. He needed them to chew. His jaw might jut out grotesquely, but he didn't care. He'd never be able to play violin with any skill at all if he had them taken out, he told her.

But while he waited for them to come in, his jaws were aching. He was going to have to suckle a bottle, he said.

He stopped, his face growing darker. The idea of nursing again triggered a frightening thought: He was alone. He had been born alone. He would die alone.

He turned on Marguerite.

He had no family, he lamented. He had no mother. He'd learned that much in therapy.

Nonsense, said Marguerite.

Her role was now over, Michael snarled back. She had relinquished it when she underwrote his therapy. She had no right to criticize.

But Marguerite continued that, while it was true the therapist now supported him in ways she used to, she had been mothering him a significant amount since therapy started.

Michael's mood shifted from fury to self-pity in a flash. His mouth quivered and his eyes brimmed with tears. He had help from several different quarters, he said. Dr. Shapiro. Other therapists and physicians that the Millers had taken him to see. But, most of all, he had Marguerite.

She was still the most important. He loved her so much. Didn't she understand? He loved her but still just couldn't live here. He needed freedom to pursue his art—his music was everything to him . . .

As his voice trailed off, he looked away from Marguerite. He needed companionship, he told her. He needed a woman. He could not live as he wanted to live while he remained under his parents' roof. Marguerite was beautiful, but he just could not continue to live there. Unless he found a woman on his own—a companion to face life with him—he was powerless to live his life the way he saw fit.

Family was important, Marguerite continued, trying to soothe his anguish. In many ways, she said, it was the most important thing of all, surrounding oneself with those who really care about each other.

Michael looked at her and said he knew she was the only one who really cared about him. He wouldn't leave home.

As they talked about Christmas coming up and wrapped a few gifts, Michael suddenly brought up Jeff's memorial service. He wanted to know how many people had attended. Marguerite recalled that there had been over a hundred, but then Michael said sadly that everyone dies alone.

The day before New Year's Eve, Michael returned from a trip to the grocery store with, among other items, a big bunch of broccoli for his mother to cook for him. Marguerite said sure, and added that it would be done shortly. Then Michael asked her to make him a baked potato. Well, that would take much longer to cook, his mother explained. Fine with Michael—he'd eat it when he finished up his broccoli.

Marguerite didn't see the logic in that and she told her son as much. Didn't he understand that he'd be done with the first in fifteen minutes and then be left waiting for his other vegetable? He would be eating very slowly, Michael said, there was so much broccoli there anyway.

When Marguerite answered that she certainly wouldn't have cooked the whole bunch for him, his face grew dark. Suddenly, he grabbed her by the shoulders and gave her a furious shake. She would do as he told her—she'd cook it all.

A flustered Marguerite regained her composure long enough to tell him he could fix the broccoli himself.

Michael refused. At the same time, he seemed to lose interest in the broccoli. Instead, he simply went to the refrigerator and got something else to eat.

Marguerite went on preparing dinner, trying to ignore her son's outburst, until he threw open a window. When Marguerite complained about the cold, he told her to put on a jacket. She ordered him to close the window. He refused. The standoff continued until Michael finally apologized to his mother for his defiance and hugged her. But he left the window wide-open.

He asked her if she wanted to go see *Brighton Beach Memoirs* on New Year's Eve. Marguerite wasn't sure, she said. Lately, she and Michael had been to the movies and theater together frequently, but Michael's tastes in the cinema as well as stage plays were not always hers. He had insisted they see the play *Amadeus* while her sister was visiting and it turned out to be unentertaining. Before she said yes to *Brighton Beach Memoirs*, she wanted to know a little bit more about the plot. She wanted to know if Michael was absolutely sure that she was going to like it.

That set him off again. He was nearly as furious as he had been when she refused to cook the broccoli. He got right up in her face and screamed. Each time she pulled away, he grabbed her shoulders and pulled her back for more.

When Marguerite's sister Gretchen had been in town a month earlier and they all went out to see *Amadeus* together, Michael got the blame because Gretchen didn't like the play. Michael always got the blame for dragging his mother to bad plays or movies and never got credit for taking her to good ones.

He screamed. He waved his hands in the air, pacing, eyes flashing.

Was that what she meant? That *Brighton Beach Memoirs* had to pass muster with Aunt Gretchen before they were allowed to go see it?

The kitchen window was still wide-open and Marguerite could see their next-door neighbor, Dr. Charles Song, barbecuing in his backyard. He had company standing all around. She knew they must be overhearing Michael's harangue.

He might have wanted to go see *Amadeus*, he shrieked, but he *never* recommended it to either Marguerite or her sister. Coming with him to see the play had been their decision, not his. He would not stand there and be guilty over their mistakes.

Marguerite left the kitchen. She tried to retreat to the living room couch, but Michael followed her. He yanked her up to face him. When she tried to look away, he grabbed her chin and angled her face up toward his so that she could not squirm out of his line of vision. He wanted an apology from Marguerite. He wanted an apology for saying he was the one who made them all go. He had already apologized to his aunt for the play's crude parts. Now it was Marguerite's turn to apologize.

Just to bring an end to the ridiculous argument, she apologized for something she regarded as absurd. She told him that she never intended to hold him responsible for making them sit through such a disgusting play.

Once he released his grip, Marguerite went to the phone and called Roy at the office. She told him of Michael's latest temper tantrums. As soon as she hung up, Michael was hovering.

He was furious again. All Marguerite ever wanted was to keep both of her sons under her thumb at all times, he raved. All she ever wanted was to keep them as compliant and helpless as babies. She didn't want them to grow up. That was why Jeff degenerated. She was the reason that he wound up in a mental hospital. Marguerite could not leave Jeff alone. She would not allow him to grow up.

He died a failure because that was the way Marguerite wanted it, Michael said with a shudder.

The holidays were heavy with the memory of happier times when Jeff was alive and the strong family ties that once characterized the Millers. When they were over, a sense of relief came over the Miller household. January and the promise of a new year seemed to brighten Michael's spirits considerably.

He entered the living room one morning after the first of the year, dressed in suit and tie. He bent over his mother, smiling his puppy-dog smile, and apologized sweetly for the mean things he'd said before. Then he gave her a loving hug. She thanked him.

She told him that she blocked most of the awful things he said about her out of her mind. Secretly, though, she sometimes wondered if any of them could possibly be true. But how could any of his accusations—the mean manipulation, the smothering behavior, the carping, the guilt games . . . how could any of it be true?

Michael went out walking the neighborhood for an hour or so in his suit and tie. When he returned, he was tense.

Without a word, he rushed by where she sat in the living room. When she looked up, he was pacing through the house, his shoulders back as if he were marching and his jaw contorting as if his wisdom teeth were hurting him again.

He finally came back in the living room and asked her to look in his mouth to see what he had done. The teeth had come in, he told her, and he had filed them down.

Marguerite tried not to act too surprised. She told him she was sorry that it had come to that and offered to help him if there was anything she could do. She did not run the risk of suggesting a visit to the dentist again to have the teeth pulled.

Instead, she gave him a big hug and smoothed his hair. Michael hugged back and then left the room, not saying a word.

The next day Marguerite was out on the front porch looking at the yard when Michael came out and stood next to her. Her father had been a good man, he said. She loved him very much. Marguerite acknowledged this with a small smile and went back to the house. Michael followed her in and put his arm around her waist, saying, "There is a God," then unclasped her and left the room.

As soon as he was gone, Marguerite ran to the phone. She got Dr. Shapiro on the line and asked for an update. He was acting strangely again. What should she do? What was going on with Michael?

Michael needed to be close to someone and he wasn't getting

close to anyone, he told her. There was genuine poignancy in his inability to break through to someone, anyone, outside of his family/psychiatric circle. He needed to get on with his education, get a job, perhaps expand into some professional or semiprofessional aspect of music. He was a smart kid. He deserved more.

But Dr. Shapiro had some disturbing news too. Michael had taken to blaming Roy again for much of his trouble. He could not seem to communicate with his father very well at all. Michael had asked Dr. Shapiro to meet with Roy and lay out some of his concerns.

Michael was going through some sort of adjustment that Shapiro could not quite put his finger on, he continued. Michael was talking to his violin, for instance, which sounded stranger than it actually was. Such things happened during therapy and were often distorted when taken out of context, he explained.

What Michael wanted very much was Dr. Shapiro's approval, he concluded. That much seemed clear. And, for the moment, Shapiro was prepared to give him just that: his approval.

Michael's attitude toward his psychiatrist had cooled by mid-February. Once, he had been fired up whenever he came home from his sessions. Now Michael spoke of Dr. Shapiro less and offered fewer details to his mother about what had gone on in therapy.

The one thing he did share with her was his interpretation of his discussions with Dr. Shapiro about creativity. Michael told Marguerite that he thought Shapiro believed that creativity and sex were utterly interdependent.

Michael had once been fairly family-oriented, Marguerite observed. But then she noted he skipped family meals at first and then slid deep into a bitter, dark frame of mind.

One Friday morning, he got up early and told her he was leaving home. Then, just as abruptly, he said he wasn't. Then he dashed out the door and started up the station wagon. As he hit the gas and burned rubber getting out of the driveway, he stuck his head out the window of the car and yelled that he was going away to get married.

Before he could back out into the street, Roy was out the front door and jogging to the car to try to stop him. He tried to open the car door, but Michael locked it just as he saw his father make a grab for the door handle. He left Roy standing in the street as he roared down the Hill without looking back.

Two hours later, Dr. Shapiro called the Millers. He'd heard from Michael. He was driving around in Pasadena and checked in just to let the psychiatrist know that he would be driving up to Encino in time to keep his regular 11 A.M. appointment.

A few moments after finishing her conversation with Shapiro, the phone rang again. When she answered it, Michael was on the other end. He was still in Pasadena. He had decided he wasn't going to keep the appointment with Dr. Shapiro, after all.

Michael did keep his next appointment.

When he got home from his psychiatric visit, he sat down with Marguerite and talked seriously and logically to her for the first time in a long time. He talked about Dr. Shapiro's suggestion that he get out of the house more and hit the social circuit—meet some girls. Michael wanted his mother's opinion.

He also wanted her opinion about Jeff. Her real opinion. He'd been thinking about his older brother a lot, wondering what he could have done to save him if he had stayed at home instead of going off to Menlo College. He wondered what might have happened if he had been there to help him past his suicidal anger.

He told his mother he was beginning to understand what psychoanalytic counseling was really all about. It hurt. It was not easy, this headshrinking business that everyone poked fun at on television and in the movies.

"I'm beginning to feel again," he said. "It's painful."

On the first day of March it rained and the fireplace in the front room leaked. The ashes from the fire the Millers had burning the night before were wet and the hearth was a soggy, sooty mess.

Michael didn't go to his Tuesday morning appointment with Dr. Shapiro. Instead, he talked with him on the phone. They were only on the phone together for an hour, but Michael wound up agreeing to pay for an eighty-minute session.

He spent the rest of the day brooding again about Jeff. He seemed to move in slow motion through the house. When Marguerite went out to weed in the garden, he joined her for about forty minutes.

In the evening, Michael took it upon himself to call another psychotherapist he had visited before he started going to Dr. Shapiro. He wanted to talk with him, he said. Before going to bed, he turned to his mother and asked her if she thought the other doctor was a bigot. Marguerite said no, she didn't think any of them were bigots.

On Wednesday, March 23, Marguerite counted mah-jongg tiles. She was getting together with her sister and some friends soon to play a few games and it would never do if the set was incomplete.

At about 10:15 A.M., Dr. Shapiro called. Marguerite welcomed the call. Michael was making her nervous, she told him.

He was quiet. Sometimes he just stood and stared at the wall. His movements were slow, like a ballet dancer racked with indecision about which step to take next. When he did speak, it was usually to announce something he planned to do—go to the backyard, walk the dog, anything. Then he would simply do nothing.

Despite his sluggishness, he remained snappish and impatient. When he accompanied Marguerite to the store, he jumped every time she turned the steering wheel or put on the brakes. Shapiro listened patiently and counseled the same thing: patience.

Michael was receptive enough to promise his mother that he would take the mah-jongg set to Marguerite's sister's house in Santa Monica the next day.

Roy couldn't do it. He had a board meeting in the evening at Arcadia Hospital. And Marguerite had an American Nutrition Society lecture. She was in charge and had to get there early enough to put out collection boxes for donations. She wasn't going to have time to deliver the mah-jongg set herself. And Michael would be out near Santa Monica for his regular appointment with Dr. Shapiro anyway. So he was the logical choice.

He had to promise he would get the tiles there. He did understand that his mother was depending on him, didn't he?

Michael nodded. He understood.

The mah-jongg tiles did get delivered.

But Marguerite Miller did not leave home for the lecture by 5:30 as she had planned. In fact, she didn't leave at all. March 23, 1983, was her final entry in the journal she kept concerning her son's mental and emotional roller-coaster ride through hypnotherapy, biofeedback, hypoglycemia, macrobiotics and psychotherapy.

By the time homicide detectives were rereading the diary five days later, Marguerite Miller's body was at a Claremont funeral home, being prepared for burial on the Saturday between Good Friday and Easter Sunday. And her only living son was on his way by Los Angeles County Sheriff's bus to the Torrance courthouse to answer charges that he raped and murdered his own mother.

___ 15

At 9:30 A.M. Monday in South Bay Municipal Court, a clean-shaven, tousle-haired Michael Miller rose at Judge Benjamin Aranda's command and stood beside his attorneys. Clad in a rust-colored turtleneck, gray sweatpants, white tennis shoes and handcuffs, the gaunt young figure with the haunted, deep-set eyes let his lawyers do the talking. He spoke just one word during the truncated proceeding. When asked if he agreed with his attorney Thomas Nolan's request for a two-week continuance on his arraignment, Michael uttered a barely perceptible "Yes."

He gave no plea of innocence or guilt to the charges of rape and murder.

In his only other action on the Miller case, Aranda imposed a gag order. Nolan and his partner, Stephen Miller, argued successfully that authorities had already talked too much to the media about the case. South Bay Assistant D.A. Richard de la Sota conceded that it had been a high-profile case. Aranda decided that it was time to muzzle detectives, coroners, lawyers and court employees before Miller's chances for a fair trial were put in genuine jeopardy.

The forty-three-year-old Aranda sympathized with Roy Miller, even though they were social, cultural and political opposites. Miller, a conservative Stanford-educated Republican, was the son of well-heeled college graduates in the stable, upper-middle-class community of Claremont. Aranda, a liberal Democrat who worked his way through Loyola Law School, was the son of divorced immigrants who lived in a blue-collar town in Imperial Valley.

Aranda and Miller had family values in common. Aranda felt profound sympathy for the tall, stooped man who had just lost his family and stood alone at the back of his courtroom. Aranda had vowed never to let his own family self-destruct the way his parents' had. Family became everything to him. After he and his wife had had seven children of their own, they adopted four more. Four years hence, in 1987, Aranda's fierce devotion to family values would gain such notoriety that Ronald and Nancy Reagan would invite him and his entire family to the White House as part of a celebration of the Great American Family.

For the moment, the only contribution he could make to the sanctity of the American family was the granting of some measure of privacy to the man who had lost one son and his wife and now stood to lose his one remaining child to justice. Fueled by Aranda's gag order, Miller's two attorneys launched a campaign to turn public attention away from the questions arising from their client's crimes by accusing the news media of exploiting the Millers' tragedy.

Later that same day and in the days to come, Michael Miller met in the Los Angeles County jail with his attorneys, his therapist and his father. During visiting hours, he talked with friends and relatives over a telephone receiver, separated from them by a sheet of bulletproof glass.

As his therapist, Sumner Shapiro got permission to meet with him one-on-one. To prevent sheriff's deputies eavesdropping on their conversations during these not-so-private sessions, Dr. Shapiro took to conversing with Michael in French. The young man's fluency did not alter Shapiro's opinion about the precarious position of Michael's mental state. Michael carried "a lot of strange baggage," Shapiro reported years later. Following conversations with his former patient, Shapiro gave Nolan and Miller the ammunition they needed to return to court with an insanity defense of their client's murderous actions.

In papers filed with the court two days after the aborted arraignment, Shapiro was quoted as being "of the opinion that Miller has been and is presently suffering from severe mental disorders evidenced by manifestation of acute psychotic behavior and suicidal tendencies . . . and is in need of immediate and intensive psychiatric treatment and observation."

After a jury found John W. Hinckley, Jr., not guilty of trying to assassinate the President and sent him to St. Elizabeth's Mental Hospital instead of to prison, Attorney General William French Smith asked Congress to essentially eliminate the insanity defense. In support of the bill that would make it all but impossible for a defendant to pay less than the full penalty for his crimes, Smith testified:

"Mental disease or defect would constitute a defense only if the defendant did not even know he had a gun in his hand or thought, for example, that he was shooting at a tree."

Reagan himself thought that the law ought to be changed to read "guilty but insane" instead of "not guilty by reason of insanity."

TV and newspapers continued raising questions about Michael Miller's sanity, but aided by the gag order, Nolan and Miller fought back. There were signs of progress on the media front. In the Thursday edition of the Millers' hometown newspaper, the *Palos Verdes Peninsula News*, publisher Hugh Ralston ordered an editorial printed with the title "Useful Silence" that reflected, to a large degree, the containment policy of Miller and Nolan, F. Daniel Frost and Gibson, Dunn and Crutcher, as well as the insular attitude of the Palos Verdes citizenry. Applauding both the police news blackout and Judge Aranda's gag order, Ralston's editorial went on to urge a further cloak over the events that led to the murder and rape of Marguerite Miller:

> We hope our newsgathering and reporting brethren elsewhere will not now be tempted into either trying or

judging these awful events in the public press or on TV
at these present and early stages of the unfolding of a
shattering series of sad events.

We think there have already been too many irresponsible and thoughtless quotes tossed around in the last 72
hours by no doubt well-intentioned people who would
have been far better advised to have kept silent.

Most importantly, none of all this helps that poor,
devastated widower in his terrible, tragic time, so why
don't we all just keep out of the public prints?

The same day that Dr. Shapiro filed his declaration that Michael
was suffering from acute psychotic behavior and suicidal tendencies, Ronald Reagan came to Southern California for a five-day
visit. While some speculated that he might have come to console
his lawyer and friend, Roy Miller, Reagan's schedule appeared to
be business as usual. He phoned Los Angeles television station KHJ
on Wednesday during a five-hour "jobathon": a kind of classified-
ad-of-the-air gimmick designed to fight the city's record 11.5 percent unemployment rate.

"I want to call and congratulate all of you there . . . for the
effort that you're making to find jobs for people," Reagan told the
KHJ jobathon host, Nathan Roberts. "It's a very inspiring thing to
see, that with all of the hardships of this recession, the people of
this country who can are doing as much as they're doing to help
their neighbors in the tradition that has been so typically American."

As Reagan spoke, Roberts beamed at the camera and thanked
the President, but neither said a word about the Miller murder
case. In fact, Reagan remained mum about it the entire week.
Newspaper and broadcast reporters who were pursuing the story
kept getting turned away in Washington and at the President's
California ranch. There was presidential sympathy, conveyed
through the White House Press Office, but that was all. The President had an agenda to attend to and personal matters could not be
allowed to interfere.

Reaganomics was being put to the recessionary test in the spring of 1983. In addition to his "God bless you all" message to Southern California job seekers, Reagan was in the midst of a fight with Congress over a perennially unbalanced budget, including Medicare and Medicaid spending. He wanted $5.1 billion slashed from the $70 billion earmarked in the 1983 federal budget for the elderly, disabled and mentally ill.

And Reagan had further plans for cutting the budget, getting big government off the backs of hardworking taxpayers and putting indolent ne'er-do-wells out on the street where they belonged. While governor of California, from 1966 through 1974, Reagan began an effective budget-cutting process that came to be known as "deinstitutionalization." His initial order called for the closing of fourteen outpatient psychiatric clinics, the deactivation of eighty wards in ten state hospitals and the elimination of 3,700 employees. He refused to visit the hospitals to see how his cuts were affecting the communities, but he ultimately backed down on his larger plan to eliminate the state hospitals when parents of patients began accusing him of dumping patients on communities that were completely unprepared for them. The worst cases remained hospitalized, but thousands of schizophrenics and other mental patients did leave the hospitals.

Reagan's supporters hailed the action as a double victory: not only were state costs of supporting the mentally ill reduced to a fraction of their pre-1966 level, but people who had been kept drugged behind closed doors were now allowed to "mainstream" with society. Other states began following the California example and the result was the most dramatic drop in tax-supported institutional mental health care in the twentieth century.

In 1970 the nation's mental health hospitals held 400,000 patients. In 1980, when Ronald Reagan became the country's fortieth President, the few remaining state hospitals had only 147,000 patients. As President, Reagan was now poised to transform his cost-cutting California deinstitutionalization into a nationwide policy.

The President's critics pointed out that, during that same decade, the nation's prison population nearly doubled, from 168,000 inmates in 1970 to 300,000 in 1980. Spokesmen for the mental health profession, such as Stanford psychology professor and serial murder expert Dr. Donald Lunde, blamed deinstitutionalization for the distended prison system. Mainstreaming worked for some outpatients, but for thousands who managed to function in a structured environment but suffered psychotic episodes without supervision, deinstitutionalization spelled disaster.

"I know President Reagan is a nice, pleasant man, but he has no empathy for certain segments of society," Lunde told one interviewer. "He believes that anyone who works can make it in this wonderful U.S.A.; that people who hang around mental hospitals waiting for handouts should be kicked out for their own good."

There was little doubt that insanity had been misused at times to win clemency and even acquittal for criminals. But such cases were few and far between, Lunde argued.

"Because of the country's conservative mood, and the attention focused on those cases," Lunde concluded, "insanity is now viewed as a loophole used by criminals to get out from under crimes, especially murder."

Now, in the space of one mind-numbing week, that national debate over criminal behavior and mental health policy had become a personal problem to the President's personal lawyer. While his most famous client campaigned through Southern California pushing his conservative agenda, Roy Miller was wrestling with the question of Michael's fate. After the scrutiny of the press died down and the glare of publicity had been dulled, what would the legal system that had been so much a part of Roy Miller's life and livelihood dictate as the future of his only living son? Would Michael face the death penalty, as the media had been suggesting? And, if not, would he then become one of the nation's 300,000 inmates . . .

Or one of its 147,000 mental patients?

To *Los Angeles Herald Examiner* reporter Steve Dougherty, the most curious thing about the Saturday afternoon funeral service in

Pasadena and the graveside farewell twenty miles east in Claremont later that same day was that nobody mentioned a word about the murder. There was a hush in the pews of the First United Methodist Church during the service as well as afterward, when the crowd spilled out of the church and onto the sidewalk of busy Colorado Boulevard. Talk of how she died was dismissed even after the long freeway funeral procession ended at the pastoral green serenity of Oak Park Cemetery. Of the estimated seven hundred mourners who came, Dougherty could find no one willing to ponder the circumstances of Marguerite Miller's death.

"The reality of the slaying was so, you know, almost unreal," Dougherty recalled years later. "You couldn't get your mind around what had happened to the Millers. These people obviously had a large circle of friends and, on the surface, had everything going for them. It was very hard to balance the two images."

He was not so interested in interviewing all of the mourners as he was one in particular, however. Like the dozen other reporters and news photographers on hand for the service, Dougherty expected to see Ronald Reagan and, perhaps, Nancy Reagan, stopping in to pay their respects. He waited in vain, though.

It was true that church officials had been notified that the President planned to put in an appearance, and a handful of White House security types even showed up before and during the service to ensure the President's safety, but the Reagans changed their plans and never did show. They sent their condolences instead.

During the service, Roy sat tall in the first row of pews, flanked by Marguerite's sisters and their families and friends. The massive church, with its deceptively simple brick and quarried fieldstone exterior, overflowed with the sympathetic and the curious. Roy stared straight ahead, unblinking, through the reading of a series of psalms. When Pastor Lance Martin announced the two hymns that preceded the eulogy—"O, for a Thousand Tongues to Sing" and "There Is a Balm in Gilead"—Roy mechanically stood to sing along with everyone else.

"There is a balm . . . to make the wounded whole . . . to heal the sickened soul . . ."

As the sound of a hundred or more voices faded inside the church, Pastor Martin stepped to the pulpit where he would deliver an Easter Sunday sermon the following day. He directed the attention of those gathered this afternoon, however, not to himself or the altar, but to the choir loft on the northwest side of the church. There, light filtered like a kaleidoscope through a stained-glass window onto an empty bench where Marguerite had sat along with the rest of the church choir as recently as two Sundays earlier. Marguerite had a high, sweet voice as willowy in tone as her slender body. She sang as though she meant it, and her church—along with her family—meant everything, according to Martin.

"Six weeks ago," the young clergyman began, "Roy and Marguerite and Michael were making a family banner."

It was a project they worked on together during a weekend retreat to a church camp in the San Gabriel Mountains. The felt banner, Martin explained, bore a red, white and rose replica of the stained-glass window that he pointed to in the choir loft above his head. Marguerite picked the window out as the central symbol of the Miller family because the church was "the heart of the Miller family," Martin told the mourners.

"What Marguerite placed at the center of the family banner now casts its colors over our grief, and light from the rose window is our remembrance of Marguerite," he said somberly.

Martin sketched Marguerite's life, from her birth through a happy childhood built around the trinity of home, church and school. The Bruner family moved to Claremont on the eve of World War II, when Marguerite was eight years old. She and her three sisters grew up at 469 West Eleventh Street. Roy Miller, who was ten, lived next door.

"Years later Marguerite and I stood on the sidewalk in front of her old home," said Martin. "And she told me Cupid's tale of falling in love with the boy next door."

Marguerite loved nature too: flowers and trees and birds. In her eyes, to commune with nature was to commune with the Almighty.

"Marguerite shared with her sons her love of music, her love of nature and her love of God," the minister said in conclusion.

As Martin sat, the Reverend George Mann, who would eventually replace Martin as pastor, stood at the pulpit. He read from some of Marguerite's own writings. She had written her essay shortly after leaving the funeral of one of her friends, according to Mann.

Marguerite saw a flock of blackbirds gathered on the grass at the cemetery. As she came near, several of them flew away. It was only then that she noticed that several of the birds weren't black, after all. She was able to make out colors in their wings. What she first believed to be blackbirds turned out to be birds of a different color on closer inspection.

"Life is certainly like that," said Mann. "Full of the unexpected. It has its bad times, its ups and downs. It has times of great exhilaration. Sometimes it takes turns that are not expected at all."

He waxed philosophical, his voice tinged with pathos.

"Marguerite was an altogether alive person," he said. "A spring of vitality."

But, mirroring the secular plea *Palos Verdes Peninsula News* publisher Hugh Ralston had made in his editorial three days earlier, Mann told those gathered that it was not up to them to even attempt to explain Marguerite Miller's death. Some things, he said, are better left unexplained.

"How do we explain what has happened? The answer is we do not. Some things in life God alone has to account for."

Steve Dougherty wasn't the only one who expected Ronald Reagan to show up at the funeral. Joe Gonzales, who billed himself as a cemetery maintenance man at Oak Park Cemetery in Claremont, also believed that the First Couple would be among the mourners. He brought his camera along just in case Reagan flip-flopped and made a last-minute appearance. There was a clearing for an Air Force helicopter off to the northeast behind a massive oak tree where the earthly remains of Jeffrey Miller had been laid to rest two years earlier.

Gonzales knew where the Miller family plot was, because, in addition to maintaining the graves, he helped dig them. Before the hearse arrived from Pasadena, he had already stationed himself in the best spot to take advantage of a clear snapshot of both the graveside and the open field where the helicopter would touch down. He imagined a moment, just before Marguerite's casket was lowered down beside that of her elder son's, when the President himself would step out of the helicopter and into the midst of the mourners.

But it didn't happen.

A crowd less than half the size of that which had been on hand for the memorial service in Pasadena watched Marguerite Miller's interment in relative silence. Gonzales snapped some photos indiscriminately, assuming celebrities of one sort or another were there.

When it was all over and the funeral procession that had driven all the way from Pasadena began breaking up, a tall, stiff man with creased cheeks and dark suit approached Joe Gonzales. It was Roy Miller, who had seen Joe shooting pictures and wanted to know if he could have prints made. It would mean a great deal, Roy explained, because his son had been unable to come to the funeral and Roy wanted to share the event with him.

"I thought it was funny that he wanted to share it with his kid. He made it sound like a celebration, like a birthday or a holiday or something, the way he put it," said Gonzales.

Gonzales shrugged and agreed to send the photos to Miller. Miller scribbled out his address and handed the card over to Gonzales, who mailed off the prints the following week. He didn't hear back. He assumed that the photographs, depicting dozens of bowed heads and solemn back pats, arrived safely.

Despite his continuous work at the Oak Park Cemetery, Gonzales never saw Miller again. On holidays and anniversaries, when relatives came to lay bouquets and wreaths on the graves of those they had lost, the two headstones in the Miller family plot at the northeast corner of Oak Park Cemetery remained alone and unadorned, year in and year out. Gonzales kept the grass trimmed around the edges of the polished marble markers so visitors could read the names of the mother and son who lay there, side by side, beneath the broad branches of the old oak tree.

But visitors never came.

*   *   *

Ronald Reagan spent the Saturday of Marguerite Miller's funeral at his ranch. While his sympathies might have been with Roy and the other mourners, his duty was to his audience.

His weekly radio address—a political tradition since his first bid for the presidency in 1976—was devoted to the subject of Easter, Passover and eternal human hope.

"My fellow Americans," the President began as he always did. "This week as American families draw together in worship, we join with millions upon millions of others around the world also celebrating the traditions of their faith. During these days, at least, regardless of nationality, region or race, we are united by faith in God and the barriers between us seem less significant."

He quoted from St. Paul's letter to the Ephesians. It wasn't one of the passages about family members loving one another, or about marriage and the love of a husband for a wife, or the respect that a wife must have for her husband. It was the couplet about Jesus Christ preaching peace and putting an end to the alienation that everyone—mothers, daughters, fathers and sons—feels toward each other sometimes.

"Tomorrow, as morning spreads around the planet, we'll celebrate the triumph of life over death, the resurrection of Jesus," said the President. "Both observances tell of sacrifice and pain but also of hope and triumph. . . ."

He spoke of international peace efforts made by Americans from all walks of life and went on to say, "The generation of Americans now growing up in schools across our country can make sure the United States will remain a force for good, the champion of peace and freedom, as their parents and grandparents before them have done. And if we live our lives and dedicate our country to truth, to love and to God, we will be a part of something much stronger and much more enduring than any negative power here on earth.

"That's why this weekend is a celebration and why there is hope for us all.

"Thanks for listening, and God bless you."

16

The Sunday one week after Marguerite's burial, Roy was in church for 8 A.M. services. Like his late wife, he was a member of the choir, but this Sunday he didn't sing. From the pulpit, the Reverend Mann saw Miller sitting tall and dignified in the middle of the congregation, among his embarrassed, sympathetic and curious friends and acquaintances. It seemed far too soon for the stoic widower to emerge from his grief, but Mann felt compelled to say a word of encouragement.

"Where else would you expect to see Roy Miller on a Sunday?" Mann asked, provoking a ripple of approval among the uncomfortable parishioners.

Likewise, his neighbors up and down Via Visalia might have expected to see a For Sale sign go up in front of the Miller house. But no such sign ever appeared. Roy Miller did what he had always done best. He persevered. To most outside observers, the life of Palos Verdes' own tragic figure remained pretty much unchanged. Roy Miller got up each day at dawn and drove down the Hill to his office in downtown L.A. Each evening, barring one of his many board or business meetings, he drove home early enough to catch the nightly news. Otherwise, he rarely ventured outdoors, but that was normal. Marguerite was the one who was always puttering in the shrubbery, and now the gardener she had hired kept up the yard by himself.

At the office, Miller instructed his staff and associates to carry on without making a fuss. He thanked them for their concern and good wishes, but they all had their jobs to do and his own misfortune should not be a consideration when it came to conducting Gibson, Dunn and Crutcher business.

The time of year—tax time—demanded that the firm redouble its efforts. Before April 15, the 1982 tax return of Miller's two most important clients was due at the White House. And though subordinates handled most of the nuts and bolts, Roy Miller's signature would be affixed at the bottom of the most scrutinized Form 1040 in the world. There was little question that Roy—or someone in the firm's tax division—had his work cut out for him.

The Reagans' tax returns had been the subject of intense scrutiny. Mrs. Reagan had been roundly criticized for wearing designer clothes and then either donating them to museums for a tax write-off or failing to declare the free use of her lavish wardrobe as taxable income. Now Roy Miller's judgment was being questioned in the newspapers. There seemed little doubt that everything from his arithmetic to his interpretation of the Internal Revenue Code would be questioned.

Roy had also been in and out of court on other matters involving the Reagans in late 1982 and the early months of 1983. Problems had cropped up surrounding the sale of the Reagans' Pacific Palisades home. In December Miller took the stand against Mrs. Ann Yarbrough, a seventy-four-year-old great-grandmother who tried buying the Reagans' home for $1.4 million on the strength of a false financial statement.

In another case, just one month earlier, Miller had helped convict two other con artists who attempted to buy the Reagan home. That pair pleaded guilty to falsifying escrow papers for the President's home and using Miller's signature on false documents. The two men wound up getting one- and two-year prison terms.

Roy Miller, a man who fancied himself a stickler for abiding by the letter of the law, would soon see to it that the old woman who tried unsuccessfully to con Ronald and Nancy Reagan out of their home would be similarly punished. When she admitted in court that she conspired with her husband to swindle more than $300,000 from two banks and the President and his wife, Mrs. Yarbrough was ordered to undergo a ninety-day psychiatric evaluation.

"I was going to live in Reagan's home," Mrs. Yarbrough said at one point. "It was owned by Reagan and it has historical value."

She was found to be sane and returned to court. Partly on the strength of Roy Miller's testimony against her, she was sentenced to three years in prison for grand theft.

But well before Mrs. Yarbrough went to prison, Roy Miller had other unanticipated legal business to attend to that did not involve the First Family. He had to preserve what remained of his own family. Stephen Miller and Tom Nolan, the two criminal litigators he hired to defend his son, were developing a strategy to keep Michael from going to the gas chamber.

It seemed fairly simple: Michael Miller was insane.

Richard Kushi, jail program director for the L. A. County Department of Mental Health, examined Michael two days before Marguerite's funeral. The young man was depressed, but not so much about his mother. He told Kushi the reason he was down in the dumps was his brother's death.

When Kushi went to his cell a little over a week later, on April 8, Michael had recovered from his depression enough to demand an audience with his attorney before he did or said anything that he might later regret. When Kushi asked him to sign papers for an evaluation to see whether or not he constituted a danger either to himself or to others under state law, Michael refused.

Michael did not refuse to see the mental health experts that his lawyers had sent to see him, though. Beverly Hills psychiatrist Dr. Saul Faerstein and Pasadena clinical psychologist and USC professor Dr. Michael Maloney both spent hours with the young man, evaluating his mental and emotional capacities. Author/psychiatrist Dr. Ronald Markman also did an evaluation on behalf of the defense, though he spent far less time with Michael.

At Michael's April 11 arraignment, his attorneys again asked for a postponement. This time, they said they needed more time because Michael was not competent to stand trial. In support of their argument, they offered the written opinions of Maloney and Faerstein. Faerstein characterized Michael as "one of the most severely mentally ill" people he had ever seen. Maloney was equally dubious of Michael's ability to stand trial.

"He answered questions with difficulty," Maloney wrote in his report to the defense attorneys. "He often appeared confused and stared straight ahead. His behavior seemed relatively out of control at times. He queried the examiner about whether therapists might be able to enter the courtroom with guns and shoot him."

The prosecutor in the case remained skeptical and said as much to Judge Aranda.

"What we are talking about here is whether he understands the nature of the charges against him and the nature of the proceedings—not whether [he] was legally sane at the time of the crime," said Deputy District Attorney Richard de la Sota. "Those are two completely different issues."

Judge Aranda was not ready to concede Michael's insanity. He ordered a neutral psychiatrist to conduct further tests and set April 29 for a mental competency hearing before Torrance Superior Court Judge Thomas Fredricks. Aranda picked another Beverly Hills psychiatrist, Dr. Blake Skrdla, as the court's neutral expert.

On April 21, eight days before the competency hearing, Skrdla spent three hours in Module 7000 of the Los Angeles County Men's Jail, talking with and observing Michael Miller.

Skrdla found him preoccupied with discussion of his old hypnotherapy and past motivational tapes he'd listened to. While he was coherent, Michael showed little or no ability to make judgments and showed no insight into his mental condition. He dwelled, instead, on his brother's suicide.

"He was my best friend," Michael told Skrdla.

At first, Skrdla found a friendly, cooperative and polite young man with above average intellect, but soon Michael's mind and manner wandered. By the end of the three-hour interview, the cracks in Michael's socially appropriate façade had deepened. Michael's normally bland surface now was either frozen, staring into space, or grimacing and rolling its eyes. Skrdla sensed a deep depression.

"He would not be able to answer the questions," said Skrdla. "And it would take sometimes several minutes to get back to the trend of what we had been talking about."

Michael insisted he did not hallucinate, nor was he crazy. Mental problems were the result of improper diet, he said. He told Skrdla he had to have three cloves of garlic and half an onion to detoxify himself after every meal.

In his notes, Skrdla scribbled: "He could offer no plan for his future, except to state: 'I think I need my father. We need each other—looking ahead, not looking back.' "

He denied ever having hallucinations and insisted that he did not have a mental disorder, but admitted having "bad thoughts" at times, even though he could not describe what they were. He complained of being "lonely" but denied having ever been suicidal.

He refused the neuroleptic drugs that his doctors prescribed, calling them "chemicals" unfit for humans.

Michael knew about the pending murder and rape charges and understood his legal status, but whenever Skrdla tried to focus him upon events leading to the murder, he became painfully slow, detached, bewildered, and preoccupied with his diet and health. Skrdla later estimated that Michael took three times longer to interview than an average patient.

Michael Miller should not stand trial, Skrdla concluded. Michael Miller was schizophrenic and belonged in a hospital.

"Mr. Miller is believed to be presently mentally incompetent to proceed with trial within the meaning of Section 1368 of the Penal Code," he wrote in the three-page opinion he gave to Judge Fredricks. ". . . Because of an active major mental disorder, it is not believed that he is able to rationally and consistently cooperate with an attorney in the discussion, planning and presentation of a defense.

"Treatment in a closed psychiatric hospital is suggested until he has shown sufficient improvement to be capable of standing trial."

Michael had let his beard grow during his month-long stay in the L.A. County jail. He entered Judge Fredricks' courtroom on April 29 carrying a yellow legal pad and a red Bible, his hair standing high and wild, a small tuft of whiskers on his chin. Throughout most of the proceedings, his eyelids were either closed or rode at half-mast over waxen pupils. In almost a parody of the male model he once aspired to become, he wore the same seasonally stylish pair of dark slacks and light cable-knit sweater over his 145-pound, six-foot-three-inch frame that he had worn two weeks earlier.

As in all of his previous hearings, Michael's father was absent.

Despite his attorneys' best efforts, the hearing was open to the public. Tape recorders whirred and camera shutters clicked as two hours of testimony began.

"Dr. Faerstein, have you had occasion to examine Michael David Miller?" attorney Stephen Miller asked, once the first psychiatrist was sworn in.

"Yes, I have," answered Faerstein.

"When have you examined him?" asked Miller.

Faerstein saw him twice, he said: on March 31 for four and a half hours and again on April 8 for two hours. His assessment came out on the stand like legal catechism:

"Are you familiar with the California statutes which govern competency to stand trial?" asked Miller.

"Yes, I am," said Faerstein.

"What are those standards?"

"The standards as defined in Sections 1368, et seq., state that 'an individual is competent to stand trial if he's presently able to understand the nature and the purpose of the legal proceedings taken against him and if he's presently able to cooperate in a rational manner with counsel in presenting a defense,' " recited Faerstein.

"Having examined Michael David Miller, do you, Dr. Faerstein, have an opinion with respect to Mr. Miller's present competency?"

"Yes, I do."

"What is that opinion?" Miller asked.

"It is my opinion that he is presently not competent to stand trial," said Faerstein.

Faerstein said he had rarely made eye contact with Michael and had a tough time establishing rapport. Among other things, Faerstein found Michael "bland, detached, disassociated at times, unpredictable. . . ." At times, he said, Michael was so detached that Faerstein wasn't sure Michael even knew he was there.

"I found that during the examination with me he evidenced thought blocking, which is a freezing of speech and thought so that there's no communication for a period of time," he said. When he did talk, he'd zip from one topic to another, going off on tangents with no focus at all.

"It's a tendency to skirt the issue," Faerstein explained. "To 'beat around the bush,' so to speak. That is a characteristic of a thought disorder, as well as a symptom of other disorders, but specifically of schizophrenia."

He could go quickly from spacy to restless, his face switching from a bland mask to a twisted grimace without warning. Michael was delusional and given to irrational statements and desires, said the psychiatrist.

"As an example, he talked about being reunited with his family. And we know that two of the members of his family that he wished to be reunited [with] were deceased."

It was all but impossible to get Michael to focus on the murder and rape charges, because all he wanted to talk about was food and nutrition. Other prisoners might grumble that jail food tasted terrible, but Michael really meant it when he said the cooks were trying to kill him.

"He actually believed that they were poisoning his body. That he had to purge his body of these poisons," said Faerstein. During one of his more lucid moments, Michael asked Faerstein to bring him some garlic so he could detoxify his body.

When de la Sota had his turn at cross-examining Faerstein, the first thing he wanted was a definition of schizophrenia.

"Schizophrenia is a major mental disorder in the category of psychosis, in which there is a severe disturbance in thought process, affect and behavior," said Faerstein.

There was no way of telling when it began, but Michael had been suffering from it for a long time, Faerstein said.

"I believe it's a chronic disorder in his case," he continued. "From what I know about him now, I can state with medical certainty that the onset of this illness was at least several years ago."

"You mentioned his statement that he wanted to be reunited with his family," said de la Sota. "Did he use the word 'family'?"

"He used the word 'family,' and he specifically talked about his mother and his brother," said Faerstein.

"Now, his mother and brother are both dead, obviously," said de la Sota.

"Yes."

"Did that indicate to you that he didn't comprehend that they were dead, or that he wanted to commit suicide?"

"Both were suggested by that," Faerstein answered. "I did feel at that time that there was a real possibility of him wanting to kill himself, based on the history of the family, based on his present condition, based on that wish which he expressed."

Michael should have been on suicide watch while in custody at the county jail, according to Faerstein.

"But when he talks about going back out into the garden, going home and working in the garden with his mother," he said, "that's less of a wish to be reunited in heaven than just a belief she's at home and nothing happened to her."

Michael Maloney saw Michael twice on April 6, once on April 7 and once again April 27, just prior to his competency hearing.

When Stephen Miller asked the psychologist how long he thought Michael had been suffering from schizophrenia, Maloney answered:

"It probably existed in an insidious way or in a less remarkable way as long as two or three years ago. I state this because of some material I reviewed today, actually."

The first time that he saw Michael, he had no information about him at all, other than what he had read in the papers or seen on television. Then, just before swearing in as a defense witness, he had an opportunity to browse through Michael's own journal.

"Today I was reading a diary, which I believe is dated about a year ago," Maloney said. "And in that diary he is talking about the fact that he was treated unfairly by his parents because they taught him to believe in Santa Claus and the Easter Bunny and so forth. And he had very long descriptive writings about how unfair this was, how unjust it was, how he had been mistreated.

"I think that his condition or the condition that we see today really dates back through that period of time. But he certainly wasn't disorganized the way he is now. Even his writing, his syntax, his logic, was much better then than it is now."

When he examined Michael in jail, Maloney gave him the verbal portion of the Wechsler Adult Intelligence Test. He did well—better than average actually. But Michael couldn't concentrate long enough to take the portion of the test that measured his motor skills.

The Minnesota Multi-Phasic Personality Inventory—a 550-item questionnaire that measures mood, mind-set and attitude—was even more revealing.

"There are two, I think, very interesting conclusions," said Maloney. "One is that the MMPI is a very structured test. It has items like: 'I like mechanics magazines: true or false.' And you put a mark in a little place. And he functions very well in that kind of thing, as long as he doesn't have to decide too much."

The other conclusion was the same one Faerstein and Skrdla arrived at without conducting any formal testing.

"The results indicated a single clinical evaluation on scale 8, which is schizophrenia," said Maloney. "And it's not an exaggerated profile. There are no data to suggest that the individual doing this is trying to look bad, but it's a clear elevation on the one single scale."

Maloney kept careful notes during his jail interviews with Michael, jotting down verbatim as best he could everything Michael said. When he asked Michael if he knew what function his attorneys performed, Michael answered:

"I didn't do it. In my heart, I didn't want to hurt my mom. This diet is killing me. If you don't do it in your heart, you don't do it."

"After that I questioned him as to what was going to happen in this case," Maloney testified.

Michael started to answer, "They probably—" before lapsing into one of his speechless pauses. Then he said, "They could let me out."

Before Maloney said anything else to Michael, the psychologist explained to him that faking incompetency was not going to gain him anything.

"One of the things we always have to consider in these cases: Is this person being straightforward? Are they faking it? And I wanted to remove any motivation that this may be a way out of this case," said Maloney.

Despite Maloney's careful explanation that incompetency meant a prolonged stay at state hospitals like Patton or Atascadero until Michael was sane enough to stand trial, Michael's chief concern was whether Patton and Atascadero had garlic. Maloney said that Michael just didn't appreciate where he was and the consequences of his actions.

"For a while, he was very much into going down the fire escape of the jail instead of going through with this whole process," said Maloney. Michael seemed to appreciate the fact that his brother was dead, but his mother was a different story, according to Maloney.

"On one occasion he clearly seemed to indicate that [she was dead], because he said, 'I took my father's wife away,' " said Maloney. "At another point, he did indicate to me something similar to what Dr. Faerstein had talked about. And that was that he wanted to go home and this time he would do well, in terms of working in the garden and so forth."

Like Faerstein, Maloney found Michael unable to discuss any topic for any length of time, unless he was spoon-fed very specific structured questions, one at a time.

"For example, I still don't have an appreciation after talking with him for some six hours what happened when his mother died," said Maloney. "And I don't think that it's an issue of his just not wanting to talk about it. When I start pushing into that area, his behavior does seem to deteriorate."

In the sworn declaration that he wrote for Miller and Nolan prior to taking the witness stand, Maloney said he first met Michael in the jail dietician's office. There were long pauses when he stared and then he would become agitated, speaking very quickly and wandering around the room.

"And he opened various doors, turned instrument switches on, put a Kleenex over his hand and started to pull cupboards open," wrote Maloney. "His behavior seemed relatively out of control at times. I was able to get him to respond to various structured test items, but when the structure of my questions or the situation diminished, mental control appeared to deteriorate."

Dr. Ronald Markman's diagnosis was short, concise and the same as that of his colleagues. Michael was schizophrenic.

"It is synonymous with what most laypeople would use the term 'crazy' for," he testified.

Where Markman's testimony differed from the others was in his acknowledging that Michael was right there, in the courtroom, and not some abstract being that the lawyers, psychologists and journalists were all addressing in the third person.

"You could watch him right now," he invited. "His eyes are closed. Now, that could mean that he's concentrating on what's going on, except that he has avoided looking at anything that's going on during the proceedings. And one of the major inputs that an individual has is visual: to be able to look around and see what's happening in conjunction with the other senses that are functioning. He has tended not to do that and remained relatively stiff throughout the proceedings."

Michael sat with his head turned slightly to one side, as if in a trance. If he was aware that Markman was talking about him, he acknowledged nothing. In fact, throughout the testimony of Faerstein and Maloney, Michael had only emerged from his trance a couple of times to whisper something to his attorney.

"I asked the attorney about what the discussions were on and they happen to be about food and what would be made available for him to eat," said Markman.

Markman's own interview with Michael had gone much the same way. He seemed composed, but after the first twenty minutes, he just disintegrated.

"He began walking around like a caged animal," said Markman. "He started brushing his teeth. He started worrying about allergies that he had towards dairy products. And many of the responses that he gave me to pertinent questions had to do with diet."

Another of Michael's eerie schizophrenic symptoms was that what he did say at any given moment was not necessarily consistent with the way he said it.

"So that he could be talking about something serious and be rather lighthearted or superficial, and at another time, he could be talking about something superficial and look very depressed," Markman explained.

None of this necessarily meant that he was incompetent, said Markman.

"Not every person who is schizophrenic is incompetent to stand trial, and not every person that's incompetent need necessarily be suffering from schizophrenia," he said.

"I do feel that he understands the charges that are pending and is aware of those charges. He is aware of a limited relationship between himself and the legal system with which he's caught up right now. But he doesn't have an appreciation of the proceedings themselves as they go on, and he doesn't have the capacity, in my opinion, to cooperate with counsel."

De la Sota burrowed in on the task of showing Michael Miller to be sane enough to stand trial for murder, but he was especially intrigued by Markman's analysis of the accused's courtroom catatonia.

"You were sitting at the side of the courtroom and kind of watching him closely, were you not?" asked de la Sota.

"Yes," Markman answered.

"And part of that time—he apparently is now, sitting there as if he were asleep," said de la Sota. "And he did that a good part of the time. What do you think about whether that is a genuine kind of reaction or whether that's just a way to make us think that he can't cooperate with us?"

"If I had not seen him yesterday, it would be a difficult question to answer," Markman answered. "But I think, based on my examination yesterday, I think that his posture here and the demeanor is fully consistent with that picture."

Finally, Judge Fredricks' own neutral expert took the witness stand. Dr. Skrdla, too, reiterated what he had written a week earlier about Michael's fitness to stand trial.

"The way he talks at times, it's almost as though these proceedings are very perfunctory and that somehow it will all be dismissed eventually," Skrdla told de la Sota.

Michael was schizophrenic, he said. He belonged in a closed psychiatric hospital—at least for a while. Until he showed improvement, Michael David Miller was not capable of standing trial.

Michael's eyes were still glued shut when testimony came to an end.

Judge Fredricks found Michael Miller incompetent to stand trial and gave the L.A. County Mental Health Clinical District a week to recommend a facility that might restore Michael's sanity. District Chief Donald Lee recommended Atascadero State Hospital, about two hundred miles north of Los Angeles in San Luis Obispo. The hospital had a treatment program specifically aimed at restoring defendants' competency to stand trial, according to Lee. In addition, Atascadero had much better security than the state hospital at Patton in Southern California, where more than five hundred patients had escaped in the previous six years.

On May 6 Michael was back in court. This time, so was his father.

His wedding ring still visible on his left hand, Roy Miller stood and told Judge Fredricks that he wanted his son to go to Patton instead of a hospital five hours away. In a clear, steady voice, he said:

"It is vitally important to Mike's restoration and rehabilitation . . . that he have the strong local support of his family and friends. . . . I say this on the basis of the feeling that my wife and I both had about mental illness—that strong family support is necessary to recovery."

After Roy sat down, Donald Lee stood and told the judge he still had a slight preference for Atascadero, but neither he nor de la Sota would object to Patton.

Fredricks suspended all criminal proceedings against Michael and ordered a competency report from state mental health officials within ninety days. Michael spent his twenty-first birthday in a locked and guarded men's dormitory at Patton, an hour's drive from downtown Los Angeles.

— 17

Patton officials admitted Michael as a patient a week later on May 16, but it was another six months before they found him fit to stand trial.

"Mr. Miller described an uneventful, pleasant childhood which was tainted by his relationship to his 4½ year older brother," wrote a staff psychologist in his admission notes.

Michael had described his relationship with Jeff as close enough to be like one of identical twins. While Jeff was the achiever, Eagle Scout and more of a linear thinker, Michael was different, more reactive than proactive. He told the staff psychiatrist that he was never as good as his brother.

When Jeff died, Michael took on Jeff's fascination with religion, perhaps to mirror his brother's personality and, in doing so, understand him better. He said that his family was very "puritanical" and that there was no room in their lives for the sins that were natural to humanity. To support his theories, Michael quoted many passages from the Bible to the psychiatrists. They noted his analytical strengths, but they also found that the passages he chose were almost always contradictory and yet Michael didn't seem to perceive it that way.

The psychologist concluded without hesitation that Michael had a great deal of trouble remaining anchored in reality, preferring instead to eschew insight into his troubled self in favor of a feeling of spiritual freedom. Basically, he thought that if he kept the faith, things would work out in his favor in the end and he could go on and devote himself to doing God's work.

Despite his missionary zeal and his evangelical eyes, Michael didn't dedicate every waking minute to God. Always, there was his preoccupation with food. His ideas about nutrition were often bizarre, but his psychiatrist refused to call them delusional. He linked Michael's food obsession with his jealousy of Jeff. Michael felt his parents neglected him in favor of Jeff, the psychiatrist concluded, so he somehow came up with the belief that he could even the score by going on various questionable diets, ranging from chocolate and garlic to goat's milk and cheese. If he lived up to his mother's precept of the properly nourished young man, he would become better than—or, at least, as good as—Jeff.

Even though he continually complained that his many food allergies were being triggered by his incarceration, his bed-wetting had ceased and his nervous tics were decreasing too. Still, with each fuss he made, Michael was utilizing two surefire parental attention-getters, food and religion, to distract from the more immediate issues of his legal predicament and mental condition his psychiatrists posited. Now that time had passed, they could occasionally get him to stray from these two topics and they felt that he did understand the charges against him on a merely intellectual level. Emotionally, he remained unconnected to the situation.

Exploring the possibility of pyromania, the psychiatrist asked him about setting fires and playing with matches.

"He remembered incidents of firesetting in his backyard, trash cans and the toilet," he noted. "Although Mr. Miller remembered having occasionally been abusive towards animals, he claims that he was not really cruel towards them."

Three months passed and the Patton committee charged with reviewing Michael's case wrote in its report that his mental condition had improved, but not by much.

On July 14 the six-person committee recommended that Michael remain at Patton another ninety days.

Three months later, there was yet another funeral for yet another important person in Michael Miller's life. Once again, Michael did not attend. Rheo Blair died of renal poisoning. His passing came as a shock to all but a handful of his most trusted friends. According to his brother, Norman Johnson, Blair had always believed that the truth about his failing health might deal a severe blow to his ever-expanding health and nutrition empire. He had secretly undergone dialysis treatment for several years, but the one kidney that had been keeping him alive since he was nine years old finally failed on October 6, 1983.

In late October Patton's review committee again met on the Michael Miller case. This time, they found him fit to stand trial.

In preparation for the impending court fight, Stephen Miller and Tom Nolan called Saul Faerstein back into service. The psychiatrist was given full access to all the available records: Michael's diary from November 1980 through February 1983; school records dating all the way back to elementary school; Jeffrey's hospital records; Marguerite's diary; police, court and mental hospital reports; and Michael's own notes about himself and his predicament since he was first taken into custody hours after his mother's death.

Faerstein also spent three more hours interviewing his client at a conference room in Patton State Hospital.

Judge Fredricks scheduled a December court date to hear from Patton's medical director before going ahead with the trial process. On November 29, one month before the hearing, Faerstein submitted his sixteen-page analysis of Los Angeles Superior Court Case No. A904176: *People v. Michael David Miller*. In it, he concluded that Michael Miller could certainly stand trial, but he was not sane . . . and may never have been.

Faerstein's report noted all the problems that Michael had had since the beginning. He noted the problems Michael had concentrating and his aggressive and hurtful behavior with other children in grade school, where the need for constant and individualized supervision brought him a diagnosis of hyperactivity. School documentation included reports that recorded the thirty-point drop Michael had in his intelligence quotient between the second and sixth grades and showed a pattern that Faerstein said reflected chronic emotional and mental difficulties.

External and internal events began to shape those problems as Michael progressed through high school. By the time Jeffrey died, Michael had already been treated by Rheo Blair, Dr. James Julian and the American Institute of Hypnosis. Yet he also continually heard his dead brother talking to him, and these aural hallucinations had actually increased right up to the present day, Faerstein noted.

Jeff was as critical of his little brother in his spectral incarnation as he had been in real life. The word "idiot" frequently reverberated inside of Michael's head, always in the deprecating scold of his older brother's voice.

Michael blamed his brother's death on his therapists as well as on Marguerite. She had smothered Jeff, he concluded.

"Michael began to fear that this smothering influence might someday kill him as well," Faerstein concluded, and went on to say that Martino had encouraged Michael to think of his mother as the enemy.

Martino's tapes contained lessons on a variety of topics pertaining to the therapy, like sexuality, separation from parents, religion and self-motivation, but their primary focus in therapy was Marguerite. Faerstein noted that Gamsky's *Smother Love* tape had been a main topic between therapist and patient and had helped Michael combine the idea that he was being dominated by his mother with his own confusing new sexuality.

Faerstein credited the number of individuals trying to treat Michael between the years of 1979 and 1982 with influencing their patient's confusion. For it was during this time that his delusions and psychotic episodes increased, fed by the barrage of information he was taking in about his maturing mind and body and relationships.

During the months he spent in New York in spring 1982 when

he was supposed to be attending acting classes, he frequently just sat in his hotel room listening to the Gamsky tapes over and over, Faerstein noted. When he came back to Los Angeles in May 1982, he again thought about killing his therapists.

But the next month, Faerstein reported, Michael began his treatment under the care of Dr. Sumner Shapiro, the psychiatrist he'd selected because he could speak French. Michael was still in the afterglow of his French girlfriend and idealized anything French. Dr. Shapiro and Michael did in fact speak in French a few times, but soon Michael was holding forth in sessions in English, and pretty foul language, at that.

During one visit, he saw a young girl walking outside Shapiro's office and asked the doctor:

"Is that your daughter out there? She's awful cute. I'd like to fuck her."

Michael began showing up at some sessions in a silk bikini bathing suit with a towel around his middle. At other sessions he appeared wearing just a towel. On one memorable day, he was in his bathing suit and asked to use the bathroom. When he returned he announced that he had inserted a hot dog in his anus, Faerstein wrote in his report.

But Shapiro's manner remained nonjudgmental. Michael grew so comfortable with the psychoanalyst that he came to feel that Shapiro's family was his own. He talked obsessively about Shapiro's initials, S.S., and how those initials might hold some special meaning for Michael.

He told Shapiro that he was wasting away and that he needed sex desperately. At one point, he even asked Shapiro, "If I can't get a date, would you let me screw you?" He said he thought his own mother and father never made love, and that he thought he could provide the much needed love in his mother's life by sleeping with her.

But the bizarre behavior Dr. Shapiro witnessed was not the only sign of Michael's mental collapse. Obsession crept into every fissure of the young man's cracking personality. Michael listened over and over to the tape of his brother's memorial service as if it were one of Gamsky's self-help tapes. He was absorbed with all his tapes. Maybe they had hypnotized him, he suggested.

Diet consumed him too. He spoke passionately to Shapiro about garlic and onions, celery, raw beef heart and liver. But at times, his teeth hurt too much to chew. His wisdom teeth were coming in painfully and had become yet another of his obsessions. At some of his sessions with Shapiro, he would pound on the psychoanalyst's office door, scream, roll his eyes and complain about his teeth. He wanted them out and he wanted his father to pay for the operation.

In the summer of 1982 a simple class reading of *Oedipus Rex* for his Greek mythology course at UCLA even turned into obsession— as it turned out, a very dangerous one. The story of the Greek monarch who kills his father and marries his mother triggered in Michael increasing ideas of incest with his mother. Those ideas preoccupied him from boyhood right up until the day she was killed, according to Faerstein.

When he was still in the second grade, Michael thought of undressing his mother after he had seen a copy of *Playboy* magazine. Throughout his childhood, he thought about having intercourse with his aunts and at least one of his cousins. When he was twelve, he actually did try having intercourse with a cousin.

The Monday before Marguerite died, he drove to the United Methodist Church in Pasadena to pick up a tape of a church service he had missed, and on the way he began thinking about a carnival that had been held at the church. There had been goats at the carnival, Michael told Faerstein. He wondered whether he could find himself a goat wandering free in Topanga Canyon, some fifty miles to the north near Dr. Shapiro's office, and have sex with it. But Michael had shocked himself with this idea, Faerstein wrote, and in order to purge himself of these thoughts about the goat, he began to drink goat's milk.

Michael didn't actually eat any dinner that night, choosing instead to cruise around in his car, trying to locate a couple of his female acquaintances, Faerstein continued. He didn't find the girls, so he drove to Dr. Shapiro's, parked in the garage and slept there in his car overnight.

The next day, he cruised around again listening to the tape of Jeffrey's memorial service. On Wednesday, the day before his mother died, Michael remembered driving somewhere with Marguerite and arguing loudly with her about her erratic driving. He felt smothered and confused.

By later in the afternoon, he felt exhausted, Faerstein wrote. Michael started having violent thoughts about blood and the weapons he'd gotten from his grandparents and fantasized about what it would be like to kill his mother and father. He wanted them dead because they couldn't have children anymore.

Michael cited that, in nature, female animals past the age of childbearing are no longer of value to the species. Even though he wanted Marguerite to have a little sister or brother for him, she didn't. If he got rid of her, though, his father might remarry and have little stepsiblings for Michael.

Faerstein's conclusion to his report reflected the conviction he felt at the end of his interviews with Michael. While the legal decision had to be left up to the judicial system, the facts about his subject's mental and emotional condition were crystal-clear:

"[Michael Miller] has not reached a level consistent with restoration to sanity. His conduct remains confused, impulsive and directed by psychotic thinking. He will require continued hospitalization in whatever setting the court chooses following the disposition of this case. The diagnosis at the present time remains chronic schizophrenia superimposed on a schizotypal personality disorder."

Faerstein told the court to note that Michael had never been treated with the drugs developed for diagnosed schizophrenics during his pretrial incarceration. The doctor mentioned that he didn't understand the reason for this decision but went on at length with a recommendation for a course of antipsychotic drug treatments as the most "humane" solution. This would demonstrably improve Michael's illness, he stated, and, when combined with psychotherapy, might give Michael a more hopeful but still "guarded" prognosis.

Finally, Faerstein warned what could happen if Michael did recover: "Michael Miller's schizophrenia protects him at present from the rational acceptance and realization of the severity and consequences of his deeds. Should he ever regain such a level of rational and logical thought that he would understand the enormity of his deeds, he might very well be overcome by the sense of guilt and horror at the meaning of his deeds. He might then become so depressed that he would present a suicidal threat."

A substantial number of reporters still showed up whenever a Miller hearing was announced, but the initial media frenzy over the bizarre case of Michael Miller had dampened somewhat with the passage of time. When Patton State Hospital's medical director took the stand on December 28, the courtroom was dotted with journalists, but the circus atmosphere of cameras and microphones and claustrophobic hallway press conferences was missing.

The psychiatric analyses and crucial reports from Patton had been successfully suppressed by the defense attorneys, so that what was revealed on the witness stand in open court tended to be terse and undetailed. Dr. August M. Kasper testified just long enough to let Judge Fredricks know that Michael could now be tried for rape and murder.

Michael himself showed up for the hearing in a dark blue suit, white shirt and tie, his hair neatly trimmed and combed. A lopsided smirk crawled across his wide-eyed face through much of the proceedings.

The first thing Dr. Kasper wanted to make clear, however, was that Michael Miller might be competent to stand trial, but he was still mentally ill.

"A person can be far more psychotic than Michael and still maintain the ability to stand trial," Kasper told the judge.

He explained. Michael could understand and respond in a word or two at times, if the question put to him was simple and straightforward, but when he had to speak at any length about something, his speech had no continuity.

"He might be talking about his brother and then extolling the virtues of lettuce and tomatoes," said Kasper.

His moods swung wildly, especially when he spoke of his parents.

"He'd be speaking of them as if he loved them deeply and then speaking of his hatred for them," said Kasper.

Nevertheless, he said, Michael was now able to grasp the gravity of the charges against him. He had improved "to the extent that he doesn't talk about [his obsessions] anymore, but I believe the obsessions are still there," said Kasper.

Judge Fredricks ruled Michael competent. Minutes later, sheriff's bailiffs shuttled him out of Judge Fredricks' fifth-floor courtroom, downstairs to South Bay Municipal Court on the third floor and into Judge Benjamin Aranda's courtroom so that he could finally be formally arraigned. Clutching his red Bible, Michael pleaded innocent in clipped words to charges that—almost exactly nine months earlier—he had raped and murdered his mother.

On March 27, 1984, two weeks before Michael's preliminary hearing, Dr. Michael Maloney filed his own report with Miller's defense team, supplementing Dr. Faerstein's assessment of Michael's sanity.

Maloney tried the venerable Rorschach test on him first.

He got an unusual array of responses to the inkblots, ranging from "a frog, bird or skeleton" on one card to "hips and a bust, some sort of arms and dangling things . . . looks like an X ray of the pelvic region" on another.

Michael observed "anatomical things, [judging] from the colors" on one card.

On yet another, he saw "buffaloes climbing out of a green something with two penises in the bottom."

After the inkblots, Maloney readministered the same Minnesota Multi-Phasic Inventory battery that Michael had taken in the days immediately following his mother's murder.

Maloney noted that Michael's responses were obviously calculated to ensure that he would be judged psychologically sound and in a positive frame of mind. But despite his best efforts, Michael came out high on four of the ten scales that an MMPI evaluator uses to determine an abnormal psychological profile. His evaluation showed an individual who was angry and full of resentment, with obsessive tendencies and a predilection for anxiety.

While the tests indicated that Michael was certainly mentally unbalanced and did suffer from a personality disorder, they did not show him to be psychotic. In fact, it went on to describe his diagnosis as fitting perfectly the mold for "schizophrenia, residual type, subchronic."

Interviewing the young man was always a challenge. It could become irritating even for a man trained to be tolerant. Maloney described him as "a very naïve, rigidly defensive individual." Michael would laugh while discussing his mother's death, for example. And though he wasn't specifically laughing at her, the chuckles always seemed to come at the most inappropriate times.

Echoing what he had told Faerstein and many others in the last few months, Michael told Maloney during the interview that Marguerite had been a smothering parent. Throughout their conversation, Michael kept bringing up the tape he'd been given by Martino and Gamsky. He was haunted still by the feeling of suffocation he'd had every time he came in contact with his mother, he told them. And he said that he'd yearned for sisters and for a healthy, happy brother. He also said he'd considered killing his father.

Maloney was continually frustrated with Michael's slippery way of avoiding or ignoring the line of questioning. He'd flit quickly from one thought to another, unconcerned with making sense and disregarding his many non sequiturs. When Maloney would ask him repeatedly about a crucial aspect of the murder, Michael tossed in trivial questions of his own about Maloney's daily life to derail him. Maloney noted that all of these comments were also made in the context of Michael's own life and referred to his thoughts about his mother, his family and Michael himself.

One important detail Michael did remember clearly was the twenty-four hours leading up to the murder. He had been over it enough times with enough counselors, lawyers and shrinks to repeat what happened without too much mind-wandering: how he gathered knives around his bed the evening before, believing that his father would come in and provoke a confrontation; how he wet the bed, got up, showered, and made his father a high-carbohydrate breakfast in hopes that it might kill him while he was driving; how he "got all those weird feelings" while sitting on the edge of the bed talking to his mother once Roy had gone to the office.

Michael was feeling as strong as he'd ever felt that morning. He even had a hard-on, he told Maloney. Michael recounted his story of going to sit beside his mother on the bed where she was sleeping. He looked down at her and tried to think out exactly what she meant to him. He realized she was the most beautiful thing he'd ever seen and his heart swelled with gratitude for the many wonderful things she'd taught him.

He'd asked her if he could crawl into bed with her for a minute. He felt dizzy—that was his explanation. But she was annoyed by his request.

"She said, 'No, get in your own bed,' " he told Maloney.

He couldn't, he told her. His bed was wet. He continued sitting on the edge of his mother's bed and waited for her to get up.

Marguerite grew uncomfortable, got up and went to the phone. She called her brother-in-law's office to see if it was all right for Michael to deliver the mah-jongg set at her sister Marilyn's house. When she hung up, Michael wanted her to look at his teeth.

So dutifully, Marguerite went to get a flashlight so she could see his teeth better. While she was occupied, Michael fetched the fishing club from his room and hid it under his robe. Marguerite returned, checked his teeth for him and then went to use the bathroom. Michael went into the living room, where he proceeded to take off his robe and pajamas, which he left on the living room carpet. Then he took the club and hid in his mother's closet.

When Marguerite opened the door and saw him there, she refused to look at him. Michael then recalled he "went out and felt weird and did weird stupid evil things." Right then he was envisioning that she was the same woman, but very old and wrinkled, he told Maloney. So he called out to her but she only said, "No, this is something to tell Dr. Shapiro." So he pulled her down to the floor with him, smothering her with his body and trying to put his penis into her. When she realized what he was doing, she said again, "This is something to tell Dr. Shapiro," Michael said.

When Maloney asked him what he could have been thinking about at the time he was forcing himself on his mother, Michael simply said, "Jeff had tried to strangle Mom and that's why he was sent to Edgemont."

The last words he remembered his mother saying were: "What are you trying to do?"

He knocked her down, but didn't know whether she was unconscious or not. He remembered that she did seem to continue to try to resist him, beating at his chest and shoulders as he straddled her. By the time he tried to enter her, she had lost her fight and he had lost his erection. All he could do once he was inside her was urinate. He remembered watching the urine spill out of her and onto the rug.

Then he dragged her body from the living room back to the bedroom, laying her faceup on the bed. He smothered her with a pillow, forcing the remaining air out of her lungs. Then he performed cunnilingus. He was once again able to get an erection, and this time when he entered her, he ejaculated within about sixty seconds.

Throughout this grotesque sexual ordeal, he remembered telling the still, limp form that had been moving and talking to him just a few minutes earlier: "Mom, I love you, I love you."

Afterward, he showered. Then he dressed in sweatpants and turtleneck, ate what he described as a "mini-meal" of cauliflower, eggplant, potato, rutabaga, a raw egg and a tablespoon of tofu.

He stared out the back window of the house, facing east, as he silently munched his breakfast. The sun rose above the tree line, gliding up and over the red rooftops of Palos Verdes and making the dusty leaves and branches glitter—renewed for yet another day.

From time to time, he returned to his parents' bedroom, pushing a little more air out of his mother's lungs and making sure the pillow was down tight over her face.

Around noon, he noted that he was running low on eggs and other groceries. He left through the front door, double-locking it behind him. Then he loaded the mah-jongg set into the car and drove down the Hill to Mrs. Gooch's Health Foods to stock up for the coming week before continuing on to Encino and his appointment with Dr. Shapiro.

He was late for the appointment and had to make another for the following day, but he did drive by another health food store in Brentwood and do some browsing before he delivered the mah-jongg set to his aunt in Santa Monica, just as his mother had asked him to do the previous morning.

He was exhausted by midafternoon. He went into his cousin Bill's room and escaped into a long, deep sleep.

He didn't awaken until the next morning.

And he never returned home again.

~ 18

On April 9, 1984, South Bay Municipal Judge Benjamin Aranda opened the long-delayed preliminary hearing to see if the district attorney had enough of a case to warrant Michael Miller's trial for rape and murder.

Aranda's first order of business was to ban the media. He heard and rejected arguments from the reporters and their lawyers that the hearing ought to be open to the public. De la Sota endorsed an open hearing, citing the stories that had been published to date as fair, evenhanded reporting that stuck to facts. But Aranda sided with Miller and Nolan, who feared the media might stoop to tabloid tactics, fanning the embers of public outrage and preventing their client from receiving a fair trial.

First Amendment protests didn't help. Aranda's bailiff told reporters they would have to cool their heels outside in the hallway while Aranda heard the prosecution's case.

Once Aranda was sure the courtroom was cleared of everyone but lawmen and lawyers, Palos Verdes Estates Police Officer Karen Belcher took the stand as de la Sota's first witness.

She recalled the night of March 24, 1983, and walked the court through her official report on the discovery of Marguerite's body, as well as Officer Joe Hall's report of what happened that night.

Stephen Miller pored over both reports, found the only major discrepancy and jumped on it with both feet.

"Officer Hall's report indicated that he had found old pry marks on a sliding glass door located on the north side of the residence," he said when it was his turn to cross-examine Belcher. "Did you read that in the report?"

"I observed that," said Belcher.

What she observed, she said, were some scratch markings near the handle of the sliding door between the Millers' master bedroom balcony and the outside deck overlooking the driveway. The markings that Joe Hall mentioned in his report were oxidized and obviously quite old, said Belcher. They had probably been made months or even years earlier and she didn't bother to include that information in her report because it didn't seem important.

Miller tucked her testimony away for future reference and gave the nod to de la Sota to call his next witness.

"Please raise your right hand," said the clerk. "You do solemnly swear the testimony you are about to give in the cause now pending before this court shall be the truth, the whole truth and nothing but the truth, so help you God?"

"I do," said Roy Miller.

For identification purposes, de la Sota had the elder Miller point out his son sitting at the end of the defense table in his blue suit. The passage of time coupled with Roy's own cerebral nature might have accounted for his precise speech and nearly mechanical actions, but any emotional breakdown de la Sota might have anticipated while Roy Miller was on the witness stand never materialized. He was more exact and less rattled than some people seemed to get over receiving a parking ticket.

Once he had Michael identified, de la Sota asked Roy about the morning that Marguerite was killed.

"Did Michael fix you breakfast?" de la Sota asked.

"He fixed me what I called this 'mini' breakfast of two pieces of buttered raisin toast and some oatmeal," answered Roy.

"At that time was your wife up and about?"

"No. She was in bed."

"Do you remember what Michael was wearing when you saw him there at about 6 A.M.?"

"No. I remember he was neatly attired and I am not sure whether he was dressed in daytime clothes or whether he was in a bathrobe. But I did make a mental note that he was neatly attired."

"Your wife you said was still sleeping at about that time?"

"Well, she had stirred. We communicated slightly, but she was still in bed."

In the kitchen, Roy remembered the conversation between father and son going like this:

"He told me that he was fixing me some breakfast. And I said, 'Well, that is very nice,' and I appreciated it. But, you know, 'This is my morning to go to the Economic Round Table and I am going to have a breakfast there as I customarily do on Thursday morning.'

"And he said, 'Well, I haven't fixed very much. Perhaps you could have this to tide you over.'

"So I thanked him for the toast that he brought first. And then he said that he had some oatmeal. And I said, 'Well, I could have a little bit but I am not going to be very hungry now because I am going to be having breakfast later.' "

What he did nibble was so loaded down with sugar and butter as to be virtually inedible, said Miller. He nodded politely at his son's odd benevolence and drove off to the office. He didn't return until after 10 P.M.

"When you got home, did you enter the front door?" asked de la Sota.

"Yes."

"And let me ask you this: Did things seem to be as they should have been when you got home? The lights on or off—that kind of thing?"

"Yes. There was a light on, which was operated by a timer."

To de la Sota's pleasant surprise, he was getting total cooperation. Roy Miller seemed to remember everything in meticulous detail.

"Can you tell us what you saw as you entered the house?"

"Well, I saw to the left into the living room a large badly stained blood spot on the carpet and some, either clothing or towels. And then closer to the chest on which the lamp sat that I mentioned, there was a large—well, not a large, about a twelve- or fourteen-inch wooden club that we had called a fish club that had been a relic that Marguerite's parents had had in their family from Alaska. And I think that had some blood on it. I saw a pair of broken glasses which I recognized as Marguerite's or looking like her glasses and that, as I recall, were perhaps partly on the oriental rug in the entryway and partly on the tile."

"How far into the house did you go?"

"About one or two steps."

"Did you turn on any other lights or anything whatsoever?"

"No."

"Did you ever go beyond the one or two steps inside the house?"

"No."

"What did you do when you saw those things lying in the positions that you have described?"

"My heart sank. I called out my wife's name twice."

"Was there any answer?"

"No, there was no answer."

Miller stepped back, shut the door, locked it, went next door and called the police, he said. It wasn't until Karen Belcher and Joe Hall arrived and checked out the Miller house that he learned of his wife's death.

"Other than that, I do not think they told me anything," he testified. "In fact, they told me that they were going to refrain from telling me anything more."

"So they used the word 'dead' rather than 'had been killed'?"

"I think I asked if she is dead and they said 'yes.' "

"And you were given no other details at all. Is that correct?"

"Well, I think there is one officer that told me that we need to keep this search confidential because the person who did it knows what happened and nobody else does, and we would just prefer to keep it that way."

One person that Roy did tell about Marguerite's death was her sister, Marilyn Adkins. When he called with the news around midnight, he testified, Michael was still asleep.

"We discussed whether to wake him up and tell him," Roy recalled. "And we decided at that point that maybe we would just wait until morning and tell him in the morning."

When Roy did call him in the morning, Michael acted shocked.

"As I can best recall his response, it was in a tone of amazement and disbelief: that that is just terrible," Miller remembered. "I told him that I had been requested by deputies Beck and Sett to [ask Michael to] come to the Palos Verdes police station and submit himself for questioning."

When he showed up, "he looked like he had come off an English moor," said Roy. "He looked like he was agitated and windblown and just very upset." Michael embraced his father, then asked him if he was going to be with him during the questioning.

"And I told him no, the officers said that they had wanted to question him alone," said Roy.

The next time he saw his son was at the jail the following Sunday—Easter Sunday—less than twenty-four hours after burying his wife.

"Forgive me for asking," de la Sota asked, "but I assume from the time you left on the Thursday morning at around 6:30, you never saw your wife alive again?"

"That is right," said Roy.

De la Sota signaled the judge that he had no more questions. Far from being a belligerent, emotional or unreliable witness, Roy Miller was turning out to be utterly credible, and utterly credible for the prosecution.

Then Stephen Miller began his cross-examination, and the careful structure of his defense of Michael Miller's actions began to take shape.

"Did there come a time when Michael began to be treated by a psychiatrist?" he asked.

"Yes," answered Roy.

For the last eight months of Marguerite's life, Michael saw Dr. Sumner Shapiro "almost daily," Roy testified.

"By that, I mean each weekday for a forty-minute session, although there were occasions, when Dr. Shapiro went on vacation or if there was a holiday or if Michael didn't want to go or . . . he either decided he wouldn't make it or he didn't make it—there were times that he didn't see him."

The weeks leading up to Marguerite's death, he missed more and more appointments, Roy said. Shapiro even tried to accommodate Michael by scheduling double appointments, but even that broke down near the end. Sometimes he would be very late and miss part of his appointment. Sometimes he just didn't show up at all.

"And in fact, Michael told us two or three times and with increasing intensity that he didn't think he wanted to see Dr. Shapiro anymore, and it took too much time and he didn't think that he was—he questioned whether he was doing him any good," Roy testified. "But he still continued to make his appointments most of the time, although sometimes it would take Marguerite going with him in order for him to go."

Shapiro told the Millers their son had been improving and that was just what they had concluded on their own. But as the second anniversary of Jeff's death approached, the improvement all began to unravel.

"Two to three weeks before she died there were a number of indications that gave concern, that were rather strange and unusual," Roy remembered.

He seemed unusually agitated at times. He didn't keep appointments. He lost his keys. In fact, during the weeks leading up to his mother's death, his fastidious neatness declined to the point that his room "seemed like it had been hit by a cyclone," according to Roy.

The same preoccupation and indifference to everything around him that he showed when he first came home from New York now resurfaced. If his parents asked him something, the question could go unanswered for seconds and minutes at a time.

"And he seemed very, very concerned with decisions which, while perhaps . . . important, seemed to be blown all out of proportion," Roy testified. "He would get agonized over what orchestra to join or what not to join: the Palos Verdes Symphony or the Carson Symphony; what courses to join, what . . . whether to sign up for a particular course of study; whether to get a job; whether to do the things concurrently; whether to have one violin teacher teach him or another violin teacher teach him or a third violin teacher teach him.

"And he was on the phone, scheduling two appointments with two different teachers for the very same day. I am not sure whether he kept both of them or not. But there was an importance and an immediacy and an urgency to resolving each of these questions, which got to the point of great agitation. And it got almost to a point of ethics or values: Should I do this or should I do that? As if there was one right answer and no other right answers. And this really concerned us deeply because it seemed that many of these alternatives were reasonable alternatives and perhaps it wasn't so much a matter of what he did, but that he do something constructive.

"I tried to tell him, 'You don't need to build Rome in a day. Select one thing that you know you can accomplish and accomplish it.' And he would absorb intellectually, but in his approach to problems he wouldn't do that."

Michael's obsessive behavior grew worse, clear up until the Sunday before his wife died.

". . . We were going to the hospital to see a friend of Marguerite's after church and Mike thought it was just so intensely important that he have *menudo* [Mexican tripe soup] for lunch, and he was vacillating back and forth whether he should have his *menudo* first or go to the hospital first. And again, the urgency and intensity and immediacy of this decision that seemed almost a life-and-death decision really kind of floored us and baffled us.

"And it seems to me explainable only in that his mental condition was just deteriorating and that it was part of this business of agitation of putting ordinary daytime decisions into value decisions and having a compelling urgency and immediacy about some things."

His son continued to unravel.

"I can think of the very morning that he served me this mini breakfast that I spoke about earlier. It was done in a context that . . ."

Roy paused briefly to reconstruct the scene in his mind.

"He had been trying to suggest ways that I might lead a healthier life and suggesting that I shouldn't eat toast because it was clogging to my system and that I shouldn't eat saturated fats such as butter. And we had had a little dialogue about that. I told him I appreciated that and I'd try to eat well."

Attorney Stephen Miller took Roy's memory as a cue to show how something as simple as breakfast could be turned around by a deranged mind.

"You are saying, are you, Mr. Miller, that prior to March 24 you and Michael had had conversations in which he intended to emphasize to you the importance of eating correctly from his point of view?" the lawyer asked.

"Yes," Roy answered. "And Michael was always concerned about his diet and continued to be throughout. But this intensified to the point of really telling me how I should be eating."

It seemed to be more than friendly advice to Roy.

"It was almost an insistence that I not eat certain things," he said. "And indeed sometimes I would go out in the kitchen in the morning to cook toast and he might have cereal. He said, 'You don't need toast. I have some cereal for you.' So then, all right, that day I might not eat toast."

But the morning that Marguerite died, Michael had a completely different attitude about what kind of food his father ought to put into his body.

". . . He not only refrained from admonishing me as he had been the days preceding, but he brought out freshly made toast that was freshly buttered with an appearance—I don't know if he had a towel over his shoulder or over his arm—but at least with a certain flair and grace, which puzzled me," said Roy. "And I couldn't really figure it out, whether he . . . had finally given in to my own admonitions or just what the situation was. But I took it for what it was worth. I didn't comment. Then he followed that with some cereal."

When de la Sota took up redirect examination, he wanted to know if Michael had ever been hospitalized for his mental condition.

"No," Roy answered.

"Had it ever been recommended to you by Dr. Shapiro that that be done?" asked de la Sota.

"No," said Roy. "We had questioned Dr. Shapiro ourselves as to whether that should be done. And Dr. Shapiro and I had talked about it. But we had also talked about the tremendous difficulty it is to hospitalize someone against his will under the present law in California, which I was experienced with to some degree in my profession. And we felt that it was probably not an alternative under the law."

"Did you ever discuss with your son his voluntary commitment to some sort of mental institution?" asked de la Sota.

"I certainly did not propose it in so many words, although it was clear to me that he would not have been receptive to it," said Roy.

During Stephen Miller's own re-cross-examination, Roy Miller implied that there may have been yet another deterrent to his conceding to commit his one surviving son into the hands of mental health professionals, despite his son's obviously deteriorating state of mind.

"Is it your understanding, Mr. Miller, that Jeffrey died as a result of a suicide?" asked the defense counsel.

"That is what the death certificate said," Roy answered indirectly and not a little bitterly.

"Very well," said Stephen Miller.

"He was being treated for mental illness and had been hospitalized for several weeks immediately prior to that time," Roy added before leaving the witness stand.

On Tuesday, April 10, the second day of Michael Miller's preliminary hearing, the proceedings almost stopped before they began.

"Your Honor, it is about 10:50 in the morning," said Stephen Miller. "I wanted to place on the record certain facts concerning Michael Miller that have come to the attention of Mr. Nolan and me within the last fifteen or twenty minutes."

Michael was "at an all-time low," said the lawyer. His wild-eyed lunacy of the previous day had given way to alternating babbling and stony silence, implying that his mental state had deteriorated once again into incompetency.

Those few observers who had been allowed into the courtroom gallery witnessed a hideously contorted face and an equally tortured body writhing between his two defense lawyers. Michael's arms and legs either flailed or folded against his torso like twisted rubber bands, and his long, slender musician's fingers seemed to have transformed into knobby claws. His mouth hung open in an animal shriek that never emerged, despite the vibrating tension of his visibly tightened jaw and neck muscles.

Tom Nolan stood and added his own observations of his client's erratic behavior.

"The only thing I would amplify for the record: A few minutes ago I got off the phone with our office and spoke to my secretary who informed me that this morning Michael Miller called and spoke to our receptionist, a woman by the name of Miss Bonnie Benson," said Nolan. "And for approximately five to ten minutes he did nothing but read straight from the Bible, had no conversation whatsoever with her.

"I would also join with Mr. [Stephen] Miller that I have been with Michael since the afternoon of March 25 of 1983 and that this is the worst condition I have seen him in," Nolan continued. "He had made numerous comments about the religious aspects and that the timing of the preliminary hearing should be in synch with what he says is God's timing for everything. I just wanted to have that for the record."

Judge Aranda turned to the prosecutor, seated at the next table.

"Mr. de la Sota?" he asked.

The tall, lanky deputy D.A. told the judge he was happy with the way the preliminary hearing was progressing from a legal stand-point. "On the other hand," he continued, "if the defendant is not cognizant of his surroundings or the proceedings, we might be spinning our wheels by proceeding at this time."

The judge was not convinced that Michael's histrionics were evidence of a relapse into incompetency and he said as much to all of the attorneys gathered in his closed courtroom.

"The court does think he is cognizant," said Aranda. "He has addressed the court as 'Your Honor' and 'judge' on several occasions. I think he is cognizant of the fact he is present in a court of law. I don't know if he realizes the reason he is present. I would say based on the evidence I saw yesterday, that he knows he is here. That is probably the reason for the deterioration that counsel had noted."

Aranda told de la Sota to call the next witness.

Thomas A. McCleary, a twelve-year veteran of the Los Angeles County Sheriff's Criminalistics Laboratory, explained how he had taken vaginal, anal and oral swabs from the body at the murder scene. In testimony similar to testimony that he and other forensic biologists had given countless times before, McCleary described the lab process he used to determine whether or not a defendant might have had sex with a victim.

"[I would] examine the slides under a microscope using a technique which basically darkens the background and makes the sperm or other cellular material kind of glow," he said. "Makes it easier to visualize."

He found semen glowing on the swabs that he had used to take body fluid samples from both inside and outside of Mrs. Miller's vaginal area, McCleary said.

The hearing broke for lunch, but there would be no reconvening. Whether he reacted to McCleary's graphic descriptions or the reality of his mother's death or just the spectral voices raging in the gray matter behind his own rolling eyeballs, Michael's courtroom antics had become too much even for Judge Aranda when the hearing resumed Tuesday afternoon. His attorneys spent as much time trying to calm their client into a receptive state as they did concentrating on the questions they put to the person sitting in the witness stand.

Aranda finally gave up. He conceded to postpone proceedings indefinitely, as long as Michael waived his right to a continuous preliminary hearing.

"Mr. Miller does waive his right in that respect," said Stephen Miller. He turned to his client in hopes that he might be lucid enough to speak for himself.

"Yes, I do, Your Honor," said Michael in a rare show of sensibility.

Aranda ordered the hearing suspended. But before he dismissed everyone and sent them out of his sequestered courtroom, he admonished the lawyers not to talk to the press or the TV cameras waiting outside.

"No doubt you will be deluged by telephone calls from reporters on this subject, so, therefore, all persons in this courtroom will be bound," Aranda warned. "There is no disclosure of any reason why this matter has been continued nor potential reason for conjecture on the part of any person in this courtroom as to why it could have been conceivably continued until this matter is resumed. The calling of witnesses or potential witnesses is not to be mentioned by any member in this courtroom."

Four months and five days passed before the preliminary hearing resumed. Michael returned to Patton for treatment and was due back in court in May, but de la Sota acceded to a postponement so that he could handle another case. It wasn't until August 15, 1984, that they all—prosecution, defense and Michael Miller— found themselves back in Judge Aranda's courtroom. Outwardly, Michael appeared no less disheveled than he had in March, but Aranda was determined to get through the remaining witnesses and finally dispose of the long-running case.

Michael's cousin was the first person de la Sota called to the witness stand.

Bill Adkins, a college student who was three years older than

Michael, remembered seeing his cousin on the morning after Marguerite died. It was between 6 and 7 A.M., he testified, and they were all standing in the dining room of the Adkins' rambling old Santa Monica bungalow.

"He had just come up from talking with his father on the phone," he said.

Bill and his parents already knew the tragic news before Michael heard it from his father, so they were somewhat braced for the grief that they expected to follow. The family members were already gathered together to help Michael take the blow. They were not braced, however, for what he actually did say when he got off the phone.

"He told us again that his mother was dead," said Adkins. "Then he threw a little bit of conversation in and then he said, basically, 'I killed her.' "

Bill Adkins took his cousin's confession as symbolic breast-beating, somehow translating his mother's murder into meaning that he, Michael, ought to have been there to protect her. No, Michael said. He insisted that he had killed his own mother.

"No, you didn't," Bill remembered telling his cousin in an attempt to comfort him.

The four of them stood awkwardly in the dining room for several moments, trying to decide what to do next. Michael had the answer.

"I should go home," he told his aunt, uncle and cousin. Bill agreed.

"And did he say anything to you after that about whether or not he had killed her?" de la Sota asked.

"No," said Adkins. "There was just basically a look on his face of despair that his mother was dead."

All three of the Adkineses volunteered to drive to Palos Verdes, but Michael insisted on driving himself. Bill accompanied his cousin as a passenger. Soon after they were in the car, Michael popped a cassette into the tape deck and turned to Bill.

"Do you mind if we listen to this?" Michael asked.

Bill motioned Michael to go ahead. For the next twenty minutes,

Adkins testified, they listened to the tape of Jeffrey's memorial service while Paul and Marilyn Adkins followed them in their own car, weaving through the early morning rush-hour traffic. Throughout the ride, neither cousin said very much. One of the few times Michael spoke was after he got off the freeway and slowed down to point out Mrs. Gooch's health food store.

"Where were you expecting to go?" asked de la Sota. "Was there any conversation about that?"

"I was expecting to go to his house," Adkins said.

Instead, once they were inside the Palos Verdes Estates city limits, Michael pulled into an underground parking garage behind the police station. An officer told them parking was restricted, so they got back into the car and drove around to the front of the station. As they entered the station, Bill grabbed his cousin's sleeve and asked, "Mike, what are we doing here?"

Michael said he didn't understand Bill's question. He ignored him, did an about-face, retreated back through the front door and walked around to the rear of the station again with a perplexed Bill Adkins at his heels.

"He never did really answer my question of 'What are we doing here at the police station?' " Adkins told de la Sota.

Adkins explained that the next thing he saw was a sea of uniforms when they walked through the back door of the station. Whether it was out of recognition or expectation, all faces seemed to focus on Michael.

"It struck me that it seemed like people knew who Mike was," Adkins recalled. "And that surprised me because he was greeted by people, and then he was escorted off. And they told me to go wait out front."

A while later, one of the officers found Adkins and asked him to fetch some distilled water from the car for Michael, but that was the last he heard about his cousin for over an hour. The next time he caught a glimpse of him, Michael was being escorted from the station by a pair of plainclothes detectives. Michael yelled over his shoulder to his cousin as he passed by: "Bill, don't sign anything!"

Sheriff's Homicide Detective Jerry Beck followed Adkins to the witness stand, explaining in explicit detail what happened in the interview room during that hour that Adkins cooled his heels in the police station lobby.

The first thing Michael told the detectives was that he had, in fact, killed his mother. Then Michael ordered Sergeant Sett to put his cigarette out and sit down before he would continue with his story and tell them both exactly what happened.

Beck didn't tape the confession, having learned from experience that a tape recorder often inhibits a person who is about to confess to murder.

"And I do not want to inhibit that person from talking freely with me," the detective added.

Beck's instincts were right. When he asked Michael to go through the statement one more time for the tape recorder, Michael refused. He didn't want to be recorded, he said.

That made perfect sense to Beck and Sett. They were both beginning to believe that what they had in Michael Miller was a first-degree-homicide suspect who might qualify for the gas chamber.

Under California law, murder committed during the commission of a second violent crime such as rape is a murder committed under "special circumstances." When a court finds a defendant guilty of special-circumstances murder, he immediately becomes eligible for one of two punishments: life imprisonment without parole, or execution. If the prosecution could convict Michael Miller of murder *and* rape, a special-circumstances finding would more than likely follow.

One item that de la Sota had entered into evidence that seemed to support that a rape might have taken place was a photo of Michael's knees. De la Sota handed it to Beck and asked him to describe it for the court.

"This is Michael Miller seated in the chair downstairs in the lockup," said Beck, describing the color close-up of a pair of legs with the pants rolled up to the thighs. "And these are his knees and lower legs. . . ."

Bright red abrasions decorated the cap of each knee—scrapes

that Beck said had gotten there while Michael forced himself into Marguerite on the living room carpet.

But when Stephen Miller had his own turn at Beck, he immediately challenged the notion that Marguerite Miller had been raped. To begin with, he pointed out, Beck's own official police report quoted Michael as saying, "I killed my mom and then I raped her."

One of the first rules of rape investigation was that the victim must be alive at the time of the sexual assault. If an attacker had sex with a victim after she was dead, it was not rape. Necrophilia might be horrible, but it was not a felony.

"The 'then' doesn't belong there," Beck protested from the witness stand as the attorney read back Michael's quotes to the detective. "That should be deleted. It was not dictated."

"So you are saying that instead of dictating to the secretary the words 'I killed my mom and *then* I raped her,' you dictated somewhat differently?" asked Miller, carefully teasing the admission of a crucial technical error out of the detective.

"I did not use the word 'then,' " Beck said gruffly.

The word "then" had been a typographical mistake, he maintained. There had been an unusual rush to get the report filed within forty-eight hours so that Michael could be arraigned immediately on the Monday after the murder, Beck explained. As a result, neither he nor Sergeant Sett had properly proofread their police report before turning it over to de la Sota.

De la Sota didn't want to file the rape charge and Stephen Miller certainly didn't want another count added to his client's murder accusation. But Beck and Sett were so certain that rape was what Michael had confessed to that they insisted on putting it into the indictment. In addition to speeding up the typing of their police report, they ordered the criminalists in the lab to expedite results from the sexual assault kit that had been taken from the murder scene so that they could show that a sexual assault had, in fact, taken place.

Jerry Beck and Stephen Miller continued kibitzing over the crucial word "then" for several minutes during Miller's cross-examination, but Beck would not budge.

"[Michael] did not use the term 'then,' " Beck said emphatically.

"You are sure of that, aren't you?" Miller asked.

"Very positive."

"And it has been, how long?"

"Seventeen months," said Beck.

"But you remember that definitely?"

Beck paused dramatically and then drilled Miller with a cool, sure stare. "It was the first time anybody had ever said to me they raped and killed their mother. And I remember it now as clear as a bell."

The duel between detective and defense counsel intensified as Miller bore down on Beck, searching for a fissure large enough in the veteran cop's rock-solid self-assurance to impeach his testimony. As Miller's line of questioning split more hairs, he hit more nerves. Beck could barely contain his sarcasm when the attorney reached a point in his questioning where he wanted to know how Beck knew which bathroom in the house belonged to Michael.

"So even at this point in time, you do not have knowledge as to which of the bathrooms in this residence Michael Miller occupied. Is that your testimony?" Miller demanded.

"He lived in the bathroom? Occupied the bathroom?" Beck asked with mock surprise.

"Utilized, sir. Thank you," Miller said icily.

"I saw no sign on the bathroom door that says, 'This is Mike's potty,' so I couldn't really tell you, sir," Beck shot back with equal venom.

After several more minutes of tense questioning, Stephen Miller finally began showing the strain of this constant parrying. When he tried pinning Beck down about the semen tests that had been conducted on Marguerite's vaginal swabbings, the lawyer's own questions began to disintegrate.

"Are you saying, sir, that you made a point of making reference yesterday to this particular piece of evidence on your direct examination in this preliminary hearing, that on March the 25th that evidence was taken by the criminalist under your direction to the laboratory, correct?"

Beck cast Miller a blank stare before looking past him to the prosecutor's table for help. His shoulders shrugged and a befuddled expression was scrawled across his face.

"I am going to object," said de la Sota. "I lost the question somewhere."

Miller let out a breath and the tension between him and Beck broke for just a few moments.

"I don't blame you," he said to de la Sota. "Let me withdraw it. I am sorry. You are absolutely right. It was very poorly phrased."

Miller pulled himself up and recast his question.

"My question is: Did you say to him in order to get this rape count included in the complaint or words to that effect, we have to have—we must show semen?"

"No, I don't think I would. And I don't recall saying that," Beck answered.

Their verbal jousting resulted in a draw, but Miller seemed to have gotten what he wanted with Beck. By the time the brawny homicide detective left the stand, the defense counsel had managed to cast substantial doubt on whether Michael had actually raped his mother while she was still alive.

Stephen Miller also questioned whether Michael's confession could be used against him. He implied that Beck and Sett did not bother to look for any other suspects once they learned that Michael had been seeing a psychiatrist. He briefly recalled Karen Belcher to the stand to reemphasize the fact that jimmy marks had been found on the sliding glass door into Roy and Marguerite's bedroom, but the police dismissed them as old and did not search for some other intruder once they had Michael in custody.

Further, Miller planted seeds during the preliminary hearing that Michael might not have been competent to legally understand his rights when he first confessed to the two detectives that he had, indeed, killed his own mother.

After calling six witnesses and placing sixteen exhibits into the court record, Richard de la Sota told the judge that the prosecution rested.

"Very well," said Aranda, "the people rest."

But then he added:

"There is a defense. Call your first witness, counsel."

De la Sota was prepared, even though a defense phase of a preliminary hearing was a rarity. Customarily, there is little or no defense at a preliminary hearing. Criminal defense strategists tear down the prosecution's case at a preliminary hearing while reserving their own best arguments for trial.

But Michael Miller was different. According to his lawyers, he was innocent by reason of insanity and there was no better time to show that than during the preliminary hearing, while the media was still blocked from covering the case.

Stephen Miller started by putting Dr. Saul Faerstein on the stand and asking his expert opinion of Michael's sanity.

"He thought that she again might be alive after he did what he did," the psychiatrist explained to the court. "He couldn't understand that what he was doing could even hurt his mother at some point in the commission of the act."

Michael was confused, said Faerstein. He was delusional. He was detached from reality.

". . . He was suffering from those characteristics and classical signs of schizophrenia which interfered with his ability to rationally and logically understand the consequences of his behavior," the psychiatrist testified.

"In understanding the terms 'right' from 'wrong,' let me address myself to two aspects of that because I believe that there may be more than one aspect which is of interest to the court," said Faerstein. "There is legal right and wrong and there is moral right and wrong. And I think that in terms of both of those, he was incapable of appreciating or understanding right from wrong."

According to Faerstein, Michael Miller was guiltless in the murder of his mother. Under the M'Naghten Rule, a defense lawyer must prove that: ". . . at the time of the committing of the act, the party accused was laboring under such a defect of reason, from disease of the mind, as not to know the nature and quality of the act he was doing; or, if he did know it, that he did not know he was doing what was wrong."

In 1843, during the early years of the reign of Queen Victoria, God instructed one of her subjects—one Daniel M'Naghten—to murder the Queen's Prime Minister, Sir Robert Peel. Unfortunately, M'Naghten mistook Peel's secretary for Peel and killed him instead.

Normally, M'Naghten would have been hanged. But compassion and understanding had begun to take hold in post-Enlightenment England. For the first time in British jurisprudence, the court ruled in favor of a murder defendant because he was proven insane at the time he committed his crime. M'Naghten's lawyer showed that his client suffered from delusions of persecution that prevented him from understanding right from wrong.

The rule that bore Daniel M'Naghten's name still applied more than 140 years later when John Hinckley, Jr., went on trial for the attempted murder of Ronald Reagan and when Saul Faerstein sat in a Southern California courtroom, testifying on behalf of Michael Miller.

In his cross-examination, de la Sota seemed more interested in debriefing Faerstein than debunking him. He asked him to explain what he meant when he said that Michael Miller had gone into denial over the murder of his mother.

"When I used the term 'denial,' I am using the term to represent psychological defenses that a human being would utilize to deal with the kind of overwhelming reaction one would normally expect from someone who is involved in [murder]," said the psychiatrist. "He was dealing with it in an almost distance. He was distancing himself from that act, thinking of it theoretically, abstractly: Why would anybody die?

"It is a very bizarre reaction when being told your mother has died, especially considering that he might have known what had happened or what his involvement might have meant. I saw what he was doing at that point. He was not dealing with it in a real way, in an emotional way that would have been appropriate."

De la Sota persevered. Hadn't Michael felt guilty enough to have made a confession?

"I don't believe he felt guilty in a normal sense," said Faerstein.

"I think there was some primitive guilt operating at some level that may have been a driving force in his making a confession.

"But I think an individual who is experiencing guilt as we know it, after the commission of the offense, would not have picked up the mah-jongg set and driven off to his aunt and uncle's . . . to have delivered it [and] taken a shower."

Dr. Ronald Markman echoed Faerstein's findings when it was his turn on the witness stand.

Schizophrenics experience the same impulses as sane people, he said. The difference is that they lack the ability to control those impulses. If they have an impulse, they do it regardless of circumstances or consequences.

"The hallmark of the condition is that the condition controls the behavior rather than the individual controlling the behavior," he said.

Judge Aranda had heard enough. He ended the hearing and made his decision the same day. Michael Miller would go back upstairs to Superior Court to stand public trial sometime after the presidential election in November.

But, until then, his gag order on all evidence and testimony would remain.

— 19

Michael Miller's trial took place on Tuesday, November 27, 1984, three weeks after the anticlimactic landslide reelection of Roy Miller's most famous client to a second term as President. The trial of his son for murder was equally devoid of surprises.

After a day of deliberation, defense motions and expert testimony from Drs. Faerstein, Markman and Maloney about Michael's sanity, the trial itself took less than an hour. When it was over, many of those who had come to watch the puzzling story of the disintegration of a perfect American family left as baffled as they had been when they first came. Veteran reporters who had covered dozens of trials were uncertain whether what they had just witnessed was a trial or merely clever legal posturing.

A week ahead of time, Michael had entered an unusual double plea: not guilty and not guilty by reason of insanity. His lawyers waived his right to a jury trial. Instead, they opted to have Judge Cecil Mills act as both their client's judge and his jury. They didn't know what to expect from him, but his reputation for compassion guaranteed at least an even chance.

Mills was a gruff-speaking bear of a man—a former county marshal whose rancher father had also been a uniformed lawman on the Oregon border fifty years earlier. He grew up on a five-thousand-acre cattle ranch in the northeastern corner of California, breaking horses and riding the rodeo circuit when he was still a teenager. After he injured a shoulder, he gave up busting broncos for busting criminals.

His speech was slow and unmodulated—a soft twang in open court that could lull the inattentive to sleep. His kindly drone often ran syllables together, so that "what's your" comes out "whatcher" and "in the morning" sounded like "inamornin."

Cecil Mills looked and acted like a good ol' boy, but he was not. When his voice changed from a kindly country twang to a hard-edged command, so did everything else about him. He would remove his glasses and sit forward at the same time that his sibilant speech gave way to a boom.

When some flippant first-time felon appeared in his courtroom, bearing both an alias and a smart-assed sneer, he would growl, "I don't care whatcher a.k.a. is today. I wanna know what name yer mama gave you when you were born."

He believed in open court and a practice of law as plain as the food he ate. He allowed cameras in his courtroom and he placed no bans on reporters coming and going during Michael Miller's trial. The full story of what had happened the day Marguerite Miller died appeared as though it would finally be aired in public.

But neither Richard de la Sota from the D.A.'s Office nor Tom Nolan and Stephen Miller, counsel for the defense, planned to call any witnesses beyond the three psychological experts. Neither side was prepared to offer any new evidence. No one took the stand to quibble over how Marguerite Miller met her untimely end. Instead, both sides based their cases on the confidential reports of psychiatric experts, undisclosed prosecution and defense exhibits and the sealed witness transcripts from Judge Aranda's preliminary hearing.

For the TV crews and newspaper reporters who had returned to the courtroom for this final revelatory scene in the Michael Miller case, the only real revelation was Michael Miller himself.

The defendant, who had now spent two birthdays in custody, seemed more rumpled and gaunt at age twenty-two than at any of his previous public appearances. After twenty months in jail and mental institutions, he looked and acted the part of a raving lunatic. He hunched over his omnipresent Bible through most of the proceedings, mumbling verses under his breath. He appeared quite oblivious to everything around him. At one point, he threw his hands into the air and hollered, "Jesus, Jesus, Jesus, Lord!"

Judge Mills, who had planned a speedy and straightforward proceeding, was unprepared for Michael's ravings. At one point, he had to halt the pretrial formalities in order to have Michael escorted from the courtroom. After Michael was calmed down enough to return, the judge rescinded his own order allowing cameras in the courtroom after Nolan and Miller had convinced him that Michael's outbursts might be aggravated by the presence of TV crews.

When Michael returned to the courtroom, a woman bailiff sat next to him at the end of the defense table, more a baby-sitter than a guard. She had a soothing effect on him. Michael seemed to ogle her as much as his Bible. Through the remainder of the proceedings, she became "almost like a teddy bear" to him, one observer noted.

The judge moved things along swiftly after Michael's "Jesus" outburst. De la Sota and Michael's two attorneys popped up to comment or object from time to time, but Judge Mills did most of the talking.

Over defense objections, he accepted Michael's confession as uncoerced and legitimately obtained by the two sheriff's detectives, but he rejected de la Sota's second felony count, explaining that the evidence was simply not conclusive enough that Marguerite had actually been alive at the time she was raped. If she was dead, he reminded the prosecutor, by definition she could not have been raped. A victim had to be alive to have suffered rape. Otherwise, it was necrophilia.

Mills also rejected Michael's first not guilty plea. He was clearly the person who killed Marguerite Miller. He did accept the second plea, though. The judge was convinced that Michael was not guilty by reason of insanity.

Mills immediately found Michael to be criminally insane and

sentenced him to Patton State Hospital for a maximum term of life or until Patton's experts and the courts could agree that he was fit to return to society.

The saga of Michael Miller had come to an end. The defendant threw his head back and shouted "Hallelujah!"

Roy Miller watched him solemnly from a spectator's seat. When the ordeal was over, he went to the defense table, where he hugged his son once more before the bailiffs led the young man away. Then Roy squared his chin and confronted the news media.

"I just want to say that I am glad the case is behind us and we can now begin a new chapter in our lives," he said in a quavering voice, reading from notes he had scratched on a yellow legal pad during the proceedings. "I hope this case and others like it will encourage citizens to address themselves to ways of addressing mental illness, and treating it in a way constructive to those afflicted, to their families and to the public generally."

He took no questions following his brief and final public word on the trial of his son for the murder of his wife. Roy Miller escaped the klieg lights and microphones and caught up with de la Sota out in the hallway. He personally thanked him for dealing compassionately but evenhandedly with his son.

Then he was gone.

"There's only one way you can tell the keepers from the patients at Patton: the ones with the keys on their belts are sane," quipped one of the Miller family's friends.

Fearful staff members, who are assaulted almost daily by Patton's criminally insane, might argue with that assessment. Stabbings or "shaftings" are a routine hazard of working there. The lackadaisical, the inattentive and the laissez-faire don't last long at Patton.

"I was assaulted twice, once when I had a chair thrown at me," said one staff member who worked at Patton through most of the 1980s. "I know an art therapist who was sexually assaulted."

"There were several rapes on the grounds," said a former female employee. "One of the psychologists was even raped and bruised up. You learn to wear functional clothing. You don't wear scarves, for example. They can be wrapped around your neck. There's a real awareness of people."

By the time he became a permanent resident at Patton, Michael Miller had already learned the ropes. Judge Mills gave him credit for 602 days served before committing him to the 360 acres of bungalows and institutional buildings nestled at the base of the San Bernardino Mountains one hundred miles southeast of Los Angeles.

When it first opened a century ago, Patton was known as the Southern California State Hospital for the Insane and Inebriates. It did not receive its current name until 1927, when the state legislature rechristened the institution Patton State Hospital—not named for General George Patton, as most people believe, but for Harry W. Patton, one of the early members of the hospital's board of trustees.

At its height in the 1950s, Patton housed over five thousand patients in an independent agricultural community that produced most of its own food and provided most of its own support services. Patton employed a staff of nearly two thousand, who helped in-mates work the dairy, chicken and pig ranch, vegetable gardens, fruit orchards, laundry, shoe shop, tailor shop and furniture shop, in addition to the wards and medical units.

The hospital was a tough place. Treatment was often primitive and included lobotomy and electroshock therapy. But most of the time, the keepers and the kept coexisted in peace. Besides, Patton was far enough away from urban centers, and the problems of its troubled population were so removed from mainstream California, that most citizens paid scant attention.

Things began to change in the 1960s, when the state fire marshal declared eighteen of Patton's buildings unsafe. No funds were allot-ted to rebuild, and the evicted patients had nowhere to live. By the time Ronald Reagan became governor in 1966, the hospital had shipped thirty-five percent of its population elsewhere. The following year, Reagan ordered the hospital to fire 237 psychiatric technicians. In 1968 he cut 212 more from the payroll.

"Employee morale dropped. During the next few years, employment at Patton was on a roller coaster, but mostly downhill," wrote journalist Harvey Feit in a short history of the hospital that the *San Bernardino Sun* published in 1981.

"Almost unnoticed among the rumors and cutbacks was the arrival at Patton in January 1968 of 60 maximum security prisoners from Atascadero State Hospital—possibly the first large group of dangerous criminals to be housed at Patton," Feit continued. "In early 1973, Reagan announced a plan to phase out all state hospitals for the mentally ill and retarded over a 10-year period."

Community leaders protested and the governor backed off. The facility with its $12-million payroll remained open.

Nevertheless, Reagan's deinstitutionalization policies had begun to catch on. He signed the Lanterman-Petris-Short Act into law in 1968—a law that civil libertarians hailed as a declaration of independence for the mentally ill. Under the LPS Act, as it came to be known, the state could no longer warehouse the mentally ill indefinitely or involuntarily in a state institution.

What sounded good on paper, however, became an excuse to offer less state-subsidized aid to the retarded and mentally ill. The state even began to shut down mental hospitals altogether. People who lapsed into schizophrenia, depression or any of dozens of other categories of psychoses had no place to go unless friends or family helped them.

Even then, if they denied their illness, the LPS Act forbade friends or family to commit them against their will beyond seventy-two hours without court approval. Roy and Marguerite Miller learned firsthand the limitations that the law imposed on parents when they tried to get help for their troubled but stubborn and uncooperative sons. They could not be committed without their consent, or the embarrassing, expensive and time-consuming intervention of the courts.

Slowly, through the 1970s, the insane left the hospitals for halfway houses and underfunded outpatient community treatment programs. Many began living on the streets.

By the 1980s, when Michael Miller arrived as a permanent resident, Patton State Hospital had changed dramatically from the relatively serene sanctuary it had been in the 1950s. The dairy and the orchards and the cobbler shop were gone. The chain-link perimeter was dotted with checkpoints and guarded by armed guards employed by the state Department of Corrections. The patient population hovered around the one thousand mark and were diagnosed as dangerous to themselves and others when uncontrolled by psychotropic drugs. Few of those inmates wound up there as the docile inebriates or quietly despairing psychotics of old.

"Patton is all form and no substance," said one of several former employees who would only speak about the hospital on condition of anonymity.

By the time Michael Miller became a permanent resident, Patton had once again become a warehouse for the very worst, least predictable and most expensive kind of patient. By the end of the 1980s, the staff outnumbered the patients and the annual payroll stood at $71 million.

"It's not like *One Flew over the Cuckoo's Nest*," said a former Patton medical staff member who described her own tenure at Patton as "being sentenced in hell."

"There are a couple of units of heavily medicated, crazy people," she said. "Some are so sad because the quality of life is gone for them.

"But a lot of people who are there are people who just wigged out and committed a crime rather than go to some private hospital somewhere. If they had stayed at home on their medication or checked into a hospital for a couple weeks, they still might be on the outside."

Most of them were going crazy for years while everyone around them looked the other way, said another Patton staff veteran.

"The public needs to know that it is a lot better to make their investments in better mental health early rather than later, when it becomes far more expensive in a lot of ways," she said.

Michael wanted out of Patton as soon as he was in. On March 5, 1985, nineteen days before the second anniversary of his mother's death and only four months after his sentencing, he filed

a handwritten petition with Judge Mills, charging that his detention was illegal.

"I am not a danger to myself," he wrote in a large, careful scrawl.
"I am not a danger to others. I am being forced to take psychotropic
medication against my will."

He had never been forced to take it before, he complained.
According to Michael, his attorneys had never mentioned whether
he was a danger to himself or to others during his sanity hearing.
That was reason enough for Judge Mills to address the issue now.

He'd had enough, said Michael. He wanted out.

Judge Mills wasted no time. He ruled that Michael would remain
at Patton for the foreseeable future.

Roy and occasionally other relatives and friends continued to
drive down to Patton to visit on weekends.

Dr. Shapiro visited once. He also shipped Michael several inspi-
rational tapes and an audio version of *Moments of Insight*, his book
about some of his more interesting cases. He explained that he
hoped the tapes might help hasten Michael's recovery. He billed
Roy Miller for the tapes, but Shapiro was never paid. In fact, Miller
quickly cut off all communications with the psychoanalyst after his
son's court case wound to a close.

Roy paid for his son's defense, but balked about paying his
psychiatric bills. On April 10, 1985, he formally invoked a state
law that required the county to pay for Michael's expert witnesses
who helped with his insanity defense. Los Angeles County taxpayers had to pay Dr. Faerstein $3,075, Dr. Markman $1,700 and Dr.
Maloney $1,360.

On January 10, 1987, Michael tried to escape from Patton. Two
days later, he was transferred to Atascadero State Hospital two
hundred miles north of Los Angeles. The state's first facility designed to house the criminally insane, Atascadero was much better
equipped to handle escape attempts.

One year later, Michael was transferred back to Patton. He was
kept on a heavy daily regimen of antidepressants, sleeping pills and
antipsychotic drugs that kept his schizophrenia in remission. The

drugs did not seem to help his personality, though. He remained as impulsive, obssessive and demanding as he had been before he ever saw the inside of a mental hospital. When he talked about his mother's murder, it was without a trace of visible emotion.

By the winter of 1988, his condition had improved. Michael stopped boycotting group therapy and started obeying ward rules. He even struck up a strange, symbiotic friendship with another patient. It looked to the staff as though Michael depended too much on the other inmate, always asking him if he, Michael, was behaving in a seemly fashion, but even that relationship seemed to improve his mental outlook. He seemed less narcissistic, more communicative and better able to take responsibility for his actions. But he was still speaking of suicide.

On April 28, 1989, Michael mustered enough confidence to write Judge Mills again, demanding a habeas corpus hearing.

"I have a legal right to go to court for a sanity hearing once a year," he wrote.

He was right, of course. Technically, the law required a staff review every six months. The following month, an interdisciplinary team of four hospital staff members did review his case again.

He and the one inmate he had befriended were no longer comrades. Their symbiotic relationship blew up and so did Michael's halting progress toward mental stability. This time, his prognosis was worse than it had ever been since he first came to Patton.

He had taken up smoking whenever and wherever he pleased. He refused to take showers. He wandered out of his ward without permission. He hid under his bed rather than go to therapy or meals. He missed more than half the meetings he was supposed to attend.

Michael had become manipulative again. If he couldn't get permission to do something from one psychologist, he'd go to another with the same request. He made undisguised and indiscreet sexual overtures to staff members. When he was given his daily dose of tranquilizers and stimulants, he spit them out on the floor.

A year passed and he was no better. The official alerts printed on his treatment chart made him sound more menacing than a rabid coyote: self-abusive, homicidal, suicidal, sexually assaultive, an escape risk.

According to those who dealt with him every day, Michael never learned from his mistakes. He had no concept of reality and he avoided any emotional give and take. He continued to deny virtually all of his actions and pathologies, ranging from his mother's murder to his use of recreational drugs when he was in high school and college.

Judge Mills became presiding judge of the Los Angeles County Criminal Courts and moved from suburban Torrance, but the one case that he took with him when he moved to downtown Los Angeles was that of Michael Miller.

"This case is unique in several respects to me," said Judge Mills. "The sense I get was that it wasn't really predictable that this event would happen, but these parents could see something building that they were powerless to stop.

"Michael was an accident waiting to happen and this family knew that. They did everything possible to deal with him except have him committed. They had Jeff committed and after what had previously happened with him, they couldn't do that again. They were just terribly frustrated."

Though he was unaware of it, Michael Miller briefly shared an address—the L.A. County jail—with the most famous offspring of any of the American Institute of Hypnosis therapists.

A few years before, Larry Gamsky and his son Joe legally changed their last name to Hunt. On September 28, 1984, Joe, now working as the institute's bookkeeper, was arrested for the murder of a high-living yuppie named Ron Levin. A few weeks after that, he was charged with killing Hedayet Eslaminia, a middle-aged businessman who suffocated to death in a trunk Hunt was hauling from the San Francisco Bay Area to Southern California in the back of a borrowed pickup truck. The pickup belonged to his father, Ryan Hunt, a.k.a. Larry Gamsky.

The murders and subsequent trials that sent Hunt and several other well-to-do Beverly Hills preppies to prison came to be known by the name of the investment company that Hunt founded with the help of his father: the Billionaire Boys Club.

In 1992 Hunt managed to get a retrial on the Eslaminia murder, during which he acted as his own defense attorney. To the surprise of many, he convinced a San Jose, California, jury of his innocence and was acquitted. He remains in prison on the first murder, however, even though the body of Ron Levin was never found.

After his son's empire began to crumble, Larry Gamsky returned to California and remarried. He and his new wife moved to Northern California following his son's murder conviction. But, as Ryan Hunt, he did not return to the hypnotherapy business.

His partner Frank Mingarella also left the therapy business for several years, finally moving in the early 1990s to Malibu, where he dabbled for a time in video distribution—at least a partial fulfillment of his longtime goal of becoming a producer. But by the summer of 1993, he was once again in the medical business. Dr. Mingarella was back at work in West Los Angeles, working for a pain-control clinic.

Richard Martino also left therapy for show business. He became a bouncer in a West Los Angeles nightclub that featured transvestite entertainment. At the time of his death in the summer of 1992, Martino was unemployed and living with one of the young men from the American Institute of Hypnosis whom he recruited to come work for him when the institute went out of business.

Dr. Julian continued to practice medicine at his Holistic Health and Weight Control Center at the corner of Cahuenga and Hollywood boulevards. At seventy, he still championed the cause of holistic health and nutritional therapy and helped promote a campaign to limit the interference of the Food and Drug Administration and other government agencies in the licensing of controversial drugs and medical procedures, including chelation therapy.

In 1985 Dr. Bruce Halstead was arrested for cancer fraud. At his trial, the sixty-five-year-old holistic physician waved a box of bran flakes at the jury and told them, "There is a difference between treating disease and nutritional support."

The jury found him guilty of selling a dying minister a cloudy liquid he called ADS for $6,000 with the implication that it could cure his leukemia. The minister died of his disease, but not before he reported the fraud to the Los Angeles District Attorney. Following an investigation, the D.A.'s Office found several more victims of the ADS fraud—or their survivors.

"He did not promise me anything," said Melodee Wolf, whose six-year-old daughter took the Halstead treatment before she died of her cancer. "He offered me hope because he was willing to at least help."

Deputy District Attorney Hyatt Seligman saw it differently. Melodee Wolf's daughter "died less than five months after she drank that swamp water day after day, fifteen hundred dollars' worth," he said.

Halstead was sentenced to four years in prison and given a $10,000 fine. Halstead's probation officer said he was only motivated by a desire to make money.

Halstead claimed he "never once considered the issue of money" and that he was deeply sorry.

"The only remorse he showed was for the fact that he had been convicted," testified probation officer Purcell Daniels.

After the Jeffrey Miller case, Dr. Thomas Talbot Seeley left the hurly-burly of Southern California to take up practice in the Northern California town of Mount Shasta. He spent several weeks a year studying and worshipping with two gurus in India. The rest of the time he treated depression, neurosis and personality disorders among New Age psychiatric patients.

"Mount Shasta is the only world-class holy mountain in North America," said Dr. Seeley, explaining his reason for abandoning the world of psychiatric medicine in Los Angeles and moving to the same rural corner of California where Judge Cecil Mills had grown up fifty years earlier.

In June 1989 the state Board of Medical Quality Assurance placed Seeley on seven years' probation for repeated professional negligence. In one charge, he allegedly took a patient home with him for treatment instead of to an emergency facility. In another charge, he suggested inappropriate reading material to a patient which aggravated her condition. Seeley agreed to a psychiatric evaluation, drug screen testing and regular monitoring by a board representative as conditions to his retaining his medical license.

The Anne Sippi Clinic, where Seeley recommended Jeffrey Miller seek treatment back in 1980, continued to accept and treat chronic schizophrenics. Jack Rosberg's controversial confrontational methods received widespread attention and his seminars have become part of the continuing education programs for many Southern California medical professionals.

Rosberg is semiretired, but his son Michael continues as the Anne Sippi administrator. Over the years, the state Department of Social Service has investigated the clinic for a variety of infractions, ranging from rats, cockroaches and poor hygiene to loose drug control and physical abuse of patients. The department has no record of Anne Sippi being under investigation for another questionable patient death since Jeffrey Miller's.

Father Ed Cordero left both Patrick House and Jersey City after Jeff died. He returned to parish work, hearing confessions and administering the sacraments. His heart failed while serving communion during Mass one Sunday morning in the late 1980s. Whatever secrets might have passed between the priest and the Dartmouth student were buried with Cordero.

The Reverend Freddie Lindblad still sold Rheo Blair's protein mix out of his rented one-bedroom bungalow in Bell Gardens, but the rest of the health food king's empire crumbled within months of his death. His masseur, Richard Backlund, wound up with his furniture, proceeds from one of Blair's houses, a grand piano and Blair's sixteen-millimeter projector, but the bulk of his estate went to his brother, who had only a passing interest in nutrition and cared even less about bodybuilding.

Helena Salt and her husband retired to a senior citizens' community in New Jersey. In Helen's bedroom the nightstand, dresser and walls are festooned with pictures of Drew. She still has all of the music he wrote and hopes to convince someone to record it someday, so that she can resurrect some of her late son's dream of becoming famous.

On April 19, 1988, the probate file on Jeffrey Bruner Miller was finally closed. His mother's estate was settled the same day.

Marguerite left a three-page will, giving everything to Roy. Her property, jewelry, artwork, stock portfolio, cash and other assets came to almost $1.4 million.

Roy also formally acknowledged receipt of Jeff's final assets: $27,329 in cash, twenty shares of IBM common stock worth $1,242.50, personal effects worth $100.

On June 23, 1992, Michael Miller's annual request for freedom was considered and denied once again by Judge Cecil Mills.

As in each previous year since his murder conviction, state hospital staff reviewed Michael's history and made its anniversary recommendation to the court as to whether he should spend another year in Unit 78 of Patton State Hospital or walk out of its gates a free man. With only minor exceptions, Miller's diagnosis and prognosis remained unchanged from the first day he entered Patton.

In his two-page report to the court, one Patton psychiatrist specified the type and severity of Miller's psychoses and the four different drugs he was administered each day to control his outbursts. Then he summarized in a few paragraphs Michael's progress during his nine years of confinement:

> Mr. Miller has not made any significant progress since his last report. He remains passively resistive to efforts to work on his problems. In "Individual Therapy" and "Socialization Group" he will not discuss anything about himself in any depth. He also maintains his dependent pathological relationships with staff and peers. He continues to present himself as unmotivated to create changes in his life and unconcerned about the consequences of his behaviors. He is often non-compliant with unit rules and requires constant supervision.

He continues to minimize his past substance abuse problem. He tested positive for cocaine on Dec. 12, 1990, on a urine drug screen. No other incidents have been noted.

Yet, he remains unaware of the symptoms of his illness or how they affect his daily behavior on the unit. He has total lack of insight and appears to be only interested in securing coffee, water and cigarettes for himself. He continues to be self-defeating, selfish, compulsive and impulsive. He displays histrionic behaviors and grandiose delusions, and requires constant verbal and physical prompting to care for his hygiene and grooming.

His excessive water consumption and non-compliance with his medication regimen had led to frequent close monitoring (one-to-ones) and more than eight days in seclusion and restraints for his protection since March 5, 1992. Over the past couple of months, Mr. Miller has also become more oppositional, defiant and manipulative. Mr. Miller has completed the required hours for both the Supportive Treatment Education Program and Specialized Treatment and Rehabilitation Program, but due to the severity of his mental illness, made no significant therapeutic gains.

Mr. Miller remains mentally ill, a danger to the health and safety of others and would remain so even if furnished supervision and treatment in the community and has not been fully restored to sanity.

Recommendations to Court: Mr. Miller should be retained at the hospital for continued treatment.

The latest report, dated December 21, 1993, is just as gloomy. Now 31 years old, the tall, spectral Miller stalks the corridors of Patton State Hospital carrying a dirty coffee cup full of "inappropriate liquid resembling weak tea with particles floating in it," according to one observer.

His hair is rarely combed and his appearance is generally disheveled. Miller has attacked others, both violently and sexually, and takes four different medications several times daily to keep those impulses in check. He reeks of urine and feces.

He's intelligent, according to his counselors, but he is also manipulative, irresponsible, compulsive and uncooperative. He breaks promises almost as soon as he makes them.

In short, Michael Miller remains a danger to the health and safety of others.

Since Michael Miller's conviction, more than a half dozen cases of adolescent schizophrenia have surfaced at the First United Methodist Church. It may have been that the illness had always afflicted some families in the congregation, but nobody would talk about it—even with their pastor.

Michael still calls collect from Patton from time to time and speaks to church secretaries and ministers. He calls Dr. Julian too. He always starts his conversations coherently, but gets off on a tangent within a minute or two and soon babbles in a language only he understands.

Roy redoubled his own faith following the death of his wife and elder son. He became a trustee and later chairman of the board of the School of Theology at Claremont, where Jeff would have gone to divinity school if he hadn't drowned in psychosis. During Roy Miller's trusteeship, the School of Theology grew to an interdenominational population of over four hundred students.

Roy also came to know another family beset by schizophrenia. Jack and Jo Ann Hinckley got in touch and sympathized with Roy Miller after Michael's sentencing. The Hinckleys, who founded the nonprofit American Mental Health Fund to disseminate information about mental illness, underwent their own torrent of condemnation following the verdict that found their son innocent of attempting to assassinate the President. The couple even coauthored a book arguing that the insanity defense is not the wealthy man's escape hatch from responsibility for criminal conduct, as it is often portrayed.

Roy had no further public statement to make about mental

illness, however. In October 1985, when the Hinckleys' *Breaking Points* was published to mixed reviews, Roy Miller was not even in the country. He spent the month hiking into the Garhwal Himalayas in northern India.

He developed a limited social life along with his strong spiritual and civic-minded attitudes. He threw himself into his work and did not give up his prized clients, even after they left the White House. The Reagans sent their autographed 8-by-10-inch glossy to Roy in time for Christmas 1985. It read: "To Roy Miller, with appreciation and our best wishes, Nancy & Ronald Reagan."

Roy Miller did not sell his Palos Verdes home, continuing to live there. The yard is raked gravel now, but everything else remains pretty much the same.

He traveled on exotic foreign vacations, as he and Marguerite had once done together.

In the summer of 1986 Roy went on his second Himalayan safari, trekking with a small group into the westernmost ranges: the Hindu Kush and Karakoram Mountains of Pakistan. He visited the old silk routes followed by Marco Polo and lands conquered by Darius the Great of Persia and Alexander the Great. He shopped the bazaars of Peshawar and met with Afghan refugees thirty miles from the Khyber Pass. He stayed overnight in Hunza, where farmers eat health foods and live to over one hundred.

"He is a profoundly spiritual man and just a good human being," said one longtime acquaintance. "He has suffered more than most people will ever suffer. And he deals with it by not talking about it."

Someday, Roy has confided in those close to him, he believes that Michael will be well enough to leave Patton and come home.

Until then, he will wait.

AFTERWORD

The true story of the Millers of Palos Verdes and the tragic end to a "perfect" family has never been told until now. It was not meant to be. Schizophrenia may afflict millions, but it is not supposed to affect those in the higher social strata. Mental illness, and the violent amorality that frequently attends it, remains one of Society's last best-kept dirty little secrets, especially if it involves the rich and powerful.

On November 19, 1984, Roy Miller joined the two lawyers he hired to defend Michael in asking Los Angeles Superior Court Judge Cecil Mills to seal the court record. Richard de la Sota, the prosecutor in the case, went along with the request. Because no one raised any objection, this unusual if not unprecedented move in California jurisprudence to shut away a serious and sobering crime from public view succeeded.

In June 1992, after Michael Miller had been in state hospitals for the criminally insane for more than eight years, I succeeded in convincing the court to unseal the records in *People v. Michael David Miller*.

Ten years after Roy Miller's family tragedy, our mental health system still has no easy answers to the causes and cures of schizophrenia, and government at all levels offers very little hope—and even less protection—to families affected by the disease. A whole range of pseudo-scientific miracle workers continue to prey on frightened, desperate parents and their disturbed children. Occasionally, the government takes action against the most obvious quacks, but even the least reputable can carry on with impunity if their methods and marketing are discreet.

The Miller's story is unusual, but it is not unique. The entire family was a victim of a political and social system that would prefer to deny the very existence of schizophrenia.

Most schizophrenics are not violent. They are often the aimless men and women in rags on the street who once lived normal enough lives until body chemistry, genetics and environment conspired to defeat their humanity. They are the men and women we hear about from a friend of a friend of a friend—a broken human being who now lives alone in a separate room over someone's garage or anonymously in halfway houses.

They are the afflicted who see monsters that no one else can see; hear spiteful words and unholy mantras that no one else can hear; writhe in relentless psychic pain that no one else can feel.

During the Reagan era, first when the former actor was governor of California and later throughout the entire nation in his White House years, schizophrenics were turned out of institutions in droves, left to emigrate to the suburbs and live in city parks or beneath bus shelters. There, they made their presence known to the middle class.

Amorality and insanity were both paid lip service in America in the 1980s. Otherwise compassionate Americans uniformly accepted government's tacit rejection of any link between mental illness and criminal acts. Thousands of schizophrenics ended up in prison. Thousands more were tucked away in board and care homes until they could no longer afford it. Then they were simply put out on the street.

One schizophrenic found lasting fame outside the Washington Hilton on March 29, 1981, when he fired five shots from a pistol in a deranged plot to win the affection of actress Jodie Foster. Two bullets struck Press Secretary James Brady in the head, disabling him for life. Another struck Ronald Reagan in the chest and came within an inch of changing the course of history.

John Hinckley, Jr., displayed his madness openly to millions before, during and after his trial. And, still, the government of Ronald Reagan ignored the dire message his would-be assassin relayed about the homeless, hapless insane who dwell among us.

Ironically, Hinckley was one of the lucky ones. His parents were well off and his intended victim was famous enough that he was given the best defense money and notoriety could provide. Instead of going to prison, where Attorney General William French Smith encouraged the punishment rather than the rehabilitation of criminals, Hinckley was sentenced to St. Elizabeth's Hospital just outside of downtown Washington, D.C. To this day, he receives daily drugs and therapy there for his psychosis. If he can convince both his psychiatric keepers and a court of law that he has regained his wits, he may again walk free—innocent of his crimes because of his insanity.

Mental health professionals say that, statistically, it is likely that someone like Hinckley will be free again, once he is in his 40s or 50s. By that age, the chemical imbalances that many psychiatrists blame for adolescent-onset schizophrenia even themselves out naturally and insanity gradually disappears. All that is left of abnormal behavior is a residue of harmless eccentricity.

Until the schizophrenic reaches middle age, their disease remains a problem to the society that cannot tolerate or understand it and a mystery to the family that once thought they knew their son or daughter, father or mother.

During the 1980s, some of these tortured young adults emerged from the safe shadows of affluence, like John Hinckley, Jr., or Michael Miller, and took their unwitting revenge against those who refused to acknowledge that something was very wrong in America—that our own children were going crazy while we looked the other way.

*   *   *

Beginning in 1991, I wrote Michael Miller a half dozen times in an effort to speak with him. He never answered me. In spring 1992, I spoke with Roy Miller about the book I intended to write. He promised to get back to me. I never heard from him again.

It was not the first roadblock I had come up against in piecing together the story of the Miller family. Almost from the project's inception, Roy Miller's closest friends and associates closed ranks. There have been a few notable exceptions without whose help I could not have completed the tale. At their request, these sources have had to remain unnamed. Roy Miller has understandably tried to keep his personal tragedy private, despite its very public overtones.

His sister-in-law, Mrs. Gretchen Catterall, told me she could not break the family's silence because Roy told her that to do so might jeopardize Michael's chances of eventual release from custody.

Michael's caretakers warn that Roy should be wary about seeking his son's freedom. According to Sergeant Ed Jaakola, who oversaw the Palos Verdes Estates Police Department's role in the case, Michael will find his father and "finish the job" if he is ever released.

In August 1992, I wrote to Patton State Hospital, formally requesting an interview with Michael Miller. I was answered within days by the hospital's executive director, William L. Summers.

Michael Miller and his family "requested that he be allowed not to be called upon to visit or otherwise communicate with you," wrote Summers. They also did not want anyone on staff discussing Michael Miller's care, treatment or anything else about him.

I could tour part of the hospital, according to Summers, but not the area in which Miller lived. I was allowed to speak with staff about "broad topic areas," but I was forbidden to ask about Miller or interview anyone who ever worked with Miller.

Sidestepping the tone of noncooperation in Director Summers' letter, I took him up on his offer. Our tour lasted four hours and carefully skirted that portion of the hospital where paranoid schizophrenics like Michael Miller are housed. But madness reigns everywhere inside Patton. It is visible in the eyes of almost every inmate, regardless of the psychotropic drug or mood modifier that keeps them functioning at an ambulatory level during most of their waking hours.

Though it may be prison-like on the outside and barely subdued chaos on the inside, Patton radiates a difference from the passive gloom of a San Quentin or a Riker's Island. There is hope here, however dim. The inmate housing has cots and lockers that make the atmosphere more like that of boot camp, not Alcatraz. There are the restraints and the occasional padded room where mania can play itself to exhaustion, but there are no cells, chains or prison bars.

According to Patton officials, physical violence comes with their jobs. With some regularity, Patton employees are attacked, beaten, bitten. Workers are not required to wear uniforms, but they are discouraged from wearing scarves, necklaces or neckties. An ounce of prevention is mandatory because there often is no cure.

Insanity doesn't inhibit sexuality, nor do the drugs that inmates are required to take. Rape is attempted often. But the attackers are subdued and treated at Patton, not beaten or worse.

Michael Miller's home is dangerous and deranged, but it is better than prison.

Despite budget cuts and a punishing philosophy championed by California governors from Ronald Reagan to Pete Wilson, Patton remains dedicated to hope and cure—no matter how improbable. It still has classes and libraries and computers and canteens where the criminally insane can relearn the rudiments of civilized behavior. Some do. Some don't. But the attendants and counselors and nurses and doctors of Patton tend to wear an air of cautious faith.

Indeed, Mike Schultz, the Patton medical staff chief, said that notorious mass murderer Charles Manson might have been rehabilitated through counseling and drug therapy had he been sent to Patton instead of state prison. Dr. Schultz conjectured that Manson

quite possibly could have been treated and returned to society if a
jury or judge had found him guilty of murder by reason of insanity
rather than simply guilty of murder.

Perhaps.

But one fact is indisputable: the Mansons and Millers and Hinckleys will inevitably come again if no effort is undertaken to
understand how they came to be in the first place.

The deterrence theory of penal purgatory promoted by Ronald
Reagan and his chief legal architect, the late William French
Smith, does not work with psychotics. All the punishment we can
develop as a society will not save those who got in the way of a
madman when his undiagnosed or ignored schizophrenia first blossoms into violence.

The only way to deal with insanity is to maintain eye contact
with it and stare it down. Each time we turn away and pretend we
do not see, we risk our lives, our children's lives and all that we
have become or hope to become. With our prisons packed to
overflowing, our mental hospitals functioning on an outpatient
basis and our streets brimming with Reagan economic refugees,
more and more eyes are turning away. It is more expedient to put
things off until later.

Some things cannot wait.

Ask the murderer or the rapist.

Almost without exception they will tell you that their crime or
crimes happened because they could wait no longer. At some point,
their internal checks short circuited. Rage and lust took over.

In a culture of denial, anyone can be a victim and anarchy is
the end result.

In a culture of denial, whole families are slaughtered in unfathomable anger with the perpetrator often turning his weapon in
suicidal despair upon himself. Well-educated young men of means
rape their dates without explanation or apology and wilding teens
strike anonymously and randomly, showing no more deference to
a well-to-do jogger in Central Park than pillaging Serbian soldiers

do to the daughters of Bosnian peasants. Anonymous gangs do drive-by shootings, and return to the scene of the crime to gape as their victims bleed to death. In a culture of denial, children shoot their parents at point-blank range, and parents rape, beat, burn and bury their children. As Irish poet William Butler Yeats predicted nearly a century ago, these are the inevitable results when the blood-dimmed tide has been turned loose: Innocence is left to drown.

In such a world, those "civilized" citizens who can afford to do so live inside security buildings or suburbs safely tucked behind guard shacks. Those of us who are able, wire our cars and our homes against intruders and peer at the barbarism outside through the periscope of our television sets. It never occurs to us that we are prisoners of the sad, hopeless and angry marauders we have barred so completely from our lives. It never occurs to us that those bloodthirsty barbarians may, in fact, live among us and sleep beneath our roofs, their hearts beating with our blood and their spirits tortured with our despair.

We live in a time of unprecedented technological wonder, but also in an era of cultural paganism unmatched in this century. We can describe in detail the symptoms of social decay, but struggle for explanations of the causes.

Violence surrounds us. It always has.

But violence, at least in the West, has been carefully and methodically subdued in these latter days of the twentieth century. For many of us, violence is merely an edited TV report of a disaster, a reenacted rape scene played between movie stars or a vicarious clash of heroes on a football field. The tragedy is excised with the gore, and all that is left is a dangerous, often murderous fantasy— free of conscience, free of consequence.

But sex and violence are never free of consequence. There is always a price to pay. Civilization is a thin veneer of universal rules that can be violated at any time. Sex and violence are human. They coexist with love and compassion and go unacknowledged and unmanaged at our peril. Mankind is just as much animal as angel—a fact that must be constantly confronted and brought into balance by an ever vigilant and empathetic citizenry.

To fail to do so is to invite insanity into our lives, there to dwell until it devours us and all that we hold dear.

—Dennis McDougal
January 1994